the Jewelled kitchen

The Jewelled Kitchen

A stunning collection of Lebanese, Moroccan & Persian recipes

BETHANY KEHDY

DUNCAN BAIRD PUBLISHERS

LONDON

This book is dedicated to my late grandparents,
Kehdy Farhoud Kehdy and Adla Kehdy

The Jewelled Kitchen
Bethany Kehdy

First published in the United Kingdom and Ireland
in 2013 by Duncan Baird Publishers, an imprint of
Watkins Publishing Limited
Sixth Floor
75 Wells Street
London W1T 3QH

A member of Osprey Group

Managing Editor: Grace Cheetham
Editor: Alison Bolus
Managing Designer: Manisha Patel
Picture Researcher: Emma Copestake
Production: Uzma Taj
Commissioned photography: Šárka Babická
Food Stylist: Emily Jonzen
Prop Stylist: Lucy Harvey

A CIP record for this book is available from the
British Library

ISBN: 978-1-84899-062-3

10 9 8 7 6 5 4 3 2 1

Typeset in Steinem and Andover
Colour reproduction by PDQ, UK
Printed in China

Publisher's note: While every care has been taken
in compiling the recipes for this book, Watkins
Publishing Limited, or any other persons who have
been involved in working on this publication, cannot
accept responsibility for any errors or omissions,
inadvertent or not, that may be found in the recipes
or text, nor for any problems that may arise as a
result of preparing one of these recipes. If you are
pregnant or breastfeeding or have any special dietary
requirements or medical conditions, it is advisable to
consult a medical professional before following any of
the recipes contained in this book.

Notes on the Recipes
Unless otherwise stated:
Use medium eggs, fruit and vegetables
Use fresh ingredients, including herbs and chillies
Do not mix metric and imperial measurements
1 tsp = 5ml   1 tbsp = 15ml   1 cup = 250ml

Note on Latinization
Representing Arabic in Latin characters is not a
straightforward process at all. As this book covers
the expanse of the Middle East and North Africa, I
have presupposed an MSA (Modern Standard Arabic)
pronunciation for all words transliterated throughout
rather than adopting the vernacular or colloquial
dialect of my country, Lebanon, which is how I would
pronounce the words day to day. That said, in some
instances, a regional variation favouring the vernacular pronunciation notable to Lebanon, may still be
present. I have tried my best to be as consistent and
faithful as possible to the Arabic phonetics and to the
best of my knowledge while trying to maintain a balance and accessibility for the non-native speaker so not
to alienate them.

culinary reflections

beirut, circa 1985. My delicate, fidgeting fingers in the bone-breaking grip of my grandfather's (*jeddo's*) hand, his other hand firmly clasps the daunting, gold, lion-faced ornament mounted on his signature walking stick. As the foot of the stick beats against the asphalt, the thumping sounds are in sync with our steps. Together, we pace down a war-ravaged street in Fassouh, Ashrafieh, en route to my kindergarten. Along the way, we pause by the corner shop where we are greeted by the ruddy-cheeked owner, Rizkallah. Here, my jeddo spoils me with sweets that my young self adored so much. Most notable amongst them were Tutti Frutti and one we knew as Ras El Abed, with its fez-shaped crunchy outer fortification concealing a soft, meringue interior. As Rizkallah puts them on the counter, my jeddo gestures me to choose from any one of the sugar-loaded pyramids populating the chilled cabinet. "*Jus ananas, jeddo*", I proclaim – "pineapple juice, grandfather". He then pierces the inconspicuous aluminium-masked porta with the straw, before passing it to me.

The sweets are reserved for *récré*, but only if I am a well-mannered girl who has eaten all her tartine for lunch. This could be Arabic bread spread with *labneh* (strained yogurt) and dotted with olives, or perhaps cheese and cucumber, ham and cheese or cheese and jam, my grandmother's (*teta's*) favourite. Returning home with the sandwich uneaten isn't something I even dare to consider. Worse still would be to abandon it in the rubbish, for somehow the school *maitresse* will discover this ultimate sin and bear news of it to my teta, much to God's outrage. "*Allah 'atena akel ya te'breene, fee gheirna 'am b jou'o.*" – "God has blessed us with food, others are starving."

These are my earliest memories of food, and the fear of my teta's wrath, which is a plausible reason as to why my plate is never given a second to entertain a crumb.

The crumbs that led me to the kitchen

At home in Beirut, we could always expect a soul-stirring rendition from the seasons' star characters as they rehearsed on the stove top before asserting themselves centre stage on our kitchen table. Our meals consisted of many of the quintessentially Lebanese home-cooked dishes, from the basic to the intricate. My teta's social foundation schedule, as active as olive oil in a Lebanese kitchen, meant that certain days would be reserved for simpler dishes like *mujadarah*, *musaqa'a* or *mutabaqa*. Mutabaqa, meaning "layered" in this instance, is a Lebanese relative of ratatouille, and was sometimes made too often for my jeddo's palate. It often triggered the complaint, "*Taba'te 'a albna ya mara*" – "You've caved in our hearts with this dish woman". Playing on one of the several meanings derived from the root word *tabaqa*, it was a coy effort to express his underwhelmed appetite.

Regardless of what was on the table, though, as the clock struck noon, you could count on my grandfather to stroll over from his nearby law office every day of his married life. Lunch over, he would listen to the news on his radio box, read a book or do some writing before his dreams hijacked him into a gentle afternoon siesta.

On Saturday mornings or during the school holidays, I would shadow my teta as she went about her grocery shopping. First, we would whizz over to Hanna *al laham* (Hanna the butcher); both his body and his store still strong and upright, their façades evidence of time's great pilgrimage. "*Ahlan b sit Adla,*" – "Welcome Madame Adla," he would greet her, a prelude to a short exchange of words about the well-being of each other's families before the serious business of shopping began, signalled by Hanna's request, "*O'moreené ya sitna*" – "Your orders, Madame". In her stern voice, bereft of hesitation, teta would question the meat's source and time of slaughter. "*Bta'refné ya Hanna ma be'bal gheir b ahsan shee.*" – "You know me, Hanna, I am only satisfied with the best."

At the greengrocer, she would shamelessly bury her hands right to the bottom of the vegetable pile, pulling out several contenders before picking the most worthy. In no way would she be outsmarted by the grocer's conspiracy to keep the older vegetables most exposed. Tomatoes would get a full, twirling, close-up inspection as though they were a model at a casting. Aubergines would be fondled to test their tenderness, and often tossed back in disappointment. On bad mornings, I would hear her discontented muttering: "*Te'te'te, shou hal bda'a ya Rizkallah! Ndahle bas yejeek ahsan!*" – "Such terrible quality of produce! Give me a ring when you get better!" she would announce, before turning on her heel and marching me out of the shop.

Cherished gifts from the land

I was four years old when my parents separated. Born in Houston, I returned to Lebanon with my father, while my siblings remained in the US with my mother; it was a long time before we would all rendezvous again.

My mother was a beautiful, all-American Texan with golden blonde hair, shimmering, ocean-blue eyes and eyelashes that, when fluttered, could get her into Fort Knox. My Lebanese father was tall, robust and olive skinned, with large, piercing eyes. A hard-working, handsome, twenty-something lawyer meant I spent most of my time soaking up the attention of my grandparents. My long, lean and imposing jeddo, with his chiselled cheekbones and a smile that, even in memory, can still light up my heart, was a renowned lawyer and author across the Arab world. His was a fascinating story of hard work, triumph and unmatched determination, deserving every blotch of ink on the flickering pages of Lebanon's history books. "His presence could shake a room," was something I often heard said about him. My grandmother, born to the only commercial tobacco farmer in Lebanon at the time, grew up along the shores of the northern town of Batroun. Stern and articulate, she never missed a beat, and it was said she could read a person and their motives in the glimpse of an eye. Family was the central focus of our life and I was always surrounded by the people who played a pivotal role in my upbringing: my grandparents, aunts and uncles.

My mother returned to Lebanon for a little while with my sisters in tow, and, as the civil war swelled with fury and pain, we entrenched ourselves in our ancestral village of Baskinta, in the foothills of Mount Sannine. My father set up a dairy farm where we spent the next five years embracing the land, its bounty, its unpredictable nature and the general, all-round, rugged goodness.

During the summers, my sisters and I would run in the terraces, hide in the pine forest, explore caves, swing from trees and compete to see who could jump the highest. Quite often, we were bribed to water the orchards, make cheese and help to bring in the harvest in exchange for pocket money that we squandered on junk food, usually a Snickers bar and a Pepsi. My idea of fun was to set up shop just outside the house, my toy wagon overflowing with seasonal produce: corn, chickpeas, apples, anything I could sell to ghostly foot traffic. Needless to say, my only customer was my jeddo.

In the autumn, my father and grandmother, would make jam, tomato purée, ketchup, apple vinegar, pickles and other *mouneh*, or preserves. My siblings and I would often help with the shelling of the pine nuts and the chickpeas. If the chickpeas were harvested while they were still green, we enjoyed them like sugar-snap peas, otherwise they were left a little longer to wither, then laid out to dry on the roof. Once dry, we would all join together, stepping and grinding to split the pods and release the seeds. The results of our labours were stored in the mouneh room, a full-sized chamber dedicated to the winter's provisions.

We surrendered our appetites to the supremacy of the land and the generous array of ingredients it would gift to us. No matter how dire the situation became in our war-torn country, our kitchen table always remained plentiful – a representation not of my father's pocket but rather his appetite and zeal for life. So it was in the mountains of Lebanon that my connection with the land and with the food that came from it was truly nurtured.

The peal of Taco Bell

By the age of ten, I suddenly found myself back in Houston with my mother, newly born brother and sisters, meeting another side of my family that I had only heard of or seen in pictures. In the US, I learned to befriend Taco Bell, Wendy's and Jack in the Box. I fell in love with Campbell's soup (the mushroom imposter one, to be precise), SpaghettiOs and Ramen noodle soup.

The few wholesome dishes I can remember eating were a rocking bowl of chilli and some sizzling, hickory-smoked ribs that my grandfather would make every so often. Of course, there was always Thanksgiving dinner, but even then, the green bean casserole was made straight from the tin. My mother's exhaustive work schedule meant she had less time to cook for us, but when she did, she relished making any of the Lebanese dishes she'd picked up from my father, grandmother and aunts. Often, she would treat us to a meal at the local Greek restaurant, which was the next best thing. And so, in many ways and like a spinning globe, my life had been flipped upside down, if food is any good indicator.

Home is where the belly is

My raging appetite for home soon steered me back to Lebanon once again. By now the 15-year-long civil war in Lebanon was blown out like a trick candle and the country was trying to rebuild itself.

My French and Arabic had been temporarily buried away and I had become a born-again American. A vain teenager by now, I was completely preoccupied with calories and dizzied with the task of reducing my intake of fat to zero, if I could only figure out how while still chewing food. I consumed countless fat-free fads like a glutton consumes cake.

It wouldn't be long before the unrelenting spoon in my father's hand would rekindle my cravings. Living in Lebanon and spending summers in the south of France, my distant love affair with real, honest food would find its way back to my heart.

Eventually, my siblings followed suit to Lebanon and, as the eldest sister, I was promoted to chief household feeder. It's here that I really began to appreciate my love for cooking and for feeding others. More importantly, though, I discovered a cheap and rewarding form of therapy.

Back Stateside again

Fresh into my twenties, I wandered back Stateside, hoping for a bigger poke at life. I drifted aimlessly, chasing lands with flashing neon signs to nickname home. It took a few extended pit stops in Montreal and Houston before I cosied up in Miami with my British flame, now husband, Chris.

Between finding houses for people to buy, flats to rent and mortgages to sign, I managed to gain a reputation as both a wild child and a snow trader to the Inuit. With a heavy workload ahead, I would spend long, therapeutic Saturdays cooking the foods of my homeland, not just to nourish us through the week, but also to satiate the longing. As I whisked, chopped and stirred, as I smelled, tasted and watched others savour each bite, I could fleetingly stumble across that comfortable feeling of belonging. Barbecues were ablaze nearly every weekend; stray friends, relentless sunshine and unceasing home-cooked Lebanese food meant we almost had it all figured out. And it was during those days in Miami that the idea of a cookbook came to exist, one day in my retirement.

As time passed, we moved on to the even sunnier shores of Maui, Hawaii, where I managed Lahaina Store Grill and Oyster Bar. Chained to the gates of a 500-seater restaurant, I gained force (and weight) by eating island-sized portions of oysters, tuna (poke) and seafood chowder.

But Island Fever would soon catch up with Chris and me, chucking us into the chills of London on an early February morning. Between the aching temperature drop, a brand new culture and a very naked wardrobe, I struggled to brace myself against the screeching and howling winds of change. So, I cooked and I cooked, because that was all that made sense, and here I am now writing that cookbook but not yet retired.

Aromas drifting from the past

The Middle East cradles an ancient cuisine; one of the oldest in the world. It is a cuisine engraved in the tablets of history, although foreign policies, the clash of civilizations and a concern to travel to the region, have kept it but a whisper beneath the dust.

Of course, that's not to downplay a much-deserved tribute to pioneering cookery writers who have championed the cuisine of this region, notable amongst them Claudia Roden, Paula Wolfert, Charles Perry, Arto Der Haroutunian, Anissa Helou, Najmeh Batmanglij and Margaret Shaida. However, the cuisines have not yet achieved the celebratory recognition of the food of France, Italy, Spain, India or China.

Set the clock back several hundred years however, and there was a time in Europe when Middle Eastern food was more than trendy. During the Middle Ages, Islam was the most advanced civilization in the world, contributing vastly to the advancement of Europe in the spheres of science, technology, medicine, art, architecture and food. Over time, with Muslim expansionism and the Crusaders' travels to the Holy Lands, trade expanded and flourished, and spices and exotic ingredients flowed along the Spice Routes, greatly influencing the European palate. Christmas pudding, gingerbread, coffee, almond paste, rice pudding, cinnamon, nutmeg and saffron can all be traced through the pages of old cookery books.

Over the last decade, mezze has settled well on Western dining room tables, and almost everyone knows its main ambassadors: hummus, tabbouleh and vine leaves. But there still exists a vast and distinct culinary heritage that remains unexplored: wholesome stews, exotic casseroles and a range of home cooking that routinely welcomes home hungry school children and soothes the appetites of tired workers. These are the dishes that feed the peasants and the affluent alike, and many are dishes that have drifted in straight from the past.

Culinary footprints

With Arabic being the common language of the territories that make up the Middle East, most dishes across the region share the same name, with their diversity concealed in the seasonings and preparation methods. This also lends a friendly culinary rivalry between the countries of the region, where the few dishes that are specialities of a particular country become integral to its national identity. Take *musakhan*, for instance. While popular in both Palestine and Jordan, ask a Palestinian and they will swear it's their own culinary treasure.

Middle Eastern food has also been influenced by visiting cultures, as peoples from both East and West have danced and mingled on Middle Eastern soil, each leaving behind a footprint from its own tradition without troubling the fundamental flavours. For example, Persian, Iraqi and Gulf cuisines share many similarities and, while they also show traces of Mediterranean influences, they are, in particular, more abundant in meat, overflowing with rice dishes, and have taken much of their use of spices from India.

The Mediterranean cuisines of Turkey, Lebanon, Syria, Palestine, Jordan and North Africa use prolific amounts of pulses, grains, nuts, citrus fruits, garlic, fresh herbs, allspice and to some extent olive oil.

Eating the Middle Eastern way

In a Middle Eastern kitchen, fresh ingredients are celebrated in tune with the seasons or conserved as part of the ritual of preservation; simple yet clever. Real home-style dishes revolve around humble vegetables and grains, which are used to extend the limited amounts of meat that may be available. While an abundance of invigorating spices prevail in the cuisine, heat for the most part does not dwell in it. Exceptions can be found in some of the dishes of North Africa, Turkey, Palestine and Yemen.

Garlic, lemon and fresh herbs feature heavily and there is an affectionate respect for marrying sweet and sour tones with the use of verjuice, pomegranate molasses and citrus fruit. Yogurt is enjoyed on its own, as labneh, or as an integral part of many dishes – so much so that it's hard to imagine this cuisine without it. Of even more significance, though, is the use of bread. Not only nutritional, it's served with every meal, however humble or lavish, and used interchangeably with or even replacing cutlery (for most in the region, eating many of the dishes without bread to mop up the juices is inconceivable). Moreover, it's also considered a gift from God, to be cherished and honoured. So intricate to the culture is bread, and the ritual surrounding its breaking, that a well-known proverb demonstrates the intimacy and unbreakable bonds of friendship it represents: "there is bread and salt between us".

The generous table

Religion and landscape have contributed to the strict notions of hospitality in the Middle East, lavishing this ancient culture with virtues, customs and overwhelming etiquettes. A Middle Eastern meal is a titillating contradiction to the rigid, three-course Western meal. In fact, it begins well before anyone sits down at the table. Guests are always greeted with tea and a selection of dried fruit, nuts and pastries to unfasten their appetite for the real feast.

The meal that follows is relaxed and fluid and, depending on location and social class, diners may gather around a table or a *sofrah*, which may be as simple as a cloth laid out on the floor. The table is adorned like a glistening Byzantine empress, with a wide variety of dishes, served in a quick procession. Guests may use bread instead of cutlery to scoop up food from the communal dishes or from their own plates. One can expect to be urged towards second and third helpings, so a wise diner eats less on the first helping. The more you eat, the more pleasure and pride your host experiences, feeling they have done their job well in taking good care of you. Desserts are not usually eaten after a meal, although guests may enjoy fresh fruits and sweet pastries with their tea. This overwhelming generosity is not only the preserve of the wealthy; genuine hospitality is shown right across the social scale, sometimes even beyond a family's means.

A culinary marriage

Growing up, I repeatedly heard my father quote the Chinese philosopher, Confucius: "Study the past if you would define the future." This would become a philosophy to which I prescribe, especially when contemplating Middle Eastern cuisine. I am as fascinated by the history of our cuisine, its ancient recipes, techniques and rituals, as I am by the superb new dishes it can inspire.

This philosophy, though, is not always welcome when approaching such a deep-rooted cuisine. More than once, I have come up against relatives who have challenged the most miniscule alteration I have made to a dish, outraged by the fact that I dared to call it by the same name. "This is not how you make *moghrabieh*!", "No, no, you cannot put cumin in *kebbeh*! What, are you crazy?" You see, although Middle Eastern and North African culinary traditions celebrate an abundance of regional variations that have been passed down over the years without precise measurements, each family and each village has become chained to its own set beliefs.

A few brave chefs have begun dabbling with modern Middle Eastern cuisine, among them Greg Malouf, though this is still a fairly new concept. The result is that we now have a large blank canvas to begin working on, and this is what excites me: cooking the foods of my childhood while knowing that there is a vast expanse of wonder and innovation to look forward to. All we need to do is to grasp the opportunity without fear or hesitation. We are not disrespecting our past or our traditions but, rather, admiring where they have brought us and, when coupled with our present, where they might lead us.

The jewelled kitchen

Developing the recipes for my first book has been both a revelation of the Middle Eastern and North African culinary traditions and a tantalizing glimpse at the possibilities that lie ahead. I like to think of this book as an ode to the treasured dishes of the past, embracing a creative and contemporary approach. I hope it will ignite (and feed) your curiosity as it has inspired and excited my own.

Over the following chapters you'll find ideas for marvellous mezze, poultry, meat, seafood and vegetarian dishes. Some of these beautiful dishes can be thrown together from scratch in a matter of minutes, while more ambitious dishes are made easy with clear instructions and clever cooking techniques.

I have also indulged the sweet tooth of my childhood to tempt you with recipes for irresistible desserts and delicate pastries. The final chapter will help you master the cornerstones of the cuisine, with recipes for breads, dips, condiments, spice mixes, stocks, cheese and pastry, as well as advice on how to prepare and cook rice and chickpeas perfectly.

With this book you can explore the Persian love of herbs and fragrance, the hearty and comforting dishes of the Mediterranean, and the rich variety of ingredients celebrated by the cuisines of the Gulf, as you turn humble ingredients into a beguiling array of spectacular, contemporary dishes.

The Middle Eastern & North African pantry

All of the authentic ingredients used in this book are readily available online or from specialist grocers, but you may feel unsure about using some of the more exotic ingredients such as *mahlab* or Aleppo pepper. Don't worry. The glossary at the back of the book will help you learn more about how to source, prepare and store any unfamiliar ingredients, as well as suggesting suitable alternatives.

It's always best to use high-quality ingredients. Remember, too, that all ingredients are not born alike. A tomato in Britain will taste entirely different from one in, say, Lebanon, and that can affect the harmony of a tomato-based stew. An aubergine you purchased this week can taste very different from the one you enjoyed two weeks ago. The length of time your spice has been sitting on the shelf will, more or less, determine the quantity required, as its potency reduces over time. And then there is the fluctuating taste of lemons, some more acidic than others, while some of us have more or less tolerance for sour flavours. And let's not forget the level of spice: if you are not an avid lover of spicy food and a dish sounds like it's going to be too hot, reduce the quantity of spices and adjust as you cook. It's all a matter of taste.

The breath of inspiration

Recipes, elaborate instructions, precise measurements; this is the stuff that fumbles me. For while I am very aware that many do not feel comfortable without these specifics, I become stifled, flustered in my own domain, stumbling as I try to stay true to a recipe.

Middle Eastern recipes are passed down over the centuries, most often from mother to daughter or within the female community, but precise weights and measures are rarely part of the instruction. A large spoonful of this, an Arabic coffee cup of that, a squeeze of lemon, just enough water ... these are the units of measure in a Middle Eastern kitchen, with the emphasis on constant tasting and adjustment.

In the Middle East and North Africa, cooking truly is an instinctive art form. In the Middle East we say a good cook has *nafas* which, directly translated, means "breath", but when used in the context of cooking means "flair"; for there is an association with the sense of smell, too – of inspiration.

Although I have given precise measurements throughout, nothing is rigid or set in stone (baking aside). So rather than slavishly using scales or measuring jugs instead rely on the most powerful tools at your disposal: your senses. Listen to the bubbling liquid, look at the vibrant colours, feel the texture but, above all, smell the aromas and taste your dish as you cook – you can't taste too much. Only then will you be able to see if your meal needs more nurturing or if it just wants to be left alone.

Whether you are cooking for your immediate family or a crowd of friends, the objective is to create an enjoyable meal that evokes comfort and happiness. As you've heard many others say, cooking is meant to be fun, not serious. Run with your senses and, most importantly, enjoy yourself.

Cooking and eating are among life's greatest pleasures and as my uncle always says to me, "*Kelé w nsee hammeek*" – "Eat and you shall forget your worries."

mezze

Silky Chickpea & Lamb Soup

SERVES 4
PREPARATION TIME: 30 minutes,
  plus preparing the starter, soaking
  the chickpeas and making the
  preserved lemon (optional), and
  making the stock
COOKING TIME: 1½ hours, plus
  cooking the chickpeas until tender
  (optional)

2 tbsp rye flour (optional)

2 tbsp strong bread flour (optional)

350g/12oz lamb shank

¼ tsp ground cardamom

¼ tsp ground cumin

¼ tsp smoked paprika

¼ tsp ground coriander

¼ tsp ground cinnamon

700g/1lb 9oz tomatoes

20g/¾oz salted butter or smen

1 onion, finely chopped

4 garlic cloves, roughly chopped

5cm/2in piece of root ginger, peeled
and finely chopped

2l/70fl oz/8 cups Vegetable Stock
(see page 211)

a pinch of ground saffron (optional)

125g/4½oz/½ cup dried chickpeas,
soaked overnight and cooked (see
page 215), or 250g/9oz/1 cup tinned
chickpeas, drained and rinsed

250g/9oz/1⅓ cups brown lentils,
rinsed

1 bay leaf

1 wedge of Preserved Lemon (see
page 212), rind rinsed and finely
chopped, or zest of half a lemon

1 tbsp finely chopped coriander
leaves, plus extra for sprinkling

sea salt and freshly ground black
pepper

a few pitted dates, to serve

1 lemon, quartered, to squeeze

warm Arabic Bread (optional, see
page 217), to serve

During the holy month of Ramadan in North Africa, this silky textured soup is the first dish with which the fast is broken. It goes well with Pan-Fried Squares (see page 149).

1 If you are using the starter, which will give a thicker, smoother soup, early in the morning of the first day, put 10g/¼oz of the rye flour and 10g/¼oz of the strong bread flour in a mixing bowl and mix together. Pour over 1 tablespoon lukewarm water and mix well. Cover the starter with kitchen paper and set aside in a warm place (22–25°C/72–77°F).

2 During the morning of the following day, "feed" the starter with the remaining flours and about 2 teaspoons lukewarm water, stirring very well to combine. Set aside, covered as above, for a further 8 hours.

3 Rub the lamb shank with the cardamom, cumin, smoked paprika, coriander and cinnamon and season with some salt. Set aside.

4 With a sharp knife, cut a cross in the skin of each tomato, then put them in a heatproof bowl and cover with boiling water. Leave to stand for 2–3 minutes or until the skins have split, then drain. Plunge into cold water to stop them cooking, then peel off the skins and discard. Slice in half and scoop out the seeds, then finely chop the flesh.

5 Melt the butter in a heavy-based saucepan over a medium heat. Add the onion, cover the pan and reduce the heat to low, then leave to sweat, stirring often, for 5 minutes or until softened.

6 Increase the heat to medium, add the lamb and any loose spices and sear for 3 minutes on each side. Add the garlic and ginger and cook for a further minute until aromatic, then add the tomatoes, stock, saffron, if using, chickpeas, lentils and bay leaf.

7 Cover the pan, increase the heat to high and bring to the boil, then reduce the heat to medium-low and simmer, covered, for 1 hour or until the lentils are soft and the meat is tender. Discard the bay leaf.

8 Remove the lamb from the pan and cut away the meat into small bite-sized pieces, then return the meat to the pan with the bone. You can extract the marrow with a narrow spoon or skewer, if you like.

9 Dilute the starter, if using, with 100ml/3½fl oz/scant ½ cup water, stir well, then slowly pour it into the pan, stirring for about 20 minutes or until the mixture has thickened. Stir in the preserved lemon and coriander and season with pepper. Ladle into bowls, sprinkle with coriander and serve with dates, lemon quarters and warm Arabic Bread, if you like.

Kishk, Lamb & Kale Soup

SERVES 4
PREPARATION TIME: 10 minutes
COOKING TIME: 20 minutes

50g/1¾oz salted butter

1 garlic bulb, cloves separated and finely chopped or crushed

1 tbsp Aleppo pepper flakes or crushed chilli flakes

1 tsp ground allspice

2 tbsp dried mint

400g/14oz minced lamb

150g/5½oz kale or spinach, finely chopped

125g/4½oz/1 cup kishk

4 tbsp pine nuts

mint leaves, to sprinkle (optional)

sea salt and freshly ground black pepper

warm Arabic Bread (see page 217), to serve

This dish celebrates the basic ingredients available to a villager in rural areas of Lebanon as well as in Syria, Palestine and Egypt during the winter months. Kishk is a fine powder made from bulgur that has been fermented with yogurt or water and left to dry in the sun for several days. Kishk can be found in some Middle Eastern grocers and can also be found under the Greek/Cypriot name trachana, which is usually served with grilled halloumi. Trachana is usually sold in a coarser grain resembling medium bulgur and can be ground in a spice grinder to a fine flour. In Lebanon, awarma (lamb confit) is usually added to the dish, but here I've used minced lamb because it's easier to source.

1 Melt the butter in a large heavy-based saucepan over a medium-low heat, add the garlic and fry for about 1 minute until aromatic. Add the Aleppo pepper flakes, allspice and dried mint and stir well to combine.

2 Add the lamb and cook for 4–5 minutes until browned, stirring often. Add the kale and mix well, letting it wilt for 1–2 minutes.

3 Sprinkle in the kishk and stir to combine. Heat through and then pour in 1l/35fl oz/4 cups hot water a little at a time, stirring well to combine and remove any lumps. Keep adding water and stirring it in until the kishk is diluted and the mixture is creamy and brothy. Adjust the amount of water based on the desired consistency of the soup. Season to taste with salt and pepper.

4 Toast the pine nuts in a heavy-based pan over a medium heat for 1–2 minutes until golden and fragrant, shaking the pan often. Ladle the soup into bowls and sprinkle the toasted pine nuts and the mint, if using, over the top. Serve with some warm Arabic Bread.

Note: The soup thickens quickly, so if you leave it for a while, it may need further diluting with hot water.

Spiced naked mini sausages

SERVES 4
PREPARATION TIME: 20 minutes,
  plus marinating
COOKING TIME: 12 minutes

200g/7oz finely minced beef

200g/7oz finely minced lamb

1½ tsp sea salt, plus extra for
  seasoning

5cm/2in piece of root ginger, peeled
  and finely chopped

2 tsp ground coriander

2 tsp white pepper

½ tsp ground nutmeg

1 mild red chilli, deseeded and
  finely chopped

½ tsp ground mahlab (optional)

½ tsp ground cloves

4 garlic cloves, finely chopped

3 tbsp pine nuts

5 tbsp white wine

3 tbsp sunflower oil

1 tbsp lemon juice or pomegranate
  molasses (optional)

8 eggs

sumac, for dusting

freshly ground black pepper

TO SERVE
tomato slices

fresh greens

warm Arabic Bread (see page 217)

Red-hot Roasties (optional, see
  page 40)

This maqaneq recipe is an ideal winter breakfast dish; just make sure you have some Arabic bread on hand to soak up every last trickle of sunshine on a plate. Traditionally, the sausages would be in casings, but shaping your own makes them more home kitchen friendly.

1 Put the beef and lamb in a mixing bowl with the salt, ginger, coriander, white pepper, nutmeg, chilli, mahlab, if using, cloves, garlic, pine nuts and white wine. Mix well, cover and leave to marinate in the fridge for 24 hours (or up to 72 hours if you are preparing ahead).

2 When ready to cook, begin shaping the meat mixture into small, finger-like sausages about 5cm/2in long and 2.5cm/1in wide, or the size of an English cocktail sausage. You should be able to make about 40.

3 Heat the oil in a wide, heavy-based frying pan over a high heat until the oil is sizzling, then add the sausages. Reduce the heat to medium and cook the sausages for 5–7 minutes, tossing them gently every once in a while, until cooked through. Add the lemon juice, if using.

4 Carefully break one egg at a time over the sausages, keeping some space between each egg, though it's fine if they just touch. You may need to do this in two separate frying pans. Let them settle for the first minute, then tilt the pan a few times to get the egg whites running before basting the eggs with the juice from the pan so they cook through. Season to taste with salt and pepper.

5 Cook for a further minute until the eggs have set to your liking, then sprinkle with sumac. Transfer the eggs and sausages to plates and serve with tomato slices, fresh greens, warm Arabic Bread and Red-hot Roasties, if you like.

eggs poached in a tomato and pepper stew

SERVES 4
PREPARATION TIME: 15 minutes,
 plus roasting the peppers and
 making the sausages
COOKING TIME: 1 hour 20 minutes

500g/1lb 2oz mixed roasted peppers
 (see Roasted Vegetables, page 216)

1kg/2lb 4oz tomatoes

2 tbsp olive oil

1 garlic bulb, cloves separated and
 roughly chopped

1 tsp Aleppo pepper flakes or
 crushed chilli flakes

2 tbsp sunflower oil

¼ recipe quantity uncooked Spiced
 Naked Mini Sausages (see page 21)
 or sliced chorizo

8 eggs

1 tbsp finely chopped parsley leaves,
 to sprinkle

sea salt and freshly ground black
 pepper

Red-hot Roasties (see page 40), to
 serve

warm Arabic Bread (see page 217)
 or any good crusty bread, to serve

This recipe for the famous dish shakshoukah is a demonstration of the North African infatuation with cooked salads. The sauce in which the eggs are poached is great to make ahead because the longer it sits, the more the flavours develop.

1 Slice off the tops of the roasted peppers, discard the seeds and cut the flesh into 2cm/¾in strips.

2 With a sharp knife, cut a cross in the skin of each tomato, then put them in a heatproof bowl and cover with boiling water. Leave to stand for 2–3 minutes or until the skins have split, then drain. Plunge into cold water to stop them cooking, then peel off the skins and discard. Slice in half and scoop out the seeds, then finely chop the flesh.

3 Put a heavy-based saucepan over a medium-low heat. Add the olive oil and the garlic and cook for about 1 minute or until the garlic is aromatic. Reduce the heat to low, add the tomatoes and Aleppo pepper flakes and stir to combine, then cover with a lid and bring to the boil. Reduce the heat to low and simmer, covered, for about 30 minutes, stirring often. Add the roasted peppers before adding salt to taste, then simmer for a further 20 minutes.

4 Put a large, non-stick frying pan over a medium heat, and heat the sunflower oil. Add the mini sausages and fry for 5–7 minutes until cooked through and golden on all sides, tossing them gently every once in a while. Pour the tomato and pepper sauce over the top and heat through for 2–3 minutes.

5 Make 8 small craters in the mixture and crack an egg into each one, making sure they are engulfed halfway by the tomato stew. Season the eggs with salt and pepper, cover the pan and cook for a few minutes until the egg whites have turned opaque and the yolks have set but are still soft. Sprinkle with parsley and serve with Red-hot Roasties and warm Arabic Bread.

kafta snugged scotch eggs

SERVES 4
PREPARATION TIME: 25 minutes
COOKING TIME: 7 minutes

6 eggs

1 onion, quartered

1 handful of mixed herbs (mint, dill, coriander and parsley leaves)

1 mild green chilli, deseeded and roughly chopped (optional)

4 garlic cloves, crushed with the blade of a knife

200g/7oz minced lamb

1 tsp ground allspice

85ml/2¾fl oz/generous ⅓ cup Greek yogurt, to serve

½ tsp dried mint

sunflower oil, for deep-frying

40g/1½oz/⅓ cup plain flour

85g/3oz/½ cup fine bulgur wheat (grade 1)

2 tsp black cumin seeds

sea salt and freshly ground black pepper

4 tsp pomegranate molasses, to serve

Red-hot Roasties (see page 40), to serve

The key to a perfect Scotch egg is a pool of velvety yolk, a moist, meaty rim, and a robust, crunchy crust achieved here with a fine-grade bulgur. Hard-boiling the eggs is a sin!

1 Fill a saucepan with plenty of water, add a generous pinch of salt and place over a high heat. Add four of the eggs and bring to a gentle boil, then cook for 3½ minutes for soft-boiled eggs, or longer if preferred. Fill a large bowl with iced water and once the eggs are cooked, drain well and immediately transfer to the iced water to stop them cooking and to make peeling easier. Leave the eggs for about 10 minutes, then peel.

2 Meanwhile, put the onion in a food processor and pulse to a rough paste. Remove the paste from the bowl and squeeze out as much of the liquid as possible if the paste appears too wet. Return the mixture to the food processor, add the herbs, chilli, if using, and three of the garlic cloves and pulse for 1–2 minutes until the mixture forms a fine paste.

3 Put the lamb in a large bowl and season with salt and allspice. Add the herb and onion mixture and mix with your hands until incorporated. Don't overwork it or the meat will toughen. Cover and set aside.

4 Finely chop or crush the remaining garlic clove, put it in a bowl with the Greek yogurt and dried mint and stir well. Set aside.

5 Preheat a deep-fat fryer to 190°C/365°F. The oil will be hot enough when a cube of bread added to the oil browns within 1 minute. Prepare three bowls: in one, sift in the flour and season with salt and pepper; in another, whisk the remaining eggs and season with salt and pepper, and in the last bowl mix together the bulgur with the black cumin seeds.

6 Roll each peeled egg in the flour mixture, then wet your hands with a little water and flatten a quarter of the lamb mixture into a very flat, thin patty. Enclose the egg in the lamb mixture, making sure it's covered and the mixture is smooth. Use damp fingers to help seal the meat together. Repeat with the remaining eggs and lamb mixture.

7 Gently roll the Scotch eggs in the whisked egg mixture then in the bulgur. Deep-fry for 5–7 minutes until golden and crisp. Using a slotted spoon, remove the scotch eggs from the oil and drain on kitchen paper. Serve warm with the yogurt dip, pomegranate molasses and some Red-hot Roasties.

minced lamb & onion crescents

SERVES 4
PREPARATION TIME: 40 minutes,
 plus making the pastry
COOKING TIME: 10 minutes

2 tbsp sunflower oil, plus extra for
 deep-frying

1 onion, very finely chopped

125g/4½oz finely minced lamb

½ tsp sea salt

1 tsp ground cinnamon

1 tsp ground allspice

1 tbsp pomegranate molasses

2 tbsp pine nuts

flour, for dusting

1 recipe quantity Savoury Pastry
 Dough (see page 213)

TO SERVE
Hummus (optional, see page 27)

Yogurt, Cucumber & Mint Salad
 (optional, see page 66)

Lamb & Bulgur Torpedoes (optional,
 see page 28)

Dynamite Chilli Cigars (optional, see
 page 38)

Spinach & Sumac Turnovers
 (optional, see page 37)

These savoury pastries are known as sambousek. They are essential to any dazzling dinner party. Pass them around with drinks and no one will ask when dinner is going to be served.

1 Heat the oil in a heavy-based saucepan over a medium heat and cook the onion until it's soft and translucent. Add the lamb and brown for about 5 minutes, stirring often. Add the salt, cinnamon, allspice and pomegranate molasses and stir well to incorporate, then remove from the heat.

2 Toast the pine nuts in a heavy-based pan over a medium heat for 1–2 minutes until golden and fragrant, shaking the pan often. Add the toasted pine nuts to the lamb mixture and mix well. Set aside to cool.

3 Meanwhile, flour the work surface and roll out the pastry dough into a large circle about 2mm/1⁄16 in thick. You may find it helps to flip the dough a few times during the rolling stage, using more flour as needed.

4 Using a pastry cutter or cup, cut out circles about 8cm/3¼in in diameter. Re-roll any pastry scraps and cut out more circles. You should end up with about 20 circles. Place about 1 teaspoon of the lamb mixture just off-centre of each circle, fold the dough over and, using your thumb and index finger, seal the edges together, thinning them as you go to create a half-moon shape. Return to the end that is furthest from you, and begin pleating the sealed edge with your fingers by making tight, overlapping diagonal folds. Repeat until all the dough has been used. (You can freeze the uncooked parcels at this stage in an airtight, freezer-safe container for up to 2 months, if you like. Allow to thaw briefly before cooking as below.)

5 Fill a saucepan one-third full with oil and heat over a high heat until the oil reaches 180°C/350°F. Test the temperature with a thermometer or by dipping in one side of the stuffed pastry – if the oil sizzles, it's ready. Alternatively, preheat a deep-fat fryer. Deep-fry the parcels in batches, if needed, until golden. Depending on the level of the oil, you may need to turn them over midway and they may take about 2 minutes per side. Don't leave them unattended, as they can quickly brown and burn. They should be a light golden colour.

6 Using a slotted spoon, transfer the crescents to a plate lined with kitchen paper. Serve with a selection of mezze dishes, if you like. You can also freeze the pastries at this stage for later use, popping them back into the oven (after thawing) for a couple of minutes until hot.

Whipped hummus with lamb

SERVES 4
PREPARATION TIME: 20 minutes,
  plus soaking the chickpeas
  (optional)
COOKING TIME: 15 minutes, plus
  cooking the chickpeas until they
  are very soft (optional)

FOR THE HUMMUS
2 tbsp tahini

2 tbsp lemon juice, plus extra if
  needed

100g/3½oz/½ cup dried chickpeas,
  soaked overnight and cooked
  (see page 215) or 200g/7oz/1 cup
  tinned chickpeas

1 garlic clove, finely chopped

3 small ice cubes

a pinch of ground allspice

sea salt

FOR THE LAMB
15g/½oz salted butter

1 small onion, finely chopped

1 tbsp pine nuts

2 garlic cloves, finely chopped

85g/3oz minced lamb

1½ tsp pomegranate molasses

a pinch of ground allspice

pomegranate seeds (see page 216),
  to sprinkle

chopped mint leaves, to sprinkle

sea salt and freshly ground black
  pepper

TO SERVE
warm Arabic Bread (see page 217)
  or Toasted Triangles (see page 49)

Hummus means chickpea in Arabic. This is a great blank canvas recipe for the simple hummus b tahini dip everyone is now familiar with (see steps 1–4). Adding lamb or preserved meat (awarma) is one serving option which is traditional in the Levant, but feel free to omit the lamb topping or allow your imagination to take over. Olive oil is not an ingredient used to make whipped hummus and is only used as a garnish.

1 To make the hummus, put the tahini, lemon juice and 1 tablespoon water in a bowl and mix until well incorporated.

2 Drain the chickpeas, then immediately loosen their skins by rinsing them under cold running water several times. Cover the chickpeas with water and swish them with your hands several times to loosen any more skins. Discard any of the loose skins. Drain the chickpeas again.

3 Immediately transfer the drained chickpeas and the garlic to a food processor and pulse for about 30 seconds. Add an ice cube to the chickpea mixture and pulse again until it's incorporated, then repeat with the remaining two ice cubes until a smooth paste is formed.

4 Pour in the tahini and lemon mixture and pulse again until it forms a smooth, well-blended purée. Add the allspice and season to taste with salt, then pulse once more for about 1 minute until all is well incorporated. If the hummus is too thick, add a little more lemon juice and/or water (being careful not to dilute the zesty flavours). Transfer the hummus to a serving bowl, cover and set aside.

5 To make the lamb mixture, melt the butter in a heavy-based frying pan over a medium heat, add the onion and cook for 3–4 minutes until soft and translucent. Stir in the pine nuts and cook for a further 2 minutes until they just start to brown.

6 Add the garlic to the pan and mix well, then cook for about 1 minute until aromatic. Add the lamb and stir well, then cook for no more than 3–4 minutes, until just browned. Pour the pomegranate molasses over the lamb mixture, stir in the allspice and season with salt and pepper.

7 Create a crater in the middle of the hummus and spoon the hot meat and any juices into the well. Sprinkle the lamb with pomegranate seeds and mint and serve with warm Arabic Bread.

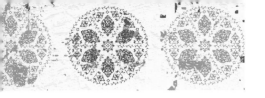

lamb & bulgur torpedoes

SERVES 4
PREPARATION TIME: 1 hour
COOKING TIME: 25 minutes

175g/6oz/scant 1 cup fine bulgur wheat (grade 1)

2 tbsp sunflower oil, plus extra for deep-frying

1 red onion, thinly sliced

2 tbsp pine nuts

350g/12oz finely minced lamb or beef

1 tsp ground cinnamon

1½ tsp ground allspice

1 tbsp pomegranate molasses

2 tsp sea salt

½ tsp ground cumin

1 tsp dried marjoram

1 tsp dried basil

1 tsp crumbled dried edible rose petals

7–8 mint leaves, finely chopped

1 large onion, quartered

freshly ground black pepper

Yogurt, Cucumber & Mint Salad (see page 66), to serve

warm Arabic Bread (see page 217), to serve

Kebbeh is the name for a family of dishes known in Lebanon and Syria where they are the national dish. They are widely popular across the Middle East, and in Iraq in particular. Traditionally, meat was ingeniously stretched to help nourish a large family by pounding it with very fine bulgur to form a fine paste. Kebbeh varieties are plentiful across the Middle East: served raw with fresh mint and spring onions in a dish somewhat similar to steak tartare and essential to an authentic mezze; spread on a baking tray and layered with onion slices and pine nuts before being baked; moulded into a variety of shapes, such as these small torpedo-shaped croquets (named "Syrian torpedoes" by the British soldiers in Syria during the Second World War because of their shape), which can also be served as part of a mezze menu; or cooked from raw in yogurt or a tahini mixture for a more hearty, winter-warming dish. There are also vegetable and seafood versions of kebbeh. Our family recipe, which I share with you here, has a higher bulgur-to-meat ratio than traditional recipes and I have taken some inspiration from Southern Lebanon by using a herb and spice blend called kammouneh, which is used in a local variation of raw kebbeh called kebbet frakeh. For the best results with this recipe, ask your butcher to prepare the meat from either the leg or the shoulder by removing the bones, skin and fat, before mincing it twice.

1 Put the bulgur in a large bowl with 250ml/9fl oz/1 cup water and leave to soak for 10 minutes. If you cannot find very fine bulgur, grind or whizz medium bulgur until it resembles fine breadcrumbs.

2 Meanwhile, prepare the stuffing by heating half the oil in a frying pan over a medium heat and frying the red onion for 3–4 minutes until soft and translucent. Add the pine nuts and cook for a further minute, then add 100g/3½oz of the lamb and cook for 3–4 minutes until browned. Add the cinnamon, ½ teaspoon of the allspice, the pomegranate molasses and 1 teaspoon of the salt, then season with pepper to taste. Remove from the heat and set aside.

3 To make the kebbeh mixture, strain the soaked bulgur and squeeze out any excess liquid. Return the bulgur to the bowl and add the cumin, marjoram, basil and remaining allspice, along with the dried rose petals and mint and mix well.

4 Put the large onion in a food processor and pulse to a smooth paste. Strain the paste, pressing with the back of a wooden spoon to squeeze out any excess liquid. Add this to the bulgur mixture along with the remaining lamb and salt. Knead well for 4–5 minutes until well incorporated, then return to the food processor and pulse for 2–3 minutes until the mixture forms a smooth, cohesive paste, stopping the processor a few times to scrape the bowl and ensure even processing.

5 Make a taste test by heating the remaining oil in a frying pan over a medium heat. Mould 1 tablespoon of the kebbeh mixture into a flat disc and fry for 2–3 minutes until golden on both sides. Remove from the heat and leave to cool slightly, then taste and adjust the seasoning if needed.

6 Divide the remaining kebbeh mixture into 24 egg-sized balls using about 1 tablespoon of the mixture per ball. Have a small bowl of iced water on hand to dip your hands into to help with any "repairs" as you mould the balls.

7 Working with one kebbeh at a time, secure the kebbeh in the palm of one hand and use the index finger of the other hand to push a hole in the kebbeh as you rotate it, creating a hollow opening for the filling. Add about 1 teaspoonful of the meat filling, or more if required, and pinch the edges closed to seal the ball. Shape points at both ends so it resembles an American football or an egg-like shape. Repeat with the remaining kebbeh mixture and filling. Don't overfill, or they may burst. (If preparing the meatballs in advance, you can freeze them at this point in an airtight, freezer-safe container for up to 3 months. Cook from frozen for about 5 minutes or until golden brown.)

8 When you are ready to serve, pour enough oil into a large saucepan to deep-fry the balls and heat the oil over a high heat to 180°C/350°F. You can test if the oil is hot enough by pinching off a bit of meat or small piece of bread and dropping it into the oil: if it browns in 1 minute then the oil is hot enough. Fry the meatballs in batches (the number will depend on the size of the pan) for 4–6 minutes or until golden brown on all sides. Use a slotted spoon to transfer to a plate lined with kitchen paper. Serve immediately or at room temperature with a Yogurt, Cucumber and Mint Salad and warm Arabic Bread.

venison & sour cherry nests

SERVES 4
PREPARATION TIME: 25 minutes,
  plus making the spice mix
COOKING TIME: 30 minutes

85g/3oz salted butter

100g/3 ½oz kataifi or sheets of filo
pastry (defrosted if frozen), very
finely shredded

250g/9oz minced venison, lamb or
beef

1 ½ tsp peeled and grated root
ginger

4 garlic cloves, finely chopped

a pinch of Lebanese Seven Spices
(see page 211)

6 tbsp kirsch

1 star anise, cracked in half

a pinch of ground allspice

250g/9oz morello cherries in syrup,
drained

1 tbsp pomegranate molasses

25g/1oz/¼ cup walnuts, roughly
chopped

sea salt and freshly ground black
pepper

*I've strayed from tradition here, as kebab karaz, as it's known
in Syria, is usually made with veal or lamb served on Arabic
bread. The sour cherry native to the Middle Eastern region is
small and dark crimson-red, and its kernels are ground to make
an aromatic powder, known as mahlab, which is used to
flavour breads and sweets. I've made the sauce with morello
cherries, although you can use fresh sour cherries when in
season, or dried sour cherries soaked in water overnight.*

1 Preheat the oven to 190°C/375°F/Gas 5. Melt 55g/2oz of the butter
in a frying pan. Remove the pan from the heat and toss the kataifi in
the melted butter, making sure to cover as many strands as you can as
you separate them into a loose pile with your fingers. Divide the kataifi
strands among the cups of a 24-cup mini-muffin pan with 2cm/¾in
cups (about 2.5g/⅛oz per muffin cup), pressing them into the bottom
and up the sides and tucking in any strands to make 24 pastry nests.
Bake in the oven for 15–20 minutes until crisp and golden.

2 Meanwhile, put the venison, ginger, garlic and spice mix in a bowl
and season to taste with salt and pepper. Mix well, then pinch off a
little of the mixture and roll it in the palm of your hands to create a ball
about the size of a golf ball. You should be able to make 24 meatballs.

3 Melt 20g/¾oz of the remaining butter in a heavy-based frying pan
over a medium heat and cook the meatballs for about 10 minutes,
turning often, until browned on all sides. Transfer the meatballs to a
plate, cover and keep warm.

4 Pour the kirsch into the frying pan, add the star anise and allspice
and mix well to get all the flavourful bits into the sauce, then boil for
1–2 minutes until it has reduced by half. Add the cherries and cook
for a further 3–4 minutes until the sauce is syrupy, stirring them
with a wooden spoon and breaking the cherries up into pieces. Add
the remaining butter and stir well to incorporate. Finally, stir in the
pomegranate molasses and sprinkle over the walnuts.

5 When the kataifi nests are ready, remove them from the pan and
transfer them to a large plate. Put one meatball into the hollow of each
kataifi nest.

6 Spoon the sauce over the meatballs and then serve as canapés. You
can wrap the nests in paper napkins before serving, if you like.

tuna tartare with chermoula

SERVES 4
PREPARATION TIME: 45 minutes,
  plus making the preserved lemon
  and grinding the saffron (optional)
COOKING TIME: 5 minutes

100g / 3½oz salted butter

1 egg white, beaten

1 tbsp clear honey

5 sheets of filo pastry (defrosted if
  frozen)

40g / 1½oz / ¼ cup sesame seeds

3 tbsp Greek yogurt

¼ tsp ground saffron or turmeric
  (optional, see page 212)

1 wedge of Preserved Lemon
  (see page 212), rind rinsed

280g / 10oz sushi-grade yellowfin
  tuna, salmon or scallops, chilled
  well

sea salt and freshly ground black
  pepper

FOR THE CHERMOULA
¼ tsp cumin seeds

1 handful of parsley leaves

1 handful of coriander leaves

2 dill sprigs

3cm / 1¼in piece of root ginger,
  peeled

1 small medium red chilli, deseeded
  and roughly chopped

1 fat garlic clove, crushed with the
  blade of a knife

1 wedge of Preserved Lemon
  (see page 212), rind rinsed

3 tbsp olive oil

sea salt

This is inspired by the Hawaiian poke I devoured on a daily basis when managing a restaurant in Maui. If you cannot find tuna, use sushi-grade salmon or scallops. Sear if you prefer.

1 Preheat the oven to 190°C/375°F/Gas 5. Melt the butter in a small pan, then pour it into a mixing bowl with the egg white, honey and a pinch of salt. Whisk until smooth and thick.

2 Remove the sheets of filo from their plastic packaging and cover them quickly with a damp kitchen towel. Place one sheet on a chopping board, brush it with a thin layer of the butter mixture, top with a second sheet and brush with more of the butter mixture. Repeat with the remaining filo sheets. The edges will crinkle as you lay each sheet, and you may need to align them gently with your fingers.

3 Sprinkle the sesame seeds evenly over the top sheet. Using a sharp knife or pastry wheel, cut the layered filo in half lengthways, then slice down the sheet every 10cm/4in, creating eight rectangles. Cut each rectangle diagonally in half. Carefully transfer the triangles to two baking sheets and bake for 4–5 minutes until golden. Transfer to a plate lined with kitchen paper to cool.

4 Meanwhile, to make the chermoula, toast the cumin seeds in a heavy-based pan over a medium heat for 1–2 minutes until fragrant, shaking the pan often. Transfer to a small food processor, add the parsley, coriander, dill, ginger, chilli, garlic and preserved lemon wedge, and pulse until it combines to form a fine paste. Drizzle in the oil and season with salt, then pulse to combine.

5 Put the yogurt in a separate bowl; add the saffron, if using, and salt to taste. Whisk with a hand blender until frothy. Finely chop the lemon wedge and stir it in.

6 Using a sharp, thin-bladed knife and a clean cutting board, slice the tuna into 1cm / ½in cubes. Divide the tuna into eight equal portions. Place a metal pastry ring about 5cm / 2in in diameter in the centre of a plate, spoon in about 1 teaspoon of the yogurt sauce, then 1 portion of the tuna, 1 teaspoon of the chermoula, and another portion of the tuna. Carefully remove the ring, then drizzle over 1 teaspoon of the yogurt sauce. Repeat with the remaining ingredients to make four servings. Season with salt and pepper and top each stack with 4 filo triangles.

artichokes with couscous

SERVES 4
PREPARATION TIME: 30 minutes,
  plus making the vegetable stock,
  and jam (optional)
COOKING TIME: 1 hour

100g/3 ½oz/ ½ cup couscous

15g/ ½oz butter

800ml/28fl oz/3 ½ cups Vegetable
  Stock (see page 211)

4 fresh artichokes, or 4 brined
  artichoke hearts

1 lemon, halved

4 garlic cloves, finely chopped

8 small anchovy fillets in oil, drained
  and roughly chopped

8 olives, pitted and roughly chopped

2 tsp capers, drained and rinsed

2 tbsp Burnt Tomato & Chilli Jam
  (see page 219) or finely chopped
  tomatoes

1 tbsp finely chopped mint leaves,
  to sprinkle

sea salt and freshly ground black
  pepper

This dish offers something for everyone. It's perfect if you want to knock something up very quickly, in which case you can use brined artichoke hearts and instant couscous. Otherwise, it's a great way to use fresh artichokes when in season, which makes for longer, but very rewarding, cooking.

1 Put the couscous in a bowl, add the butter and rub it into the couscous. Line the top half of a steamer with some muslin cloth and put the buttered couscous in the steamer basket. Pour the vegetable stock into the bottom half and place over a medium heat. Once the stock has come to the boil, place the steamer basket over it, cover and steam for 30 minutes or until the couscous is soft. Reserve any remaining stock.

2 Meanwhile, to prepare the artichoke hearts, begin by cutting off the stem close to the base and then peeling off the outer leaves of each artichoke either one-by-one or pulling off a few at a time (not too many, though, or you'll tear into the fleshy bottom). The leaves will get softer and smaller as you progress, and then you'll reach the fuzzy choke. Using a spoon or a paring knife, gently scrape out all the inner choke to leave a bowl-shaped cavity. You don't want any of the prickly hairs to remain. Quickly squeeze one of the lemon halves onto the artichoke hearts to prevent them from oxidizing and transfer them to a bowl filled with water and the juice of the remaining lemon half. Alternatively, if using brined artichoke hearts, rinse the brined hearts well and place in a bowl of water with a squeeze of lemon.

3 Toss the steamed couscous with the garlic, anchovies, olives, capers and jam. Season lightly with salt (the anchovies will already have made the dish salty) and pepper. Fill the cavity in each artichoke heart with the couscous mix. Stand the artichokes in a large heavy-based saucepan and pour over the reserved stock (diluted with more water if it has reduced: the stock should come to just below the top of the artichokes). Cook, partially covered, over a medium heat for 30 minutes or until the hearts are soft. Serve warm, sprinkled with mint.

mixed greens frittata

SERVES 4
PREPARATION TIME: 15 minutes,
 plus making the advieh
COOKING TIME: 20 minutes

1 tbsp dried barberries or
 cranberries (optional)

2 tbsp finely chopped parsley leaves

2 tbsp finely chopped coriander
 leaves

2 tbsp finely chopped tarragon
 leaves

2 tbsp finely chopped dill leaves

2 tbsp finely chopped chives

8 eggs

1 tsp baking powder

1 tsp Advieh 2 (see page 211)

40g/1½oz salted butter, of which
 15g/½oz softened and diced

1 tbsp chopped walnuts (optional)

55g/2oz feta, crumbled

dried edible rose petals, crumbled
 (optional)

sea salt and freshly ground pepper

TO SERVE
warm Thin Flatbread (see page 218)

lime wedges

Greek yogurt

side salad (optional)

This recipe is loosely based on kookoo sabzi ("kookoo" implies the use of an egg and "sabzi" means mixed greens), which is the most popular of all the Persian kookoos. An abundant and almost frivolous mix of herbs and vegetables, it's served during Nowruz, the Persian New Year festivities, and symbolizes new beginnings. Both the barberries and walnuts are optional, and are usually reserved for special occasions.

1 Put the barberries, if using, in a small bowl of water and leave to soak for 5 minutes, then drain. Use kitchen paper to pat out as much moisture as you can from the soaked barberries and the herbs.

2 Whisk the eggs vigorously in a large bowl with the baking powder, advieh, softened butter, herbs, barberries and walnuts, if using, and season with salt and pepper.

3 Melt the remaining butter in an ovenproof, non-stick frying pan over a high heat. When the butter begins to foam, pour in the egg and herb mixture and stir well, then reduce the heat and cook for 15 minutes until well risen and almost fully set on top. Sprinkle with the feta. Meanwhile, preheat the grill to high.

4 Place the pan under the grill and grill for about 5 minutes until golden on the top and just cooked.

5 Transfer to a plate and sprinkle with dried rose petals, if you like. Serve immediately with warm flatbread, lime wedges and yogurt. Alternatively, leave the frittata to cool and enjoy as a light snack with a simple salad.

Spinach & sumac turnovers

SERVES 4
PREPARATION TIME: 40 minutes,
 plus making the pastry
COOKING TIME: 10 minutes

80g/2¾oz spinach leaves or Swiss
 chard

1 tsp sea salt

1 small onion (about 55g/2oz), finely
 chopped

2 tbsp sumac

1 tsp ground allspice

2 tbsp olive oil, plus extra for
 greasing

a pinch of crushed chilli flakes
 (optional)

2 tbsp pine nuts

flour, for dusting

1 recipe quantity Savoury Pastry
 Dough (see page 213)

*The key to achieving dainty turnovers is to make the dough
slightly wet and the filling dry. Practise by making larger ones
first. The balance between onion and spinach is vital for
success, which is why I have specified the onion's weight.*

1 Wash the spinach and pat it dry, then chop finely. Put the spinach in
a bowl and sprinkle with ½ teaspoon of the salt, then rub it all together
very well until the spinach breaks down and water starts to drain out.
Leave to rest for about 5 minutes, then squeeze the spinach tightly to
remove the remaining liquid. Do this very well to ensure all the juice is
expelled, otherwise it will make sealing the parcels a difficult task.

2 Put the onion in another bowl and sprinkle with the remaining salt,
then rub it well for 1–2 minutes until it has softened. Squeeze out any
water and then add the onion to the spinach and continue mixing,
squeezing out and discarding any excess water until the mixture is dry.
Add the sumac, allspice, oil and chilli flakes, if using.

3 Toast the pine nuts in a heavy-based pan over a medium heat for
1–2 minutes until golden and fragrant, shaking the pan often. Add to
the mixture, then taste and adjust the seasoning, if required, bearing in
mind that the mixture is meant to be quite sour.

4 Preheat the oven to 200°C/400°F/Gas 6 and lightly grease a baking
sheet with oil. Roll out the dough on a well-floured work surface into a
large circle about 2mm/⅟₁₆in thick. If necessary, divide it in half and roll
it out and stamp it in two stages. For best results, you may find it helps
to flip the dough a few times between rolling and sprinkling more flour.

5 Using a 7cm/2¾in pastry cutter, stamp out about 20–25 rounds.
Place 1 teaspoon of the stuffing in the centre of each circle. Use your
thumb and index finger to seal the edge of each circle together as
though to create a half-moon shape, but stop once you get halfway.
Then, as your thumb and index continue to pinch, use your other
hand to bring over the remaining unsealed dough so the edges meet
perpendicularly. Seal, and with the help of your middle finger, lift the
dough at three points, joining them into a triangle with a peak at the
joint. Pinch together tightly, and thin out gently until you see no crease,
to ensure they stay sealed during cooking. Check that all the turnovers
are firmly sealed. (You can freeze the uncooked turnovers at this stage
in an airtight, freezer-safe container for up to 2 months).

6 Put the turnovers on the prepared sheet and bake for 7 minutes or
until golden and crisp at the edges. Serve hot or at room temperature.

dynamite chilli cigars

SERVES 4
PREPARATION TIME: 30 minutes
COOKING TIME: 10 minutes

olive oil, for greasing

250g/9oz soft goat's cheese, crumbled

1 garlic clove, finely chopped

1 small mild red chilli, deseeded and very thinly sliced

2 tsp dried oregano

1 tsp sesame seeds

1 egg, separated

4–5 sheets of filo pastry (defrosted if frozen)

75g/2½oz salted butter

sea salt and freshly ground black pepper

Known as briwat in Morocco, we have something quite similar in the Levant called raqaqat. What's lovely about this recipe is that there is plenty of cheese and not too much filo, so that the "cigar" is very creamy, with a light and crisp casing. Some of them might explode a bit in the oven, but this is fine. They are not called "dynamite" for nothing...! They can be assembled up to 4 hours ahead, then covered with cling film and kept in the fridge until ready to bake.

1 Preheat the oven to 180°C/350°F/Gas 4 and lightly grease a baking tray with oil. Put the crumbled goat's cheese, garlic, chilli, oregano, sesame seeds and egg yolk in a mixing bowl and beat well. Season to taste with salt and pepper.

2 Remove 4 sheets of the filo from their plastic packaging and cut into 18 x 10cm/7 x 4in strips. You should get 24 strips, depending on how accurately you cut them. If you are short, use part of the last sheet, too. Cover the strips with a damp kitchen towel to stop the pastry drying out while you work.

3 Melt the butter in a small saucepan over a low heat. Working with one filo strip at a time, and keeping the others covered, place a strip on the work surface with a short end towards you. Brush the strip with melted butter, then put another strip on top and brush that with butter.

4 Place 1 scant tablespoon of the goat's cheese filling at the short end nearest to you, leaving 1.5cm/½in filo on each side. Fold the strip over the filling, and fold in the sides all the way to the end, then roll away from you to form a roll.

5 Beat the egg white and use it to brush the seam, then brush all over the roll with a little more melted butter. Repeat with the remaining ingredients to make 12 rolls.

6 Put the cigars seam-side down on the prepared baking tray and bake for 5–7 minutes until lightly golden and crisp. Serve hot.

red-hot roasties

SERVES 4
PREPARATION TIME: 30 minutes
COOKING TIME: 1 ¼ hours

1kg/2lb 4oz floury potatoes, peeled and chopped into 4cm/1 ½in cubes

15g/½oz sea salt flakes, plus extra for seasoning

1 handful of coriander leaves, finely chopped, plus extra for sprinkling

2 small mild red chillies, deseeded and finely chopped

1 garlic bulb, cloves separated and finely chopped

1 tsp paprika

80ml/2 ½fl oz/⅓ cup olive oil

juice of 1 lemon

freshly ground black pepper

TO SERVE
fried eggs

Spiced Naked Mini Sausages (see page 21)

warm Arabic Bread (optional, see page 217)

I'm a diehard fan of the texture of these spicy roasties. They are my interpretation of the popular mezze dish batata harra. For the crispiest results, use floury rather than waxy potatoes. Simply serve with some fried eggs on top and with some Spiced Naked Mini Sausages and Arabic bread.

1 Preheat the oven to 200°C/400°F/Gas 6. Rinse the potatoes under cold running water for a few minutes to wash off any surface starch.

2 Bring 1l/35fl oz/4 cups water to the boil in a saucepan over a high heat, add the salt and the potatoes and cook for about 5 minutes or until the edges of the potato pieces soften.

3 Meanwhile, put the coriander, chillies, garlic and paprika in a small bowl and mix well. Season to taste with salt and pepper.

4 Drain the potatoes and return to the pan. Stretch a kitchen towel securely over the top and shake the pan for about 30 seconds or until the edges of the potatoes have fluffed up. Set aside, uncovered, to let all the moisture evaporate.

5 Meanwhile, brush a 24 x 30cm/9 ½ x 12in roasting tin with the oil, then place the tray in the oven for about 10 minutes or until the oil is sizzling hot.

6 Remove the tin from the oven and spoon the potatoes into the sizzling oil, gently turning them to ensure they are well coated. Return to the oven and roast, uncovered, for 35–40 minutes until light golden. Sprinkle over the coriander and garlic mixture, turning the potatoes to make sure they are well coated. Return to the oven and cook for another 10–15 minutes until crisp and golden.

7 Remove from the oven and transfer to a serving dish. Squeeze over the lemon juice and sprinkle with more coriander. Serve warm with fried eggs and Spiced Naked Mini Sausages, and with warm Arabic Bread, if you like.

Shipwrecked potato boats

SERVES 4
PREPARATION TIME: 10 minutes
COOKING TIME: 1 hour 10 minutes

4 large potatoes, such as Desiree, halved lengthways

4 tbsp olive oil

140g/5oz salted butter

3 garlic cloves, crushed or finely chopped

¼ tsp ground cumin

1 tsp dried coriander

3 tbsp finely chopped chives

2 tsp sesame seeds

sea salt and freshly ground black pepper

Burnt Tomato & Chilli Jam (see page 219), to serve

These were born of my attempts to deconstruct a potato cake. Here, the essence of fluffy mashed potato is retained while the crispy crust is reincarnated through the use of the much-neglected potato skin. The best potato varieties to use are Desiree, King Edward, Harmony or Maris Piper. Try the boats with flaked smoked mackerel or allow your imagination to lead you wherever you want. While the cooking time is just over an hour, the actual active time required to knock these up is about 10 minutes. Baking the potato skins is a suitable alternative if you're steering clear of frying: brush each skin with 1 tablespoon of olive oil and bake for 10 minutes at the same temperature as the potatoes.

1 Preheat the oven to 220°C/425°F/Gas 7. Brush the potato halves lightly with a little of the oil. Cover each one with foil and seal the packages tightly. Place them directly on the oven rack or on a baking sheet and cook for about 1 hour until the flesh has softened. Remove from the oven and leave for 5 minutes until cool enough to handle, then scoop out the flesh into a mixing bowl.

2 Heat the remaining oil in a frying pan over a medium heat and fry the potato skins for 2–3 minutes each side until they are crisp, then transfer to a plate lined with kitchen paper.

3 Add the butter, garlic, cumin and coriander to the potato flesh and season to taste with salt and pepper. Using a potato masher or ricer, mash the potatoes until they are light and fluffy and have no lumps, but don't mash for too long or they will be overworked and gluey. Sprinkle over the chives and mix just enough to combine. Spoon the mixture equally into the potato skins. If the mashed potato cools too much during this process and is hard to spoon, just transfer to the still-warm oven for a couple of minutes.

4 Toast the sesame seeds in a heavy-based pan over a medium heat for 1 minute until golden and fragrant, shaking the pan often. Sprinkle them over the stuffed potatoes. Serve with some Burnt Tomato and Chilli Jam.

corn on the kobab
with pistachio-saffron butter

SERVES 4
PREPARATION TIME: 15 minutes
COOKING TIME: 12 minutes

sunflower oil, for greasing

½ tsp saffron threads

85g/3oz unsalted butter, slightly
  softened

4 garlic cloves, roughly chopped

1 tbsp pistachios

4 sweetcorn cobs

2 tbsp sea salt, plus extra for
  seasoning

freshly ground black pepper

lime wedges, to serve

*Dunking corn in hot, salted water after grilling it on a
barbecue is a delicious departure from the usual boiled corn.*

1 Depending on your choice, preheat a charcoal barbecue until the
charcoal is burning white or turn on a gas barbecue to high. Lightly
grease the rack with oil.

2 Toast the saffron threads in a heavy-based pan over a medium
heat for a few seconds until fragrant, then tip them into a small food
processor with the butter and garlic. Season to taste with salt and pepper.
Pulse for about 1 minute or until smooth. Transfer to a serving dish.

3 Add the pistachios to the pan and toast over a medium heat for
1–2 minutes until lightly browned, then crush using a pestle and
mortar. Sprinkle the crushed pistachios over the flavoured butter and
stir to incorporate. Set aside until ready to use.

4 Peel off the corn husks, remove all the silky threads and rinse the
cobs well under cold running water.

5 Place the corn cobs on the barbecue and cook for about 10 minutes
until tender and lightly charred, turning them every few minutes so
they cook evenly. Corn cooks quickly, so keep an eye on it. You'll hear
the corn popping – that's normal. If you would like to cook the corn on
a gas hob, simply turn the flame to medium and lean the corn against
the flame. Cook for 4–5 minutes, turning with tongs every minute or so.

6 While the corn is cooking, put the salt in a wide, heatproof bowl large
enough for dunking all the corn at once. Add 1l/35fl oz/4 cups hot
water to the bowl and stir to dissolve the salt.

7 Once the corn is cooked, use tongs to remove the cobs from the
barbecue and submerge them in the hot water for a few seconds,
then remove. The water will evaporate quickly. Cut the cobs in half and
insert corn holders at the ends of the halves, then roll and rub them in
the pistachio-saffron butter, covering them generously. Serve with some
lime wedges.

Jewelled rice

SERVES 4
PREPARATION TIME: 30 minutes,
 plus making the rice, advieh and
 saffron liquid
COOKING TIME: 35 minutes

40g/1½oz/heaped ¼ cup currants

60g/2¼oz/1 cup dried barberries
 or cranberries

1 bitter orange, such as a Seville

70g/2½oz/heaped ¾ cup flaked
 almonds

70g/2½oz/½ cup pistachios, halved

1 tbsp finely chopped mint leaves

5 tbsp sunflower oil

1 recipe quantity Parboiled Rice
 (see page 214)

1 tsp Advieh 2 (see page 211)

60g/2¼oz unsalted butter

2 tbsp Saffron Liquid (see page 212)

The berries, nuts and dried fruits mirror the effect of precious stones in this dish, with its elaborate layers of texture.

1 Soak the currants in a bowl of water for 10 minutes until swollen. Put the barberries in a separate bowl of water and soak for 5 minutes. Drain both and pat dry separately. Set aside.

2 Peel the orange, removing all the pith. Cut the peel into very thin strips, then transfer to a small saucepan. Add enough cold water to cover, then bring to the boil over a medium heat. Blanch for 20 seconds, then drain. Repeat the blanching twice more to remove the bitterness.

3 Reserve 1 tablespoon each of the flaked almonds, pistachios and soaked currants and combine the remainder with the blanched orange strips, then mix in the mint. Set aside.

4 Heat the oil in a heavy-based saucepan over a medium heat until it is sizzling. Using a spoon, sprinkle 4–5 tablespoons of the rice across the bottom to cover the base. Sprinkle 1 tablespoon of the fruit and nut mixture over the top, then sprinkle in a pinch of advieh. Continue adding layers of rice, fruit and nut mixture and advieh, building the mixture up into a dome. Finish with a layer of rice. Avoid tipping all the rice in at once, as this will compress it, and the result will not be light.

5 Using the handle of a wooden spoon, make three holes in the rice all the way to the bottom of the pan. This forms the tahdeeg, or crispy base.

6 Melt half the butter in a small pan. Add the saffron liquid and 2 tablespoons water and mix well. Pour the mixture over the rice.

7 Wrap the saucepan lid in a clean kitchen towel and tie it into a tight knot at the handle, then use it to cover the pan as tightly as you can so that steam does not escape. (The kitchen towel will prevent the moisture from dripping into the rice, making it soggy.) Cook the rice over a medium heat for 2–3 minutes until the rice is steaming (you will see puffs of steam escaping at the edges of the lid), then reduce the heat to low and cook, covered, for 20–25 minutes.

8 Meanwhile, melt the remaining butter in a small heavy-based saucepan over a medium heat, add the soaked barberries and fry, stirring often, for 3–4 minutes to refresh their colour. Remove from the heat and set aside for serving.

9 Serve the rice and tahdeeg following the instructions in steps 5–7 for Steamed Rice on page 214. Decorate the rice with the soaked barberries and the reserved flaked almonds, pistachios and soaked currants.

carrot salad
with cumin & preserved lemon

SERVES 4
*PREPARATION TIME: 5 minutes,
  plus making the preserved lemon*
COOKING TIME: 15 minutes

350g/12oz carrots, quartered
  lengthways

¼ tsp cumin seeds

¼ tsp coriander seeds

40g/1½oz salted butter

2 garlic cloves, finely chopped

5cm/2in piece of root ginger, peeled
  and grated

1 wedge of Preserved Lemon (see
  page 212), rind rinsed and thinly
  sliced

1 tsp finely chopped mint or
  coriander leaves

¼ tsp orange blossom water
  (optional)

sea salt

*Moroccans love their cooked salads, such as this quintessential
carrot salad. Preserved lemons are so versatile and I tend to
make really good use of them. You can too – adding them is
a wonderful way to make your food shine. However, if you
don't want to preserve your own lemons, you can use the zest
of a lemon instead for a citrus note.*

1 Cook the carrots in a saucepan of salted water over a medium heat
for 4–5 minutes or until they are tender but still have a slight bite to
them. Drain and set aside.

2 Place a heavy-based frying pan over a medium heat, add the cumin
and coriander seeds and cook for 1–2 minutes until aromatic, stirring
often. Remove from the heat, transfer the seeds to a spice grinder and
grind roughly.

3 Return the pan to the hob, melt the butter and add the ground
spices, followed by the garlic and ginger and cook for 1 minute until
aromatic. Add the parboiled carrots and toss to cover, then cook for
a further 2–3 minutes until a nice sheen has developed. Add the
preserved lemon, mint leaves and orange blossom water, if using.
Toss to combine and remove from the heat. Serve immediately or
leave to cool and serve at room temperature.

monk's aubergine salad

SERVES 4
PREPARATION TIME: 10 minutes,
 plus roasting the aubergines
COOKING TIME: 7 minutes

1kg/2lb 4oz roasted aubergines
 (see Roasted Vegetables, page 216)

1 handful of mint leaves, finely
 chopped, plus extra for sprinkling

2 tomatoes, finely chopped

1 handful of parsley leaves, finely
 chopped, plus extra for sprinkling

1 spring onion, finely chopped

3 tbsp pomegranate seeds from
 ½ pomegranate (see page 216)

3 tbsp olive oil

1 tbsp pomegranate molasses

1 handful of walnuts, coarsely
 chopped (optional)

sea salt and freshly ground black
 pepper

FOR THE TOASTED TRIANGLES
2 medium-large loaves of bought
 Arabic Bread, each about
 30cm/12in in diameter, cut into
 small triangles

1 tbsp olive oil

sea salt

*This salsa-like salad goes by two native names: the debated
baba ghanouj (father of a coquet), and salatet el raheb (monk's
salad). The salad may have gained the latter name because
the monks consumed it during Lent.*

1 To make the triangles, preheat the oven to 180°C/350°F/Gas 4.
Put the bread on a baking tray, add the oil and season to taste with
salt, then toss well. Bake in the oven for about 7 minutes, or until they
are crisp and lightly golden, shaking the baking tray halfway through
the cooking time. Remove the tray from the oven and set aside.

2 Put the roasted aubergines on a chopping board. Slice off each
crown and squeeze out any juices, then cut the flesh into thin, long
strips and then into cubes.

3 Place the cubed flesh in a large shallow bowl and layer with the
mint, tomatoes, parsley, spring onion and pomegranate seeds. Sprinkle
with extra herbs and season to taste with salt and pepper. Drizzle with
the oil and pomegranate molasses and toss very gently. Sprinkle with
the walnuts, if using, then serve with the toasted triangles.

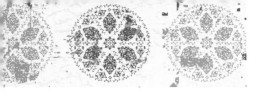

courgette & sumac fritters

SERVES 4
PREPARATION TIME: 25 minutes
COOKING TIME: 15 minutes

185ml/6fl oz/¾ cup Greek yogurt

2 tbsp tahini

1 tbsp lemon juice

½ tsp paprika

300g/10½oz courgette flesh and seeds (see page 158) or grated courgette

1 onion, coarsely grated

½ tsp sea salt, plus extra for seasoning

8 garlic cloves, finely chopped

3 eggs, beaten

60g/2¼oz/½ cup self-raising flour

zest of 1 lemon

4 tbsp parsley leaves, finely chopped

2 tbsp finely chopped dill leaves

3 tbsp sumac

¼ tsp ground allspice

100g/3½oz feta cheese (optional)

sunflower oil, for frying

TO SERVE
lime wedges

warm Arabic Bread (see page 217)

Fattoush Salad (see page 61)

These irresistible fritters come with a few subtle twists that make them different from the classic versions found across the Middle East. They are incredibly versatile and are wonderful as part of a mezze, light lunch or snack. They can be served warm or cold, which means they are perfect to prepare ahead and a great addition to your picnic basket. This recipe uses up the leftover courgette flesh from the Courgettes Stuffed with Herbed Rice recipe on page 158. You could also make it by grating the same weight in courgettes.

1 Put the yogurt, tahini, lemon juice and paprika in a bowl and whisk until well combined. Season to taste with salt, then cover and put in the fridge.

2 If you are using whole courgettes, remove the courgette ends and coarsely grate the courgettes using either the large holes of a box grater or, if you have one, using the grating blade of a food processor.

3 Put the courgette flesh and seeds or grated courgettes, the grated onion and salt into a mixing bowl, mix well and leave to sit for about 10 minutes or until the juices have been drawn out. Strain the courgette and onion mixture through a sieve, squeezing out and discarding as much of the liquid as possible. Set aside the strained courgette and onion flesh.

4 In the bowl used for the courgettes, put the garlic, eggs, flour, lemon zest, herbs, sumac and allspice and whisk until well combined. Stir in the strained courgette and onion mixture and feta, if using, and season to taste with salt, if you like (the feta will be salty).

5 Heat some oil in a frying pan over a high heat until it sizzles (test by dropping in a tiny amount of the fritter mixture, and if it bubbles around the edges the oil is hot enough). Add 2–3 heaped tablespoonfuls of the fritter mixture to the pan to make each fritter. Make sure the fritters are far enough apart so they don't touch each other. Cook for 2–3 minutes on each side until golden brown. Transfer to a plate lined with kitchen paper, covering the fritters as you make them to keep them warm. Repeat with the remaining mixture; you should get about 16 fritters in total. Serve the fritters warm or cold with the paprika and tahini yogurt, lime wedges, warm Arabic Bread and Fattoush Salad.

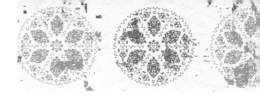

warm hummus in a cumin & olive oil broth

SERVES 4
PREPARATION TIME: 15 minutes,
 plus soaking the chickpeas
 (optional)
COOKING TIME: 30 minutes, plus
 cooking the chickpeas until they
 are very tender (optional)

400g/14oz/2 cups dried chickpeas,
 soaked overnight and cooked (see
 page 215), or 800g/1lb 12oz/4
 cups tinned chickpeas, drained and
 rinsed

2 garlic cloves, finely chopped

1 tsp ground cumin, plus extra for
 sprinkling

5 tbsp olive oil, plus extra to drizzle

2 tbsp pine nuts

1 tbsp choped parsley leaves, to
 sprinkle

sea salt

TO SERVE
warm Arabic Bread (see page 217)

Fattoush Salad (see page 61)

Spinach & Sumac Turnovers
 (see page 37)

Yogurt, Cucumber & Mint Salad (see
 page 66)

Spiced Naked Mini Sausages
 (optional, see page 21)

*This rustic winter vegetarian dish, called hummus balila, is
served warm. Served with Spiced Naked Mini Sausages (see
page 21) or chorizo it also makes a robust, non-veggie main
course. Allspice can be substituted if cumin is too powerful a
flavour for you.*

1 Strain the cooked chickpeas, reserving about 125ml/4fl oz/½ cup
cooking liquid. Put the chickpeas in a heavy-based saucepan with the
reserved liquid and garlic. If using tinned chickpeas, replace the cooking
liquid with water.

2 Heat over a medium heat and stir to combine, then bring to a
gentle boil. Once boiling, reduce the heat to low and season to taste
with salt, then sprinkle in the cumin and mix well. Cook for a further
2–3 minutes, then remove from the heat. Pour in the oil and set aside,
covered. Some of the chickpeas may have disintegrated, creating a thick
sauce-like texture. This adds to the richness of the dish but you still want
the majority of the chickpeas to remain whole. Transfer the chickpea
mixture into a mezze-style bowl.

3 Toast the pine nuts in a heavy-based frying pan over a medium
heat for 1–2 minutes until golden and fragrant, shaking the pan often.
Sprinkle the pine nuts and some extra cumin over the chickpea mixture
and drizzle over some oil, if you like. Sprinkle with parsley and serve
immediately with warm Arabic Bread, Fattoush Salad, Spinach and
Sumac Turnovers, Yogurt, Cucumber and Mint Salad and Spiced Naked
Mini Sausages, if you like.

swimming chickpeas

SERVES 4
PREPARATION TIME: 30 minutes,
  plus soaking the chickpeas
  (optional) and making the tarator
COOKING TIME: cooking the
  chickpeas until they are very soft
  (optional)

250g/9oz/1 heaped cup dried
  chickpeas, soaked overnight
  and cooked (see page 215), or
  500g/1lb 2oz/2 heaped cups tinned
  chickpeas, drained and rinsed

½ recipe quantity Tarator (see page
  220)

5 tbsp olive oil, to drizzle

½ tsp Aleppo pepper flakes or
  crushed chilli flakes, to sprinkle

1 tbsp finely chopped parsley leaves,
  to sprinkle

warm Arabic Bread (optional,
  see page 217), to serve

*The native name for this Syrian dish, hummus musabaha,
is derived from the Arabic root word sabaha, meaning "to
swim". A traditional breakfast food, the chickpeas are served
"swimming" in a pool of tahini and oodles of olive oil. The
dish incorporates the same ingredients as hummus b tahini,
but they're not whipped into a purée, which allows the dish
more texture and body. Make sure your chickpeas are super-
soft: collapsing at the gentlest touch. I've found that removing
the skins, although more time consuming, really improves
the taste and feel of the whole dish. You can prepare both
the chickpeas and the tahini (part of the tarator) in advance,
but you'll need to reheat them over a gentle heat and then
assemble the dish just seconds before serving.*

1 If using cooked chickpeas, strain the chickpeas, reserving 3
tablespoons of the cooking liquid.

2 Loosen the chickpea skins by running them under cold water several
times, lastly covering them with water, swish them with your hands
several times to loosen any more skins. Discard any of the loose skins.
Drain the chickpeas again.

3 Mash 100g/3½oz/⅔ cup of the chickpeas with the reserved cooking
liquid to create a paste. If using tinned chickpeas, replace the cooking
liquid with water. Transfer the paste to a bowl, add the remaining
chickpeas and pour over the tarator. Mix gently. Drizzle with olive oil,
sprinkle with Aleppo pepper flakes and parsley. Enjoy it on its own or
as part of a mezze with warm Arabic Bread.

chargrilled sweet pepper & walnut dip

SERVES 4
PREPARATION TIME: 20 minutes,
  plus roasting the peppers and
  standing time

500g/1lb 2oz roasted sweet pointed
  peppers (see Roasted Vegetables,
  page 216)

75g/2½oz /¾ cup walnut halves,
  roughly chopped

55g/2oz/⅔ cup fine breadcrumbs

2 tbsp pomegranate molasses

½ tsp ground cumin

½ tsp paprika

¼ tsp cayenne pepper

1 tsp Aleppo pepper flakes (optional)

2 tbsp olive oil, plus extra to drizzle

finely chopped mint leaves,
  to sprinkle

sea salt

warm Arabic Bread (see page 217)
  or Toasted Triangles (see page 49),
  to serve (optional)

The Arabic title of this pesto-like dip, muhamara, means reddened or crimsoned. This recipe is traditionally made using sun-dried Aleppo peppers, finely chopped to a coarse paste. These peppers, which hail from Syria and neighbouring Turkey, have a high oil content and a hint of earthy smokiness in their flavour. It isn't easy finding Aleppo pepper paste in the West, but Aleppo pepper flakes are readily available. The most popular recipes for this dip involve puréeing, but I prefer it chunky like this. It's lovely as a dip, spread on flatbreads, mixed into hearty stews, or tossed with pasta or potatoes (in which case you can omit the breadcrumbs).

1 Slice off the tops of the roasted peppers, discarding any seeds. Chop the flesh finely and put it in a mixing bowl.

2 Add the walnuts, breadcrumbs, pomegranate molasses, cumin, paprika, cayenne pepper, Aleppo pepper flakes, if using, and oil and season to taste with salt. Mix well, then set aside for about 1 hour to allow the flavours to develop.

3 Put the ingredients in a serving dish, drizzle with olive oil and sprinkle with mint. Serve at room temperature with warm Arabic Bread.

smokey aubergine dip

SERVES 4
PREPARATION TIME: 10 minutes,
  plus roasting the aubergines

1kg/2lb 4oz roasted aubergines
  (see Roasted Vegetables, page 216)

2 garlic cloves

5 tbsp tahini

juice of 1 ½ lemons

sea salt

olive oil, to drizzle

mint leaves, to sprinkle

seeds from ½ pomegranate
  (see page 216), to sprinkle

warm Arabic Bread (see page 217)
  or Toasted Triangles (see page 49),
  to serve

This dish, which many know as baba ghanouj, is actually known in the Levant as mutabal batinjan (sauced or tossed aubergine). This staple Levantine dip can be found in many variations where beetroot, courgette, calamari or pumpkin replace the aubergine (see Shaved Beetroot, Radish & Grapefruit Salad, page 62). Here, the idea is to add only a trace of tahini so that the seductively smoky undertones released by the flames still caress the taste buds.

1 Put the roasted aubergines on a chopping board. Slice off each crown and squeeze out any juices, then transfer the flesh to a mixing bowl. Add the garlic, tahini and half the lemon juice, and season to taste with salt. Toss the mixture together using a fork for a more rustic texture or with a pestle and mortar if you're after a creamier consistency. It's meant to have some body, so don't purée it completely.

2 Taste the dip. If it's too thick, thin it with the remaining lemon juice and adjust the seasoning to taste.

3 Transfer the mixture to a plate. Create a shallow well in the middle. Drizzle in some oil. Sprinkle over the mint and pomegranate seeds and serve with warm Arabic Bread.

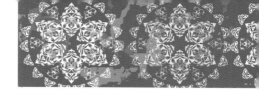

Spinach & Labneh Dip

SERVES 4
PREPARATION TIME: 25 minutes,
  plus draining and chilling the
  yogurt and making the advieh, and
  the saffron liquid (optional)
COOKING TIME: 15 minutes

2 tbsp sunflower oil

2 small shallots, finely chopped

1 onion, thinly sliced (optional)

300g/10½oz spinach leaves

a pinch of Advieh 1 (see page 211)

2 garlic cloves, finely chopped

200ml/7fl oz/heaped ¾ cup Greek
  yogurt or Labneh Dip (see page
  221)

a squeeze of lemon juice

1 tsp Saffron Liquid (optional, see
  page 212)

sea salt and freshly ground pepper

warm Thin Flatbread (see page 218)
  or Toasted Triangles (see page 49),
  to serve

*Booranis are a variety of yogurt-based dishes that are served
as sides in Iran. They are cousins of mutabal, where yogurt
is used instead of tahini. You can use any kind of green or
vegetable instead of the spinach.*

1 Heat half the oil in a heavy-based frying pan over a medium heat.
Add the shallots and fry for 8–10 minutes until soft and lightly golden.
Transfer to a plate and set aside. Add the remaining oil to the pan and
cook the sliced onion, if using, until golden and crispy. Set aside.

2 Meanwhile, put the spinach in a large saucepan and pour in 1l/
35fl oz/4 cups boiling water. Cover and cook over a high heat for 1–2
minutes until it wilts. Rinse under cold running water, then drain well
and squeeze firmly with the back of a spoon to extract as much liquid
as you can.

3 Chop the spinach finely and add to the shallots. Add the advieh and
garlic and season to taste with salt and pepper. Mix well and return the
pan to a medium heat. Stir well, cooking for a further 2 minutes, then
remove from the heat and leave to cool.

4 Position a colander over a bowl, and line the colander with two fine
muslin cloths. Tip the yogurt in, join the sides of the cloth to create a
pouch, and close by creating a tight knot. Squeeze the pouch and then
leave it to sit in the colander as the whey drains for 10–15 minutes
while the spinach cools. Discard the whey. Alternatively, if you have
Labneh Dip on hand (see page 221), you can use that.

5 Once the spinach mixture has cooled, transfer to a serving dish and
mix in the yogurt. Add a squeeze of lemon juice, then taste and adjust
the seasoning, if necessary. Put in the fridge for 1 hour to chill. Drizzle
with saffron liquid and sprinkle with caramelized onion, if using. Serve
extremely cold with warm Thin Flatbread.

tabbouleh salad

SERVES 4
PREPARATION TIME: 45 minutes

80g/2¾oz/4 cups flat-leaf parsley
  leaves (roughly 4 handfuls)

1 tbsp finely chopped mint leaves

300g/10½oz plum tomatoes, cut
  into 5mm/¼in cubes

2 small spring onions, very finely
  chopped

2 tsp fine bulgur wheat (grade 1),
  (optional)

crisp cos lettuce

½ head of cabbage

4 fresh vine leaves (optional)

¼ tsp ground allspice

juice of 1 lemon

4 tbsp high-quality extra virgin
  olive oil

sea salt and freshly ground black
  pepper

The juice of this salad, known as zoum, is cherished by diners: it's not uncommon to witness people sipping it from their plate. An authentic tabbouleh calls for prolific amounts of parsley, which forms the base of the salad. Bulgur wheat is sprinkled over the dish like salt and is not actually an essential ingredient at all. For a real tabbouleh, the most important thing is that the parsley should be cut into very fine threads as carefully as possible, and ideally the blade of the knife should only come into contact with it once. The more the blade is allowed to bruise the parsley, the more bitter it will taste, so a food processor is not a good option. Use the best oil you have.

1 Pick out and discard any discoloured or imperfect parsley leaves, and discard any stalks, which would make the salad bitter. Wash the parsley well, then place in a salad spinner and spin several times until the leaves are completely dry. Alternatively, pat dry thoroughly on kitchen paper.

2 Bunch up small amounts of the parsley leaves at a time, keeping an extremely tight grip on them, then slice them very thinly (no thicker than 2mm/¹⁄₁₆in threads) using a very sharp knife. Put in a salad bowl along with the mint, tomatoes and spring onions. If preparing for later, cover at this stage and set aside in the fridge.

3 Rinse the bulgur, if using, and drain well.

4 Separate the lettuce leaves and the cabbage leaves, and remove their central veins.

5 Arrange the lettuce, cabbage and vine leaves, if using, on a plate. When ready to serve, sprinkle the tabbouleh with the bulgur wheat, if using. Add the allspice, lemon juice and olive oil and season with salt and pepper. Taste and adjust the seasoning if necessary. Use the various leaves to scoop up portions of the tabbouleh.

fattoush salad

SERVES 4
PREPARATION TIME: 10 minutes,
  plus making the toasted triangles

4 tbsp extra virgin olive oil, plus
  extra for serving

juice of 1 ½ lemons

200g/7oz mixed green leaves

2 tomatoes, cut into thin wedges

2 small red onions, thinly sliced

100g/3 ½oz radishes, thinly sliced

100g/3 ½oz cucumber, halved
  lengthways and thinly sliced

2 tbsp finely chopped dill leaves

a small handful of parsley leaves

4 tsp sumac

75g/2 ½oz pomegranate seeds
  (see page 216)

115g/4oz feta cheese, crumbled

1 recipe quantity Toasted Triangles
  (see page 49)

1 ripe avocado

sea salt and freshly ground black
  pepper

lemon wedges, to serve

*Fattoush is a bread salad that has become synonymous with
the Middle East. It's a good choice when you want to use up
some soon-to-expire vegetables and stale bread. Bread holds
a symbolic, almost revered, status in the Middle East. Growing
up, I learnt that if I found a piece on the floor I should pick it
up, kiss it and place it somewhere it would be appreciated.
"Bread and penny never wasted": the idea is to make use
of what is available and in season. Here is one of the many
versions I've made over time.*

1 To make the dressing, put the olive oil and most of the lemon juice in
a mixing bowl and whisk together well. Adjust the sourness by adding
more lemon juice, if you like. (Note that the sumac will add a tang to the
salad, so it's best to err on the side of caution first and adjust the zing
of the salad once it has all been dressed.) Season to taste with salt and
pepper. Set aside.

2 Put the mixed leaves, tomatoes, red onions, radishes, cucumber, dill
and parsley in a serving bowl and drizzle over the dressing. Toss well,
then sprinkle with the sumac, pomegranate seeds, feta and toasted
triangles.

3 Cut the avocado in half, remove the pit and scoop out and dice the
flesh, then add to the salad and gently toss again. Taste and adjust the
seasoning, if necessary. Divide among four bowls and serve with lemon
wedges and some extra olive oil.

Shaved beetroot, radish & grapefruit salad

SERVES 4
PREPARATION TIME: 20 minutes

3 tbsp tahini

2.5cm/1in piece of root ginger, peeled and grated

1 garlic clove, finely chopped

5 tbsp verjuice, or lime juice to taste

100g/3 ½oz radishes

400g/14oz beetroots, peeled

1 pink grapefruit

1 tbsp sesame seeds (optional)

2 tbsp finely chopped dill leaves, plus extra for sprinkling

sea salt and freshly ground black pepper

warm Arabic Bread (optional, see page 217), to serve

This is another dish from the mutabal family (see page 56). Traditionally the beetroots for this salad are boiled, roughly chopped and served with a tarator dressing, but here they are served raw. If you cannot resist cooking them they can be sautéed for a couple of minutes in sesame oil. I really enjoy the earthiness and crispness of raw beetroot, and if you want a really spectacular showpiece try combining different colours and varieties. The radishes add a great contrast, with their peppery-hot tones, against the sweet-tart grapefruit and the rich, nutty tahini.

1 Put the tahini, ginger and garlic in a bowl, then season to taste with salt. Slowly pour in the verjuice, whisking quickly as you pour. Set aside. You can prepare this dressing a day ahead to allow the flavours to develop, if you like.

2 Using a mandolin on the thinnest setting, slice the radishes, then the beetroots, keeping them separate until assembly. Alternatively, you can use a vegetable peeler or a knife to make thin slices. Arrange the slices on a large platter or in a shallow serving bowl.

3 Zest the grapefruit using a zester, removing only the coloured part of the peel and leaving the bitter white pith. If you don't have a zester, use a vegetable peeler to peel, then finely chop the rind. Put the zest to one side. Peel away and discard any remaining peel and pith and cut the grapefruit into thin slices. Arrange the slices over the beetroots and radishes.

4 Sprinkle the zest over the salad and pour over the tahini dressing.

5 If using, toast the sesame seeds in a heavy-based pan over a medium heat for 1 minute until golden and fragrant, shaking the pan often. Sprinkle the sesame seeds and dill over the top of the salad and season to taste with pepper. Toss before serving and sprinkle with extra dill. Serve as part of a mezze or as a side dish with warm Arabic Bread, if you like.

pomegranate & cucumber salad

SERVES 4
PREPARATION TIME: 20 minutes,
  plus soaking the chickpeas
  (optional)
COOKING TIME: 2 minutes, plus
  cooking the chickpeas until they
  are tender (optional)

1 long English cucumber or 4 short
  Middle Eastern cucumbers

2 tbsp pine nuts

seeds from 1 pomegranate (see
  page 216)

200g/7oz/scant 1 cup dried
  chickpeas, soaked overnight and
  cooked until tender (see page
  215), or 400g/14oz/2 cups tinned
  chickpeas, drained and rinsed

zest of ½ orange

2 tbsp finely chopped mint leaves

2 tbsp finely chopped chives

3 tbsp olive oil

2 tbsp verjuice, or lime juice to taste

85g/3oz feta cheese or ½ recipe
  quantity Paneer Cheese (see page
  213), crumbled

sea salt and freshly ground black
  pepper

warm Thin Flatbread (see page 218),
  to serve

The simple ingredients in this refreshing salad provide a contrasting blend of warm, festive colours. It's a beautiful stand-alone salad and is best served with some crusty bread for a quick lunch or as a side dish to complement a Smokey Aubergine & Split Pea Stew (see page 168). Non-veggies can choose from a Leafy Lamb Kebab (see page 99) or a plate of Lamb Rice with Crispy Potato Base (see page 109). If using tinned chickpeas is unavoidable, be sure to soak them in water for 10–15 minutes and rinse them well under running water to remove as much of the tin flavour as possible.

1 Peel the cucumber(s), then use a mandolin or a vegetable peeler to slice them lengthways into thin ribbons.

2 Toast the pine nuts in a heavy-based pan over a medium heat for 1–2 minutes until golden and fragrant, shaking the pan often.

3 Put the cucumber ribbons, pomegranate seeds, chickpeas, orange zest, mint, chives and toasted pine nuts in a bowl. Season to taste with salt and pepper and toss gently.

4 To make the dressing, put the oil and verjuice in a small bowl and whisk to combine.

5 Sprinkle the salad with feta, drizzle with the dressing and serve immediately with warm Thin Flatbread.

yogurt, cucumber & mint salad

SERVES 4
PREPARATION TIME: 10 minutes

250ml/9fl oz/1 cup Greek yogurt

1 garlic clove

¼ tsp sea salt, plus extra for seasoning

1 tbsp dried mint

100g/3½oz cucumber, peeled and finely chopped

freshly ground black pepper

warm Arabic Bread (optional, see page 217), to serve

As refreshing as a cold shower on a blistering-hot day, this salad has the power to improve the character of any dish it accompanies. My favourite use for this salad is as a side dish to kebbeh (see pages 28–9) or Freekeh with Lamb & Rhubarb (see page 110), or atop cold spaghetti. It's equally lovely eaten with warm Arabic bread, as people do in the Middle East.

1 Put the yogurt in a bowl and stir in up to 6 tablespoons water to thin it a bit. The amount you need to add will depend on the brand of yogurt and the desired consistency of the salad.

2 Crush the garlic with the salt and 2 teaspoons of the mint using a pestle and mortar until it forms a paste. Add the paste to the yogurt and stir well. Add the cucumber and mix well. Taste and adjust the seasoning if necessary.

3 Cover and set aside in the fridge until you are ready to serve it. Transfer to a small serving bowl and serve sprinkled with the remaining mint. Enjoy it on its own, as a side dish or spread over warm Arabic Bread, if you like.

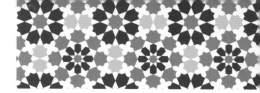

undressed herb salad

SERVES 4
PREPARATION TIME: 10 minutes,
  plus making the cheese (optional)

1 handful of walnuts (optional)

3–4 handfuls of any of the following:

mint leaves (all varieties)

basil leaves (all varieties)

tarragon leaves

marjoram leaves

watercress

radishes

coriander leaves

parsley leaves

spring onions

chives

1 recipe quantity Paneer Cheese (see
  page 213) or 175g/6oz feta, cut
  into cubes

warm Thin Flatbread (see page 218),
  to serve

The native name for this dish, sabzi khordan, literally translates as "eating greens" and it's a vital accompaniment to any authentic Persian meal. It's a light and refreshing way to begin any meal, as it awakens the appetite. It's fairly simple to create an undressed salad, just make sure that the herbs you use are fresh and in season. A dressing is not usually served, as that would steal the limelight from the real stars of the show.

1 Soak the walnuts, if using, in warm water for 5–10 minutes until they are softened, then drain.

2 Meanwhile, place your selection of herbs and salad vegetables on a serving plate.

3 Add some paneer, sprinkle with the soaked walnuts and serve with warm Thin Flatbread.

moroccan citrus salad

SERVES 4
PREPARATION TIME: 10 minutes

1 lime

1 orange

1 blood orange

1 pink grapefruit

seeds from 1 pomegranate
  (see page 216)

2 tsp roughly chopped pistachios

2 tbsp clear honey

½ tsp orange blossom water
  (optional)

¼ tsp ground cinnamon

1 tsp chopped mint leaves,
  to sprinkle

TO SERVE (OPTIONAL)
4 tbsp Greek yogurt

2.5cm/1in piece of root ginger,
  peeled and grated

Citrus salads, whether sweet or savoury, are very popular in Morocco. As in many parts of the Middle East, most meals end with a vibrant array of seasonal fruit: ruby pomegranates, oranges, apples, grapes, loquats, bananas ... It's hard to provide a recipe for such a basic salad since it really should come about by following one's instinct and mood, so regard this as more of a suggestion than a hard-and-fast recipe: it's now up to you to bring it to life in whatever way you choose. If you want to attain more savoury notes, add thin slices of red onion, a creamy cheese, olives, a dash of paprika and a drizzle of argan oil. The combination of fruits and vibrant colours will revive you at first glance, let alone at first bite. Serve with some ginger yogurt, if you like.

1 Using a sharp knife, trim the top and bottom of the lime so that the flesh is revealed. Keeping the lime upright, cut through the peel downwards from top to bottom, following the shape of the fruit, making sure to shave off all the peel and pith. Turn the lime onto its side and cut into thick wheels (not too thick, but thick enough so they are not falling apart).

2 Repeat with the remainder of the citrus fruit. Remove the pips and arrange the slices on a serving plate, so they overlap. Drizzle any juice over the citrus slices.

3 Sprinkle over the pomegranate seeds and pistachios. Put the honey and orange blossom water, if using, in a small mixing bowl and stir well, then drizzle it over the citrus fruits. Dust with cinnamon and sprinkle the mint over the top.

4 To make the ginger yogurt, if using, put the yogurt and ginger in a bowl and mix well. Serve with the salad.

poultry

Chicken basteeya

SERVES 4
PREPARATION TIME: 30 minutes
COOKING TIME: 1 hour 20 minutes

2 tbsp sunflower oil

1 onion, finely chopped

500g/1lb 2oz mixture of chicken legs
and thighs

2 garlic cloves, finely chopped

5cm/2in piece of root ginger, peeled
and grated

½ tsp turmeric or ground saffron
(see page 212)

4 eggs

1 handful of coriander leaves, finely
chopped

1 handful of flat-leaf parsley leaves,
finely chopped

juice and zest of 1 small lemon

125g/4½oz/scant 1 cup blanched
almonds

3 tbsp icing sugar, plus extra for
dusting

⅛ tsp ground cinnamon, plus extra
for dusting

1 tbsp orange blossom water

7–8 sheets of filo pastry depending
on the sheet size (defrosted if
frozen)

70g/2½oz unsalted butter, melted

sea salt and freshly ground black
pepper

*Traditionally, basteeya is a sweet and savoury delicacy made
from pigeon layered with crushed almonds and egg, enclosed
in a filo-like pastry. I decided to add a literal twist to the
recipe by shaping the basteeya into snakes.*

1 Heat the oil in a deep, heavy-based frying pan over a medium heat.
Add the onion and fry for 5 minutes or until soft and translucent.

2 Season the chicken with salt and pepper and add it to the pan. Sear
for 3–4 minutes, browning on both sides, then drain off any excess fat.
Add the garlic, ginger and turmeric and cook for 1 minute until aromatic,
tossing the chicken to coat. Cover with 500ml/17fl oz/2 cups water and
simmer for 30 minutes or until the juices from the chicken run clear
when the thickest part of a thigh is pierced with the tip of a sharp knife.

3 Remove the chicken from the broth, leaving the broth in the pan, and
set the chicken aside to cool in a bowl. Continue cooking the chicken
broth until it has reduced by about half, then whisk in the eggs one at a
time until the eggs and broth form a scramble. You may find you don't
need to use all the eggs. Set aside to cool.

4 Once the chicken has cooled slightly, shred the meat and discard the
bones. Add the herbs and lemon zest and juice to the chicken.

5 Grind the almonds to a rough paste in a food processor, then mix
in the icing sugar, cinnamon and orange blossom water and stir to
combine. Add this to the chicken along with the egg mixture. Stir to
combine. If convenient, you can prepare the recipe to this stage one
day in advance.

6 Preheat the oven to 200°C/400°F/Gas 6. Remove the sheets of filo
from their packaging and cover them quickly with a damp kitchen
towel to stop them drying out. Working with one sheet at a time, evenly
spoon 4–5 tablespoons of the chicken mixture along the long edge of
a filo sheet. Roll the pastry tightly into a long tube. Repeat with the
remaining filo sheets and chicken mixture.

7 Transfer the rolled sheets to a 30cm/12in square or round baking tin.
Starting from the outer edge, add the filo rolls as you work inwards to
cover the base of the tin like a coiled snake. Drizzle the melted butter
over the coiled pastry and bake in the oven for 25–30 minutes or until
golden brown. Lightly dust with cinnamon and icing sugar, then slice
into small, bite-sized pieces. Serve warm.

Sumac-scented Chicken Parcels

SERVES 4
PREPARATION TIME: 20 minutes
COOKING TIME: 1 hour

2 skinless chicken legs and 2 skinless chicken thighs, weighing about 700g/1lb 9oz in total

½ tsp ground allspice

6 tbsp olive oil

800g/1lb 12oz large red onions, thinly sliced

2 tbsp sumac

8 garlic cloves, peeled and crushed with the blade of a knife (optional)

4 tbsp pine nuts

250ml/9fl oz/1 cup dry white wine

250ml/9fl oz/1 cup chicken stock

4 medium-large loaves of bought Arabic bread, each about 30cm/12in in diameter, unseparated, or 4 soft flour tortillas

sea salt and freshly ground black pepper

mixed salad leaves, to serve

This Palestinian dish called musakhan is traditionally prepared to celebrate the end of the olive harvest. It's made by slow-roasting chicken with onions and sumac and then encasing it in sheets of taboon flatbread that has been lathered in freshly pressed olive oil. It's perfect for using up leftover chicken or turkey. Note that the Arabic bread for this recipe has to be bought, not made to my recipe on page 217, because home-made bread is not ideal for this recipe.

1 Season the chicken with the allspice and some salt and pepper. Heat half the oil in a heavy-based frying pan over a medium heat, then sear the chicken pieces for 5–8 minutes on each side. Remove and set aside.

2 Add the rest of the oil to the pan, unless there is still some in there, then add the onions, sumac and garlic, if using. Reduce the heat to low, and cook for 10 minutes or until the onions are soft and slightly caramelized. Add the pine nuts during the last minutes of cooking time.

3 Transfer the onion mixture to a plate and deglaze the pan with the wine, simmering for 2–3 minutes to reduce it. Pour in the stock and bring to the boil, then simmer for a further 5 minutes until the mixture has reduced by about half.

4 Shred the cooked chicken and add to it to the frying pan along with the onion mixture and mix well to incorporate with the wine broth. Leave to stand for about 5 minutes or so to soak up some of the juices.

5 Meanwhile, preheat the oven to 150°C/300°F/Gas 2. Place one loaf of bread on a work surface and spoon one-quarter of the onion mixture with some of its juices onto the centre of it. Create a parcel by folding over the edges and wrapping a long piece of kitchen string or sewing thread around the parcel lengthways, keeping the seamless side down, then twist the string lengthways to wrap it around the box shape widthways. Turn the parcel over so that the seamless side is facing up and tie the string into a bow on top of the parcel. Repeat to make the remaining parcels.

6 Place the parcels on a baking sheet, seam-side down, and bake in the oven for 15–20 minutes, or until golden and crispy. If you have any remaining juices in the pan, reserve them for spooning over the opened parcels once served.

7 Transfer the cooked parcels to four serving plates and remove the string. Serve with the salad leaves.

slumbering chamomile chicken

SERVES 4
PREPARATION TIME: 15 minutes,
  plus brining and resting, and
  making the preserved lemon
COOKING TIME: 1¾ hours

3 tbsp dried chamomile (from about
  10 chamomile tea bags)

1 onion, quartered

1 cinnamon stick

3 garlic cloves, crushed with the
  blade of a knife

5cm/2in piece root ginger, peeled
  and sliced

55g/2oz/scant ¼ cup coarse sea
  salt

185ml/6fl oz/¾ cup clear honey

1 chicken, about 1.5 kg/3lb 5oz

115g/4oz salted butter, softened

3 wedges of Preserved Lemon (see
  page 212), rind rinsed and finely
  chopped

4 tbsp roughly chopped tarragon
  leaves

140g/5oz/¾ cup couscous

1 tbsp plain flour

150g/5½oz/1½ cups broken-up
  vermicelli

3 tbsp sunflower oil

This is my version of a Moroccan dish, which produces a juicy and flavoursome bird. If you don't want to brine the chicken, add 2 tablespoons honey and chamomile to the seasoned butter in step 4 and adjust to taste with garlic and salt.

1 If you are brining the chicken, follow step 1–3. Put the chamomile, onion, cinnamon stick, garlic, ginger and salt in a large bowl. Add 125ml/4fl oz/½ cup of the honey, then pour in 500ml/17fl oz/2 cups boiling water. Stir well and leave to cool.

2 Put 2l/70fl oz/8 cups cold water in a large glass, plastic or non-metallic container, add the cooled brine and mix well. Add the chicken to the brine, then cover and leave in the fridge for 4–8 hours.

3 About 1 hour prior to cooking, remove the chicken from the brine, rinse well under cold running water and pat dry with kitchen paper. Strain the brine and reserve. Place the chicken in a colander over a bowl and leave to air-dry for 30 minutes. Pat dry with kitchen paper.

4 Put 55g/2oz of the butter, one-third of the preserved lemon and 2 tablespoons of the tarragon in a bowl and mix to create a spreadable paste. Using your fingers, gently separate the chicken skin from the flesh and dot the flesh with the butter mixture, spreading it out as much as you can. Spread a little inside the cavity too.

5 Place the chicken on a wire rack in a roasting tin and roast for about 1½ hours or until a meat thermometer registers 70°C/150°F.

6 Meanwhile, cook the couscous following the instructions on page 216, using the reserved brine for steaming, if possible. Don't salt the couscous until after cooking, and then only if you like. Reserve 125ml/4fl oz/½ cup of the brine.

7 When the chicken is cooked, transfer to a shallow serving dish, then cover it and set aside. Place the roasting tin with the juices over two burners on a medium heat. Whisk in the remaining butter and the flour. Add the reserved 125ml/4fl oz/½ cup of the brine, if using, and 125ml/4fl oz/½ cup water. Alternatively, add 250ml/9fl oz/1 cup water. Whisk in the remaining honey, the preserved lemon and the tarragon, to form a thick, pourable sauce.

8 Fry the vermicelli in the oil over a medium heat for 2 minutes until light golden brown. Toss with the cooked couscous to heat it through, making sure the mixture is hot. Pour the sauce over the chicken and sprinkle the couscous-vermicelli mixture over the top. Serve immediately.

Wild thyme chicken

SERVES 4
PREPARATION TIME: 40 minutes,
  plus marinating and resting and
  making the thyme mixture and
  bread
COOKING TIME: 45 minutes

2 garlic cloves, finely chopped

juice of 2 lemons

125ml/4fl oz/½ cup olive oil

1 chicken, about 1.5kg/3lb 5oz

1 tbsp Wild Thyme Mixture (see
  page 220)

2 loaves of warm Arabic Bread (see
  page 217)

2 tsp sumac, for dusting

sea salt and freshly ground black
  pepper

TO SERVE

lemon wedges

Garlic Gone Wild (see page 219)

Fattoush Salad (see page 61) or
  Tabbouleh Salad (see page 58)

Swimming Chickpeas (see page 52)
  or Warm Hummus in a Cumin &
  Olive Oil Broth (see page 51)

selection of mixed pickles, such as
  pickled cucumbers, pickled turnips
  and banana peppers

I grew up eating this dish from the Farouj el Lala restaurant, at that time a humble hole in the wall, in Ashrafieh, Beirut. For the best results, cook the chicken on a barbecue using barbecue grill mesh graspers.

1 Put the garlic, lemon juice and olive oil in a small non-metallic bowl, mix well and set aside to let the flavours develop.

2 Spatchcock the chicken by placing it breast-side down with the drumsticks facing you. Using a pair of kitchen shears, cut through the small rib bones around one side of the backbone. Repeat on the other side and then remove the backbone. Turn the chicken over and, using a paring knife, make a small cut in the cartilage in the centre of the top breastbone. Bend the halves backwards so that the breastbone becomes exposed. Run your paring knife or index fingers down both sides of the breastbone to separate it from the meat, then pull the bone out in one or two pieces. Trim away any excess fat and rinse the chicken. Pat dry.

3 Place the chicken on a baking tray, season with salt and pepper and pour the lemon and olive oil mixture over the top. Leave to marinate for 30 minutes. Meanwhile, depending on your choice, preheat a charcoal barbecue until the charcoal is burning white, turn on a gas barbecue to medium–high or heat an oven to 180°C/350°F/Gas 4.

4 Press the chicken between the plates of grill mesh graspers, reserving the marinade. The chicken should be sandwiched tightly between the two plates. Place the chicken on the barbecue and cook for 5–8 minutes on each side.

5 Once the skin develops a slightly pinkish colour, baste it with the marinade several times on each side for 15 minutes as it cooks. Add the thyme mixture and continue for about 15–20 minutes, basting and turning the chicken 3–4 more times until the juices run clear when the thickest part of a thigh is pierced with the tip of a sharp knife. Alternatively, put the chicken in a roasting tin and cook in the oven for 30–45 minutes, basting once or twice and adding the thyme mixture halfway through, then grill for the last 5 minutes, if possible, to crisp the skin. Test as above.

6 Peel the Arabic loaves apart at the seam and put half on a serving plate. Lay the whole chicken on top (first releasing it from the graspers, if using), then dust with the sumac.

7 Leave for 10 minutes, then serve with lemon wedges, Garlic Gone Wild, Fattoush Salad, Swimming Chickpeas, mixed pickles and the remaining bread. Use the bread to help eat the chicken.

sumac chicken casserole

SERVES 4
PREPARATION TIME: 20 minutes
COOKING TIME: 45 minutes

4 chicken legs

1 fennel bulb, quartered

2 potatoes, roughly chopped

1 garlic bulb, crown sliced off and
   bulb halved

1 onion, quartered

4 tbsp olive oil

2 tbsp sumac

½ tsp ground allspice

1 bay leaf

1 lemon, for squeezing

sea salt and freshly ground black
   pepper

Undressed Herb Salad (see page 67)
   or White Cabbage Salad (see page
   220), to serve

This is my brother Eli's take on a popular dish called djej bel furn (chicken in the oven). It exudes simplicity and home comfort and requires only a little bit of preparation before everything goes in the oven.

1 Preheat the oven to 190°C/375°F/Gas 5. Put the chicken legs in a large roasting tin with the fennel, potatoes, garlic and onion. Drizzle over the oil and season with the sumac, allspice, salt and pepper. Add the bay leaf and toss well.

2 Bake for 45 minutes or until the chicken is cooked through: the juices from the chicken should run clear when the thickest part of a thigh is pierced with the tip of a sharp knife. The vegetables should be soft.

3 During the last 10 minutes of cooking, change the oven setting to grill or heat a separate grill and move the tin into it. Grill the chicken for 5 minutes until the skin is golden and crispy. Squeeze over lemon juice to taste and serve with a salad.

Chicken & Spinach Upside-down Cake

SERVES 4
PREPARATION TIME: 40 minutes
 plus marinating and preparing the
 advieh, saffron liquid and rice
COOKING TIME: 1 hour 20 minutes

250ml/9fl oz/1 cup Greek yogurt, plus extra to serve

2 egg yolks

500g/1lb 2oz skinless, boneless chicken thighs cut into 2cm/¾in cubes

1 tbsp Advieh 1 (see page 211)

1 large onion, grated

zest of 1 lemon

2 tbsp sumac

3 garlic cloves, crushed

3 tbsp Saffron Liquid (see page 212)

1 tbsp sea salt, plus extra for seasoning

80g/2¾oz unsalted butter, diced, plus extra for greasing

500g/1lb 2oz spinach leaves, washed, drained and finely chopped

1 recipe quantity Parboiled Rice (see page 214)

freshly ground black pepper

Undressed Herb Salad (see page 67), to serve

Here I have married the classical chicken tahcheen with the spinach version. Tahcheen (arranged at the bottom of the pot) is best cooked in a wide, shallow baking dish and is suitable for making in advance. Once turned out onto a serving dish, it makes for a wonderful centrepiece.

1 Put the yogurt and egg yolks in a mixing bowl and beat until well incorporated. Add the chicken, advieh, onion, lemon zest, sumac, garlic, saffron liquid and salt, then season with pepper. Mix well, then cover and leave to marinate in the fridge for at least 4 hours. At the end of the marinating time, remove the chicken from the fridge and bring to room temperature.

2 Preheat the oven to 190°C/375°F/Gas 5. Generously grease a 2l/70fl oz/8-cup ovenproof, round, clear glass dish with some of the butter and place in the oven to heat for 5 minutes until it's sizzling.

3 Meanwhile, place a frying pan over a medium-high heat, add a quarter of the butter, and the spinach. Cook, tossing often, for a few minutes until the spinach wilts. Season to taste with salt and pepper. Set aside to cool, then squeeze out as much of the liquid as possible.

4 Using a slotted spoon, remove the chicken from the marinade and set aside. Add half the rice to the marinade and mix well.

5 Once the butter in the oven is sizzling, remove the dish and spread most of the rice and marinade mixture across the base and up the side. Add the chicken and spinach to the rice base and sprinkle with the remaining rice. Gently smooth the surface and sprinkle the remaining pieces of butter across the surface of the rice. Cover tightly with a sheet of lightly buttered foil and bake in the oven for 1¼ hours or until the base is golden. If you are preparing the dish ahead, put it in the fridge once it's covered with foil, then cook it when you're ready.

6 Remove the dish from the oven, and the foil from the dish, then leave to cool for 10 minutes. Meanwhile, place a serving plate in the still-warm oven to heat up. Serve the rice and tahcheen following the instructions in steps 5–7 of Steamed Rice on page 214, with some extra yogurt and the Undressed Herb Salad.

Chicken with caraway couscous

SERVES 4

PREPARATION TIME: 15 minutes,
plus soaking the moghrabieh and
chickpeas (optional)

COOKING TIME: 45 minutes, plus
cooking the chickpeas until they
are tender (optional)

200g/7oz/1 cup moghrabieh or
Italian fregola

4 chicken legs, about 1kg/2lb 4oz

1 cinnamon stick

1 bay leaf

1½ tsp ground allspice

80g/2¾oz salted butter

200g/7oz baby pearl onions, peeled

250g/9oz/1¼ cups dried chickpeas,
soaked overnight and cooked (see
page 215) or 500g/1lb 2oz/2½
cups tinned chickpeas, drained and
rinsed

2 tsp caraway seeds

2 tbsp plain flour

4 tbsp verjuice, or lime juice to taste

sea salt and freshly ground black
pepper

2 handfuls of baby spinach leaves,
to serve (optional)

Using verjuice (see page 209) and fresh spinach isn't traditional in this dish, which was probably brought to the Middle East by North Africans, but it bellows for a bit of greeny goodness. The pearl form of couscous used here is known as moghrabieh.

1 Put the moghrabieh in a heatproof bowl and pour over 250ml/9fl oz/ 1 cup boiling water. Stir once and set aside to soak for 15 minutes.

2 Put the chicken, cinnamon stick, bay leaf, 1 teaspoon of the allspice and 1l/35fl oz/4 cups water in a large saucepan and heat over a medium heat. Season to taste with salt. Place the moghrabieh in a steamer basket or colander set over the pan containing the chicken and broth. Cover, bring to the boil, then reduce the heat to medium-low and simmer for 30 minutes until the moghrabieh is tender but not mushy and the chicken is cooked through: the juices from the chicken run clear when the thickest part of a thigh is pierced with the tip of a sharp knife.

3 Preheat the oven to 150°C/300°F/Gas 2. Meanwhile, melt 30g/1oz of the butter in a frying pan over a medium heat, add the onions and brown them for about 5 minutes or until they are soft and light golden. Set the pan aside for later use. Transfer the onions to a large ovenproof plate, cover and keep warm in the oven.

4 Once the moghrabieh and chicken are cooked, use a slotted spoon to transfer the chicken to the ovenproof plate, cover and return to the oven. Strain and reserve the broth.

5 Add the moghrabieh to the frying pan with the chickpeas and onions. Cook for 5 minutes, mixing gently so that the grains are well coated with the browned butter. Season with the caraway, remaining allspice and salt and pepper to taste. Cover and set aside.

6 Melt the remaining butter in a saucepan over a medium-low heat. Add the flour and cook for 1–2 minutes, stirring continuously, then slowly pour in the verjuice, followed by 500ml/17fl oz/2 cups of the reserved broth a little at a time, whisking vigorously. The mixture will first thicken to a paste before reaching a creamy consistency. Season with salt and pepper, then pour half of the sauce over the moghrabieh, chickpea and onion mixture, gently mixing to combine well.

7 Preheat the grill to high and grill the chicken for 3–4 minutes, skin-side up, until lightly golden and crispy. Divide the moghrabieh into bowls and serve with the chicken, remaining sauce and spinach leaves, if you like.

Chicken & preserved lemon tagine

SERVES 4
PREPARATION TIME: 40 minutes,
  plus grinding the saffron and
  making the preserved lemon
COOKING TIME: 50 minutes

1 chicken, about 1.25kg/2lb 12oz

¼ tsp ground cinnamon

1 tbsp sunflower oil

1 large onion, sliced

3 garlic cloves, finely chopped

5cm/2in piece of root ginger, peeled
  and grated

a pinch of ground saffron (see page
  212) or turmeric

500ml/17fl oz/2 cups hot chicken
  stock

1 bay leaf

2 wedges of Preserved Lemon (see
  page 212), rind rinsed and finely
  chopped

12 black olives

2 tbsp finely chopped coriander
  leaves

sea salt

Couscous (see page 216), to serve

lemon wedges, to serve (optional)

This simple one-pot tagine dances with flavour. You can steam the couscous over the broth as it cooks (see page 216).

1 Put the chicken breast-side down on a chopping board. Using a small and very sharp knife, cut through the skin between the thigh and the body. Twist the legs gently to remove them from the sockets. Turn the bird back over and ease the legs gently away from the body. Cut through the skin between the thigh and body as far around each leg as possible, keeping the knife as close to the body as you can.

2 Pull the leg away from the body more vigorously and bend it back on itself, so you expose the thigh joint and the ball breaks free of the socket. Cut between the ball and socket to release the leg, and cut through any flesh still attached to the carcass. The "oyster" should still be attached to the thigh.

3 Place a leg skin-side up, on a board and cut off the knuckle joint at the end of the drumstick. Feel and bend the joint joining the thigh to the drumstick to locate the gap in the bone. Cut through to split the leg into two. Repeat with the other drumstick and thigh.

4 Next, take a breast and wing off the carcass in one piece. To do this, make a cut through the skin and flesh running along either side of the cartilaginous ridge of the breastbone. Cut the breast meat back, from the cavity end of the chicken down towards and under the wing joint, keeping the knife as close to the carcass as possible. Finish by cutting through the joint where the wing is attached, giving you a breast with its wing attached. Repeat with the other breast and wing.

5 Lay each of the breast-wing pieces skin-side up on the board and cut slightly on the diagonal into two, leaving about one-third of the breast meat attached to the wing. Season with cinnamon and salt.

6 Heat the oil in a heavy-based pan over a medium-high heat and brown the chicken pieces, skin-side down. Remove from the pan and drain on kitchen paper. Add the onion to the pan, cover and sweat for 2–3 minutes until translucent, then add the garlic and ginger and cook for a further 1 minute until the fragrance is released.

7 Stir the saffron into the hot stock and return the chicken to the pan. Pour the stock over the chicken and add the bay leaf, then cover and reduce the heat. Simmer for 30 minutes or until the meat is tender. Add the preserved lemon and olives to the pan and cook for another 10 minutes. Stir in the coriander and serve with Couscous and lemon wedges, if you like.

Jew's mallow with cardamom chicken

SERVES 4
PREPARATION TIME: 30 minutes
COOKING TIME: 1 hour

500g/1lb 2oz chicken breasts, thighs
   and legs

5 whole cardamom pods, crushed

1 cinnamon stick

1 bay leaf

1 onion, halved

10 garlic cloves

1 whole nutmeg

2 tbsp olive oil

2 large shallots, finely chopped

3 handfuls of coriander leaves,
   finely chopped

½ tsp ground allspice

1kg/2lb 4oz fresh or frozen,
   defrosted, Jew's mallow leaves or
   spinach leaves, chopped

½ red onion, finely chopped

85ml/2¾fl oz/generous ⅓ cup
   cider vinegar

2 toasted medium-large loaves of
   bought Arabic bread, each about
   30cm/12in in diameter, crumbled

Vermicelli Rice (see page 215)

salt and freshly ground black pepper

In Arabic, mloukhieh means "of the kings", which refers to the dish as well as the Jew's mallow leaves that are used. The sweet-scented cardamom, along with the allspice, lends heart-warming flavours to this regal dish. If you can't find fresh Jew's mallow, frozen leaves work just as well, or you can use spinach instead.

1 Put the chicken, cardamom pods and seeds, cinnamon stick, bay leaf, onion, 1 of the garlic cloves, the nutmeg and 750ml/26fl oz/3 cups water in a deep, heavy-based pan. Season to taste with salt and pepper. Cover, heat over a medium heat and bring to the boil, then reduce the heat to low and leave to simmer for about 40 minutes until the chicken is cooked through and the broth is flavourful.

2 Preheat the oven to 150°C/300°F/Gas 2. Remove the pan from the heat and strain the contents, reserving the broth. Separate the chicken from the spices and aromatics. Transfer the chicken to an ovenproof plate, then shred the meat from the bones or slice it off. Cover and keep warm in the oven.

3 Heat the oil in a deep, heavy-based pan over a medium heat. Add the shallots and cook for 2–3 minutes or until soft and translucent. Meanwhile, pound the remaining cloves of garlic into a smooth paste using a pestle and mortar or process in a mini blender. Add the garlic paste to the pan and cook for 1–2 minutes until fragrant, then add the coriander and stir well. Pour in the reserved chicken broth, sprinkle in the allspice and stir. Add the chopped Jew's mallow leaves and stir well, then reduce the heat to low and cover partially with a lid. Simmer for 10 minutes, checking that the mixture does not come to the boil, otherwise it can coagulate, rendering it inedible. Jew's mallow has natural thickening agents, so don't worry if it looks too runny initially, as it will thicken up.

4 Mix the red onion and apple vinegar in a small bowl and set aside.

5 Dish out the Jew's mallow mixture into a large serving bowl, and place on the table along with the crumbled bread, chicken, onion vinaigrette and the Vermicelli Rice, each in its own dish. Diners can then assemble their own dish to their liking, first creating a bed of rice, followed by a layer of Jew's mallow mixture with as much juice as they like, then chicken, a sprinkling of crumbled bread and finally a drizzle of the onion vinaigrette.

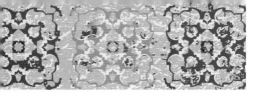

Chicken Stuffed With Cherries

SERVES 4
PREPARATION TIME: 45 minutes,
  plus making the rice and saffron
  liquid
COOKING TIME: 1¾ hours

60g/2¼oz/1⅓ cups dried whole
  albaloo or morello cherries

60g/2¼oz/½ cup dried barberries
  or cranberries

1 tbsp sunflower oil

1 onion, finely chopped

4 garlic cloves, crushed

40g/1½oz/scant ⅓ cup whole
  unsalted pistachios

¼ recipe quantity Parboiled Rice
  (see page 214)

3 tbsp Saffron Liquid (see page 212)

2 tbsp pomegranate molasses

1 tsp ground cinnamon

1 chicken, about 1.5kg/3lb 5oz

85g/3oz unsalted butter

juice of 1 lemon

sea salt and freshly ground black
  pepper

Greek yogurt, to serve

Undressed Herb Salad (see page 67),
  to serve

This dish will turn a traditional Sunday roast into something truly exotic. Trussing the chicken will ensure even cooking, as well as keeping the stuffing in.

1 Preheat the oven to 170°C/325°F/Gas 3. Soak the cherries and barberries in water for 5 minutes, then drain and pat dry.

2 Heat the oil in a heavy-based pan over a medium heat and fry the onion until soft and translucent. Add the garlic and fry for 1 minute until fragrant. Add the cherries, barberries, pistachios, rice, 2 tablespoons of the saffron liquid, pomegranate molasses and cinnamon and mix well. Season with salt and pepper to taste. Set aside until cool.

3 Rinse the chicken and pat dry with kitchen paper, then rub lightly with salt inside and out. Stuff the cavity with the cooled stuffing mixture, then sew up the cavity with a needle and strong thread.

4 To truss the chicken, place it in front of you on a cutting board, legs facing away from you. Take a 60cm/2ft length of kitchen string and place the centre point under the tail between the two drumsticks. Pull the two ends of the string up around the dip in the drumsticks, then cross them over and then under each drumstick in a criss-cross pattern, pulling the string tight to bring the ends of the drumsticks together. Now, run the string down along the sides of the chicken where the legs and thighs meet and over the inside of the wings. Turn the chicken over, pull gently, and tie the strings tightly under the neck of the bird. Tuck in the wings tips and press down the breast tip if necessary to form a neat parcel.

5 Put the chicken in a baking dish. Melt the butter in a small, heavy-based saucepan over a medium heat, then mix in the lemon juice and remaining saffron liquid. Drizzle the mixture all over the chicken and cover the dish with foil. Roast for about 1½ hours or until the juices from the chicken run clear when the thickest part of a thigh is pierced with the tip of a sharp knife. Baste with the juices every 30 minutes.

6 During the last 10 minutes of cooking, remove the foil and change the oven setting to grill (or heat a separate grill and move the dish into it). Grill on high for a few minutes to allow the skin to crisp until golden. Remove the string and serve the chicken with yogurt and an Undressed Herb Salad.

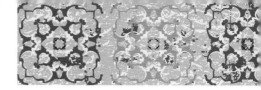

mandaean duck stuffed with nutty ginger rice
with date & apple compote

SERVES 4
PREPARATION TIME: 45 minutes
COOKING TIME: 2¾ hours

150g/5½oz/¾ cup basmati rice

5cm/2in piece root ginger, peeled and thinly sliced

235g/8½oz/1⅓ cups pitted dried dates, roughly chopped

500ml/17fl oz/2 cups unsweetened apple juice

2 star anise

1 tsp lemon juice

2 tbsp white wine (optional)

25g/1oz/scant ¼ cup blanched almonds

25g/1oz/scant ¼ cup pine nuts

25g/1oz/scant ¼ cup pistachios

1 duck, about 2.5kg/5lb 8oz, skin lightly pricked

½ tsp ground cinnamon

½ tsp paprika

½ tsp ground cardamom

½ tsp ground nutmeg

½ tsp turmeric

½ tsp freshly ground black pepper

½ tsp dried lime powder (optional)

sea salt

This recipe is inspired by the spiced duck eaten by the small Mandaean community of Iraq. Traditionally, the duck is boiled and then fried in its own fat. The spices I have used are fairly typical, but the stuffing usually includes sultanas and onions.

1 Rinse the rice several times in cold water until it runs clear, then drain well. Tip into a heavy-based saucepan and cover with 2 times its volume of water. Add the ginger and season with salt, then cover and bring to a rolling boil for about 20 minutes.

2 Meanwhile, put the dates, apple juice, star anise, lemon juice and white wine, if using, in a heavy-based saucepan over a medium heat and bring to the boil. Reduce the heat to low, then cover the pan and simmer for 10–15 minutes until the dates have softened and the compote is a thick and sticky sauce. Set aside

3 Meanwhile, toast the almonds in a heavy-based pan for 1 minute, then add the pine nuts and pistachios and toast for another 1–2 minutes until lightly browned. Remove from the heat and roughly chop.

4 Remove the rice from the heat and drain well. Add the chopped toasted nuts and toss to combine.

5 Preheat the oven to 170°C/325°F/Gas 3. Place the duck on a roasting rack or wire rack set over a roasting tin to allow the juices to drain away and the skin to crisp. Lightly prick the skin.

6 Combine all the spices, the black pepper and the dried lime powder, if using, and add sea salt to taste. Rub the mixture all over the duck inside and out, then stuff the duck with the rice mixture. Sew up the cavity using a needle and strong thread, if you like. It isn't essential, but it does yield the best results.

7 Roast the duck for 2 hours or until the skin is crispy and the meat is tender and falling off the bone, basting it all over with the rendered fat from the bottom of the pan every 20 minutes or so. When ready, carve the duck and serve slices of the meat with the rice and the compote to the side.

duck shawarma with fig jam

SERVES 4
PREPARATION TIME: 25 minutes,
  plus overnight marinating
COOKING TIME: 2¾ hours

4 tsp sea salt

½ tsp mastic powder, xanthan
  gum or about 4 small mastic tears
  ground using a pestle and mortar

½ tsp ground mahlab or ground
  almonds

1 tsp ground cinnamon

1 tsp dried mint

2.5cm/1in piece of root ginger,
  grated

8 garlic cloves, finely chopped
  or crushed

juice and finely grated zest of
  1 orange

2 cardamom pods, crushed

4 duck legs, skin on

1 tsp orange blossom water

200g/7oz/1¼ cups dried figs

1 tbsp lemon juice

200g/7oz/scant 1 cup caster sugar

¼ tsp fennel seeds or aniseeds,
  crushed

4 Thin Flatbreads (see page 218),
  to serve

Undressed Herb Salad (see page
  67), to serve

This dish was inspired by a shawarma sandwich I once had at Ilili restaurant in New York City. Shawarma is widely believed to have originated in Anatolia, Turkey, and the name is derived from the Turkish word "cevirme", meaning "turning", referring to the traditional method of cooking it on a spit.

1 Put the salt, mastic powder, mahlab, cinnamon, mint, ginger, half the garlic cloves and the orange zest in a bowl and mix well to make a rub. Crush the cardamom seeds using a pestle and mortar and add to the mixture.

2 Lightly pierce the duck skin all over the legs with the point of a sharp knife or a skewer, being very careful not to puncture the meat, as this would make it toughen during cooking. Rub the spice mixture over the legs, then cover and leave to marinate in the fridge for up to 24 hours.

3 The following day, remove the duck from the fridge and bring it back to room temperature. Preheat the oven to 140°C/275°F/Gas 1. Put a heavy-based, flameproof pan over a medium heat, add the duck and sear, skin-side down, until the fat is rendered and the skin is golden and crispy. Flip the duck over so that the skin is now facing upwards. Pour in the orange juice and orange blossom water and scrape up the browned bits from the bottom of the pan. Cover with a lid and bake in the oven for 2½ hours until the flesh just falls off the bones.

4 Put the dried figs in a heavy-based saucepan and cover with boiling water. Leave to stand for 5 minutes until the figs have plumped up, then remove using a slotted spoon, reserving the liquid. Remove the stems from the figs and chop the figs into thin strands. Return the figs to the pan with the reserved boiling water and turn the heat to medium.

5 Add the lemon juice, sugar and fennel seeds and stir well. Bring to the boil, then reduce the heat to low and simmer, stirring often, for 15–20 minutes or until the mixture has thickened. To test for readiness, remove a teaspoon of the mixture and leave it to cool on a plate so that you will know if the jam has set to your liking: slightly runny is best. If the jam is still too runny, simmer a little more, then test again.

6 During the last 10 minutes of cooking the duck, change the oven setting to grill (or heat a separate grill and move the pan into it), and grill the duck for the last 3–5 minutes until the skin is crispy and sizzling. Remove the duck from the oven and use two forks to pull the meat off the bone along with the crispy skin. To serve, put a spoonful of the fig jam in the centre of each flatbread and top with some of the juicy duck flesh and prized crispy skin. Serve with an Undressed Herb Salad.

braised duck legs

SERVES 4
PREPARATION TIME: 30 minutes,
  plus roasting the aubergines
COOKING TIME: 1¾ hours

4 duck legs, skin on

4 tsp finely chopped mint leaves,
  plus extra for sprinkling

sea salt and freshly ground black
  pepper

chopped mint leaves, to sprinkle

seeds from 1 pomegranate (optional,
  see page 216), to sprinkle

Chelow Rice (see page 214), to serve

FOR THE FESENJÂN CHUTNEY
2 tbsp sunflower oil

2 shallots, finely chopped

5cm/2in piece of root ginger, peeled
  and finely chopped

6 garlic cloves, finely chopped

4 tomatoes, finely chopped

½ tsp ground cinnamon

500g/1lb 2oz roasted aubergines
  (see Roasted Vegetables, page
  216), flesh chopped into cubes

60g/2¼oz/½ cup walnut pieces,
  roughly chopped

4 tsp pomegranate molasses

sea salt and freshly ground black
  pepper

This is a hearty Iranian stew, traditionally made with game birds and meatballs. Here, I have used duck legs instead and made the sauce as a separate chutney. You can serve this chutney with fish and chicken dishes, too.

1 Preheat the oven to 170°C/325°F/Gas 3. Lightly pierce the duck skin all over the legs with the point of a sharp knife or a skewer, being very careful not to puncture the meat, as this would make it toughen during cooking. Season with salt and pepper.

2 Put a large dry frying pan that is wide enough to fit the duck legs in a single layer over a medium heat. Add the duck legs to the pan, skin-side down, and sear for 5–10 minutes until the skin is browned and much of the fat has been rendered.

3 Transfer the duck legs to a wire rack with a roasting tin underneath to collect the fat, and cook in the centre of the oven for about 1½ hours, until the meat is cooked through and tender and the skin is golden and crispy. Meanwhile, leave the frying pan to cool. If you want the skin to be more crispy, during the last 10 minutes of cooking, change the oven setting to grill (or heat a separate grill and move the tin into it), then grill on high for the last 2–3 minutes.

4 Meanwhile, pour 250ml/9fl oz/1 cup boiling water over the cooled duck fat in the frying pan. Stir the mixture, which will have all the rich flavours of the duck, then set aside.

5 About 15 minutes before the duck will be cooked, make the fesenjân chutney. Heat the oil in a heavy-based saucepan over a medium heat. Add the shallots and ginger, then cover and sweat for 2–3 minutes. Add the garlic, tomatoes and cinnamon and cook for about 1 minute until fragrant, then pour over the reserved duck water from step 4. Bring the mixture to the boil, then reduce the heat to low, add the chopped aubergines and walnuts and mix well. Simmer for about 5 minutes, then season to taste with salt and pepper.

6 Remove from the heat and stir in the pomegranate molasses. Adjust the seasoning to taste, if needed. Sprinkle the duck legs with mint and pomegranate seeds, if using, and serve with the chutney and Chelow Rice.

Note: If you are in a rush or making this dish for a large number of guests, you can skip the searing step and simply grill the duck at the end to help crisp up the skin. Use a flavoursome stock with the chutney in place of the duck fat water from step 4.

meat

Chickpea Flour Quiche

SERVES 4
PREPARATION TIME: 10 minutes,
  plus resting and making the
  harissa
COOKING TIME: 25 minutes

butter, for greasing

2 tbsp olive oil

135g/4¾oz boneless lamb shoulder,
  fat removed, sliced into thin slivers

200g/7oz/2 cups chickpea flour or
  gram flour

1½ tsp cumin, plus extra for
  sprinkling

½ tsp sea salt, plus extra for
  seasoning

750ml/26fl oz/3 cups milk

2 eggs

¼ tsp Harissa (see page 210)

85g/3oz sun-blushed tomatoes

Undressed Herb Salad (see page 67),
  to serve

Cumin, lamb and chickpeas are a celestial pairing, and no more so than in this North African quiche-like dish, sold along the streets of eastern Morocco and western Algeria by the slice, sandwiched in a baguette. Traditionally, it's a simple combination of gram flour (chickpea flour), milk or water, eggs and a sprinkling of cumin. It's incredibly versatile and lends itself well to so many flavours, such as caramelized onions, goat's cheese, shredded artichokes, spinach, bacon, olives… you can really go wild with this. It's meant to be served slightly wet and wobbly, although some people prefer it drier and more cooked. It's gluten free, and water can be substituted for milk.

1 Preheat the oven to 180°C/350°F/Gas 4 and lightly grease a 23cm/9in round ovenproof dish with butter.

2 Heat half the oil in a frying pan over a medium heat. Add the lamb and sear for about 2 minutes until cooked through, stirring often.

3 Put the chickpea flour, cumin, salt, milk, eggs, harissa and remaining oil in a mixing bowl and pulse with a stick blender until you achieve a smooth, frothy, liquid mixture with an airy texture. Add a little salt, but not too much because the sun-blushed tomatoes you will be using are already salted.

4 Add the cooked lamb (discarding the oil and juices released after cooking) and stir to combine, then pour the mixture into the greased dish and scatter over the sun-blushed tomatoes.

5 Bake in the oven for 20 minutes. During the last 5 minutes of cooking, change the oven setting to grill (or heat a separate grill and move the dish into it), then grill on high for the last few minutes in order to brown the top of the quiche. Leave to rest for a few minutes before slicing. Serve warm, sprinkled with more cumin if you like, and with the Undressed Herb Salad on the side.

aubergine-wrapped fingers

SERVES 4
PREPARATION TIME: 30 minutes,
  plus resting
COOKING TIME: 1 hour 10 minutes

2 aubergines

5 tbsp olive oil

250g/9oz minced lamb or veal

1 onion, finely chopped

1 tbsp pomegranate molasses

1 tbsp finely chopped coriander
  leaves

¼ tsp ground cardamom

¼ tsp ground allspice

a pinch of crushed chilli flakes
  (optional)

500g/1lb 2oz/2 cups passata

3 garlic cloves, finely chopped
  or crushed

2 tbsp pine nuts

sea salt and freshly ground black
  pepper

Greek yogurt, to serve

chopped mint leaves, to sprinkle

Arabic bread (see page 217), to
  serve

These are the Middle Eastern versions of involtinis. Known as lisan el qadi in Arabic, they literally translate as "tongue of the judge". Long, thin slices of aubergine are rolled to wrap the meat. Their name was possibly inspired by the fact that Iraqis are so fond of meat that a noble judge would always expect his food to be served with meat rather than rice.

1 Preheat the oven to 180°C/350°F/Gas 4. Slice the aubergines lengthwise into 3mm/⅛in-thick slices; you should get about 16 slices. Brush each slice with oil on both sides, then put them in a baking dish (one that you can reuse later to cook the final dish in its sauce) and bake for 20 minutes, turning them once halfway, until they are cooked through and golden but not charred. You may need to cook them in batches. Transfer to a plate lined with kitchen paper and leave to one side until cool enough to handle.

2 Meanwhile, add the mince to a bowl with the onion, pomegranate molasses, coriander, cardamom, allspice and chilli flakes, if using. Season to taste with salt and pepper. Mix well to incorporate and then divide the meat into sausage-shaped portions or "fingers", 2.5cm/1in thick and 5cm/2in long.

3 When the aubergine slices are cool, lay one of them down on a work surface, with the wider end facing you. Place a veal finger at the end of the aubergine slice and begin rolling it up tightly. Continue with the remaining aubergine slices and veal fingers. Transfer the rolls to the dish, seam-side down and making sure they fit snugly. Put the passata and garlic in a bowl and season to taste with salt and pepper. Pour the passata sauce over the aubergine rolls, then cover with foil and bake in the oven for 45 minutes.

4 Remove the dish from the oven and leave to rest for at least 10 minutes. Meanwhile, toast the pine nuts in a heavy-based pan over a medium heat for 1–2 minutes until golden and fragrant, shaking the pan often.

5 Put the fingers on a bed of yogurt, then pour over the sauce and sprinkle with the toasted pine nuts and mint. Serve with Arabic bread.

leafy lamb kebabs

SERVES 4
PREPARATION TIME: 20 minutes,
  plus marinating
COOKING TIME: 5 minutes

70ml/2¼fl oz/¼ cup sunflower oil,
  plus extra for oiling

70ml/2¼fl oz/¼ cup verjuice, or
  lime juice to taste

1 heaped tbsp sumac

500g/1lb 2oz fillets of lamb
  tenderloin

2 onions, thinly sliced

12 cherry tomatoes

sea salt and freshly ground black
  pepper

Chelow Rice (see page 214), to serve

warm Thin Flatbread (see page
  218), to serve

The original name for this dish is kabâb-e barg. Barg translates as "leaf" and you need to cut your meat into long, thin strips. If tenderloin is hard to find, you can use neck fillets instead. Lime juice can be substituted for the sweet tang of verjuice. The more fat or oil there is in the marinade, the more tender the results will be. For the best results, marinate the lamb overnight and use wide skewers.

1 To make the marinade, put the oil, verjuice and sumac in a medium bowl and mix well until the ingredients have emulsified. If using wooden skewers, soak them in cold water before grilling.

2 With a sharp knife, divide the lamb fillet into 4–6 equal portions around 6cm/2½in long. Working with one portion at a time, flatten each portion slightly with the palm of your hand, then cut through at about 1cm/½in from the top, horizontally, making sure not to sever the flesh completely. Open it out to form one longer slice, and then repeat the same process in the other direction from the bottom so that you end up with one long leafy strip. Each strip should ideally be about 18cm/7in long and less than 1cm/½in thick. Trim the edges so the strip has straight lines, then use a meat mallet to soften and stretch the meat.

3 Carefully weave a wooden skewer through each strip of meat. Put 2–3 kebabs in a shallow dish and sprinkle with a little onion and half the marinade. Repeat with the remaining kebabs, onion and marinade.

4 Leave to marinate in the fridge for at least 1 hour or overnight, turning the kebabs in the marinade a couple of times during this period. Just before putting the lamb on the barbecue, shake off most of the marinade, and season to taste with salt and pepper. Reserve the onions.

5 Preheat a charcoal barbecue until the charcoal is burning white or heat a gas barbecue to high. Oil the rack. Grill the kebabs for just 1–2 minutes on each side. You can also barbecue the tomatoes and onions at the same time, using a vegetable basket, until golden and caramelized. Alternatively, cook them in a griddle pan.

6 Serve the kebabs immediately with the caramelized onions and barbecued tomatoes and with Chelow Rice and warm Thin Flatbread.

caramelized onions stuffed with lamb

SERVES 4
PREPARATION TIME: 35 minutes
COOKING TIME: 1 ½ hours

250g/9oz lamb mince

55g/2oz/¼ cup short-grain white rice or risotto rice

½ tsp ground allspice

½ tsp ground cinnamon

2 tsp dried mint

1 tbsp tomato purée

1 tbsp pine nuts (optional)

about 1 tbsp sea salt, plus extra for seasoning

4–5 large white onions

1 tbsp tamarind paste

juice of 1 lemon

freshly ground black pepper

Greek yogurt, to serve

green salad of your choice, to serve

This dish is dedicated to Aunty Suham, the mother of my dear friends Dhabia and Wid, who first introduced me to these moreish dolmas at an unforgettable feast she prepared when I asked her about some Iraqi dishes for the cookbook. Variations of the dishes she made that evening have made it into this book and I'm forever grateful to her. It's important to use large onions because the layers have more surface area, making them more suited for stuffing and rolling. The number of onions required will vary depending on how many layers you can get out of each onion. If you like them more meltingly soft, you can cook them for a little longer. The dolmas are easy to make, but you do need to make sure the onions are blanched enough to be very pliable. The stuffed onions are usually cooked with other dolmas, such as Vine Leaves with Bulgur, Figs & Nuts (see page 160) but never cabbage leaves, as they're too similar in appearance to onions, potentially confusing diners.

1 Put the lamb, rice, spices, mint and tomato purée in a mixing bowl and season with salt and pepper.

2 Toast the pine nuts, if using, in a heavy-based pan over a medium heat for 1–2 minutes until golden and fragrant, shaking the pan often. Add the toasted pine nuts to the lamb mixture and mix well to incorporate.

3 Half-fill a large saucepan with water, sprinkle in the salt and bring to the boil over a high heat. Meanwhile, slice off the tops and bottoms of the onions. Without cutting right through them, cut the onions in half lengthways, stopping about halfway through each one. Remove the skin, then gently remove the root strands and any shorter layers that will be too short for stuffing and rolling. Set these aside for use in the stuffing later. You should have 5–6 outer layers per onion to work with.

4 Once the water reaches the boil, add the onion layers that are suitable for stuffing, then reduce the heat to low, cover with a lid and simmer for 10 minutes, or until the onion layers begin to soften and come apart. You want them to be pliable enough so that they are easy

to roll. Remove the onions from the pan using a slotted spoon, reserving 500ml/17fl oz/2 cups onion broth. Set aside until cool enough to handle.

5 Meanwhile, finely chop a small onion's worth of the reserved shorter onion layers. Add the chopped onion to the meat mixture and mix well. (Any leftover onion layers can be transferred to a zippable bag and kept in the fridge for use in other recipes, or finely chopped and frozen.)

6 Once the blanched onion layers have cooled, gently separate the layers, being careful not to tear them. Working with one layer at a time, place a spoonful of the stuffing into each onion layer (the size of the spoon will depend upon the size of the onion) and roll tightly, following the curve. If you are preparing the dish ahead, you can freeze the stuffed onions at this point, if you like.

7 Transfer the stuffed onions to a deep, ovenproof, heavy-based pan, about 32cm/13in in diameter, and layer them snugly, seam-side down.

8 Put the tamarind paste in a bowl and stir in most of the reserved onion broth. Add the lemon juice and season with salt, then pour the mixture over the onions. Put a heatproof plate on top of the mixture to prevent the onions from moving around and losing their shape.

9 Put the pan over a medium–high heat and bring to the boil, then reduce the heat to low. Cover with a lid and simmer for 1 hour or until the onions have softened, the rice is tender and the juices have somewhat reduced. Remove the lid and the plate and cook, uncovered, for a further 15 minutes.

10 During the last 10 minutes of cooking, change the oven setting to grill (or heat a separate grill and move the pan into it), then grill the onions on high for 5 minutes until they are golden brown and lightly charred, adding some of the remaining reserved broth if they appear to be drying out. Serve with yogurt and a green salad.

baked kafta

SERVES 4
PREPARATION TIME: 30 minutes
COOKING TIME: 45 minutes

1 large onion, very finely chopped,
plus 400g/14oz onions, cut into
1cm/½in slices

2 handfuls of parsley leaves, very
finely chopped

1 tbsp mint leaves, very finely
chopped

500g/1lb 2oz minced lamb or beef

1 tbsp sea salt, or to taste

1½ tsp ground allspice

2 tbsp olive oil

600g/1lb 5oz tomatoes, cut into
1cm/½in slices

600g/1lb 5oz potatoes, cut into
1cm/½in slices

1 heaped tbsp tomato purée

Kafta is the Middle East's version of hamburger meat. It can be shallow-fried, moulded onto skewers for barbecuing or baked with vegetables, as here. I prefer the texture of the kafta when it's mixed by hand, but if you want to use a food processor, create the paste first in it before adding the meat. Pulse for 2 minutes, but be sure not to overwork the meat or it will be tough. For another type of kafta, try Herbed Kafta with Dukkah Tahini (see page 104).

1 Put the chopped onion and the herbs on a chopping board and continue chopping until the mixture forms a fine paste. Transfer the paste into a large bowl, add the meat and 1 teaspoon of the salt and 1 teaspoon of the allspice. Knead the mixture with your hands for 1–2 minutes until well mixed.

2 Preheat the oven to 200°C/400°F/Gas 6. Generously grease the base and sides of a 6cm/2½in deep, 35cm/14in diameter, baking dish with the oil. Spread the meat mixture across the base of the dish to a thickness of about 1cm/½in.

3 Cover the entire meat layer with tomato slices, then season with another teaspoon of the salt. Next, form a layer of onion slices and then potato slices. Sprinkle with the remaining salt and allspice.

4 Dilute the tomato purée in 6 tablespoons water, mix well and drizzle the mixture over the potato slices.

5 Cover with foil and bake in the oven for 45 minutes, basting with the juices halfway through the cooking time.

6 During the last 10 minutes of cooking, remove the foil, then change the oven setting to grill (or heat a separate grill and move the dish into it). Grill on high for a few minutes or until the potatoes are golden and crispy. Serve hot.

herbed kafta with dukkah tahini

SERVES 4
PREPARATION TIME: 45 minutes
COOKING TIME: 50 minutes

1 large onion, quartered

2 handfuls of mixed herb leaves
  (mint, dill, coriander and parsley)

2 mild red chillies, deseeded and
  roughly chopped (optional)

6 garlic cloves, crushed with the
  blade of a knife

500g/1lb 2oz minced lamb

1½ tsp ground allspice

½ tsp coriander seeds

½ tsp cumin seeds

1 tsp sesame seeds

½ tsp dried mint

½ tsp poppy seeds (optional)

160ml/5¼fl oz/⅔ cup tahini

5 tbsp lemon juice

1 tbsp olive oil

sea salt

Potato Matchsticks (see page 218),
  to serve

mixed salad, to serve

Known as kafta b tahini, this dish is particularly popular in Palestine. While not traditional, I've added to the tahini an Egyptian mix of spices, herbs and seeds, known as dukkah, which also traditionally includes nuts.

1 Put the onion in a food processor and pulse to form a rough paste. Squeeze out as much of the liquid as possible. Return the mixture to the food processor, add the herbs, chillies and garlic and pulse again for 1–2 minutes until the mixture forms a fine paste.

2 Put the lamb in a large mixing bowl. Add the allspice, season to taste with salt and knead the herb and onion mixture with the meat for 1–2 minutes until well incorporated. Don't overwork it or the meat will toughen. Cover and set aside.

3 Meanwhile, prepare the dukkah mixture by toasting the coriander and cumin seeds in a heavy-based pan over a medium heat for 1–2 minutes until fragrant, shaking the pan often. Transfer to a small food processor or grinder and grind to a rough consistency.

4 Return the mixture to the pan, add the sesame seeds and continue to cook until golden, then remove the pan from the heat. Add the dried mint, poppy seeds, if using, and season to taste with salt. Set aside.

5 Put the tahini in a mixing bowl and slowly stir in as much of 160ml/ 5¼fl oz/⅔ cup water as is needed to reach a creamy consistency. Also add a little of the lemon juice as you go, until a creamy consistency is reached and the tahini is as sharp as you like it. Make sure the mixture is runny (as it will thicken with cooking), by adding more lemon juice or water to taste. You may not need all the lemon juice. Sprinkle in the dukkah mixture and stir well.

6 Preheat the oven to 200°C/400°F/Gas 6. Meanwhile, mould the meat mixture into 16 patties, about 5cm/2in in diameter. Heat 1 tablespoon of the oil in a large ovenproof frying pan over a medium heat. Add the patties and cook for about 2 minutes on each side until browned, then remove from the heat.

7 Pour the tahini mixture over the patties, cover the pan with the lid or some foil and bake for 45 minutes.

8 Once the kafta have finished cooking, test the tahini mixture around the patties: it will have dried up a bit and the tahini will hug the patties snuggly. If you want to have more of a sauce, thin it with a little water before serving with Potato Matchsticks and a mixed salad.

spiced lamb flatbread pizzas

SERVES 4
PREPARATION TIME: 25 minutes,
 plus making the dough and rising
 time
COOKING TIME: 5–7 minutes

2 large onions, very finely chopped

4 large plum tomatoes, very finely
 chopped

1 tsp sea salt

400g/14oz finely minced lamb

1 tsp ground cinnamon

1 tsp ground allspice

1 tsp hot chilli flakes

2 tbsp pomegranate molasses

1 recipe quantity Arabic Bread
 dough (see page 217)

flour, for dusting

3 tbsp pine nuts

TO SERVE
Undressed Herb Salad (see page 67)

Harissa (see page 210)

Savoury Yogurt Shake (see page
 221)

lemon halves

Although these are known by Armenians as missahatz, by Turks as lahmacun and by the Lebanese as lahm b'ajeen, the basic idea is the same: spread meat on bread. The best flatbread pizza I've ever had, second to this recipe of course, was at an Armenian bakery called Furn Ikhshanian, in Zokak el Blat, a district of Beirut. The reason for this was their paper-thin and crispy dough. Flatbread pizzas belong to the manaquiche family, and while manaquiche are considered a breakfast food, they are enjoyed throughout the day, and there is a predominant after-club culture of tucking into these after a heavy night out! They're best when washed down with some savoury yogurt shake.

1 Put the onions and tomatoes in a bowl. Note that they must be chopped almost to a paste. Sprinkle the paste with the salt and set aside for 5 minutes, then squeeze out as much liquid as possible.

2 Put the well-squeezed tomatoes and onions in a bowl with the lamb, sprinkle with the cinnamon, allspice and chilli flakes and drizzle with the pomegranate molasses, then mix well.

3 Preheat the oven to 250°C/500°F/Gas 9. Divide the bread dough into 4 balls of equal size (about 125g/4½oz each) and dust the work surface with flour. Roll out each ball to about 30cm/12in in diameter (the dough should be paper thin). Using your fingers, gently spread one-quarter of the meat mixture evenly and thinly across each piece of dough. Sprinkle the pine nuts over the pizzas.

4 Transfer the pizzas to perforated round pizza crispers and bake in the oven for 5–7 minutes until the edges of the pizzas are golden and crispy. Alternatively, use baking sheets to slide the pizzas straight onto the oven shelves. Serve with Undressed Herb Salad, Harissa and Savoury Yogurt Shake, with lemon halves for squeezing.

lamb rice with crispy potato base

SERVES 4
PREPARATION TIME: 30 minutes,
  plus making the advieh and rice
COOKING TIME: 1 ½ hours

125ml/4fl oz/ ½ cup sunflower oil

1 onion, finely chopped, plus
  1 onion, thinly sliced

4 garlic cloves, finely chopped

500g/1lb 2oz boneless lamb
  (preferably leg), fat trimmed off
  and cut into 1cm/ ½in cubes

2 tsp Advieh 1 (see page 211)

a pinch of ground cinnamon

5 tbsp tomato purée

500g/1lb 2oz large tomatoes,
  deseeded and cut into 1cm/ ½in
  cubes

500g/1lb 2oz waxy potatoes, peeled,
  one half cut into 1cm/ ½in cubes,
  the other half sliced lengthways
  into long thin ovals about 3mm/⅛in
  thick

1 recipe quantity Parboiled Rice
  (see page 214)

chopped mint leaves, to sprinkle

sea salt and freshly ground black
  pepper

Greek yogurt or kashk, to serve

This is my take on a layered rice recipe known as Istambooli Polow. At first glance it does sound like a carb-on-carb sin, with its combination of potato and rice, but don't judge it until you have tried it. Turkey also works well instead of lamb.

1 Heat 2 tablespoons of the oil in a frying pan over a medium–low heat, add the chopped onion and sauté for 4–5 minutes or until soft and translucent. Add the garlic, lamb, spices, tomato purée and tomatoes, and season to taste with salt and pepper. Add 115ml/3¾fl oz/scant ½ cup water, or enough to cover the other ingredients, then increase the heat to high and bring to the boil. Reduce the heat to low and leave to simmer gently for 1 hour or until the meat is tender and the sauce is thick. Remove from the heat and stir in the potato cubes.

2 Place a 2l/70fl oz/8-cup non-stick saucepan with a 20cm/8in base over a medium heat, and pour in 5 tablespoons of the oil. Once the oil is sizzling, arrange the potato slices across the base (they can overlap slightly), then sprinkle over 2 tablespoons of the lamb and tomato mixture, followed by a layer of rice. Continue alternating layers of lamb and rice, building it up into a dome shape. The last layer should be rice.

3 Using the handle of a wooden spoon, make three holes in the rice all the way to the bottom, being careful not to puncture the potatoes.

4 Wrap the saucepan lid in a clean kitchen towel and tie it into a tight knot at the handle, then use it to cover the pan as tightly as you can so that steam doesn't escape. (The kitchen towel will prevent the moisture from dripping into the rice, making it soggy.) Cook the rice over a medium heat for 2–3 minutes until the rice is steaming (you will see puffs of steam escaping at the edges of the lid), then reduce the heat to low and cook for 20–25 minutes, with the lid on all the time.

5 Meanwhile, heat the remaining oil in a frying pan over a medium–low heat, and fry the sliced onion until crispy and golden.

6 Serve the rice and tahdeeg following the instructions in steps 5–7 of Steamed Rice on page 214. Sprinkle with mint and serve with yogurt and the fried onion rings.

freekeh with lamb & rhubarb

SERVES 4
PREPARATION TIME: 25 minutes,
 plus making the stock
COOKING TIME: 2 hours

30g/1oz salted butter

240g/8½oz pearl onions or small shallots, peeled

900g/2lb lamb shank(s)

½ tsp ground allspice

2 tsp Aleppo pepper flakes or crushed chilli flakes

5cm/2in piece of root ginger, peeled and chopped very finely

6 garlic cloves, crushed with the blade of a knife

1 bay leaf

¼ tsp coriander seeds

2.5l/88fl oz/10 cups Vegetable Stock (see page 211)

400g/14oz/2½ cups wholegrain freekeh or wholegrain farro, rinsed well

250g/9oz rhubarb, cut into 2.5cm/1in lengths

2 tbsp pine nuts

30g/1oz/scant ¼ cup blanched almonds

2 tbsp roughly chopped coriander leaves, to sprinkle

sea salt and freshly ground black pepper

Greek yogurt, to serve

Freekeh is my number one grain. The wheat is harvested young when the grains are soft and full of moisture. The grain is then sun-dried before being roasted over an open fire for several minutes. Once cooled, it's rubbed to separate it from the chaff. It can be purchased cracked or whole, and will often require careful cleaning to rid it of any stones.

1 Melt 20g/¾oz of the butter in a large heavy-based saucepan over a medium–low heat, and fry the pearl onions for 3–4 minutes until golden. Remove the onions from the pan and set aside.

2 Rub the lamb shank(s) all over with the allspice and Aleppo pepper flakes and season to taste with salt and pepper, then transfer to the saucepan.

3 Return the onions to the pan, and sear the onions and lamb until browned all over. Remove the shank and set aside on a plate.

4 Add half the remaining butter to the pan, along with the ginger, garlic, bay leaf and coriander seeds, and cook for 1 minute or so until aromatic. Return the lamb shank and pour over 1l/35fl oz/4 cups of the stock, then cover the pan with a lid, reduce the heat to low and simmer for 1¾ hours, turning the shank around a couple of times during the cooking time.

5 Meanwhile, put the freekeh in a saucepan and pour over the remaining stock, then cover the pan and bring to the boil. Reduce the heat to low and leave to simmer for about 45 minutes or until the stock has been absorbed and the grains are cooked through but still have a slight bite to them. If the grains have not cooked through in this time, but the stock has been absorbed, add a little water as needed. Once cooked, set aside, covered, until ready to serve.

6 Just before the lamb stew finishes cooking, melt the remaining butter in a pan over a medium heat, add the rhubarb and toss to combine, then cook for 4 minutes until just beginning to soften.

7 Spoon the rhubarb into the lamb stew and toss well, then remove the stew from the heat and leave it to sit, covered, for 5 minutes.

8 Toast the pine nuts and almonds in a heavy-based pan over a medium heat for 1–2 minutes until golden and fragrant, shaking the pan often.

9 Transfer the freekeh to a serving plate and top with the lamb stew and rhubarb. Sprinkle with the nuts and coriander and serve with yogurt.

auntie anwaar's mansaf risotto

SERVES 4
PREPARATION TIME: 15 minutes,
  plus making the bread
COOKING TIME: 1 ½ hours

30g/1oz salted butter

850g/1lb 14oz lamb shank(s)

2 carrots, roughly chopped

1 onion, quartered

10 garlic cloves, 5 left whole and
  5 pounded using a pestle and
  mortar or crushed

6 cardamom pods

1 bay leaf

1 cinnamon stick

200g/7oz/scant 1 cup short-grain or
  risotto rice

1 tsp turmeric

750ml/26fl oz/3 cups Greek yogurt

1 egg

1 tbsp cornflour, if needed

3 tbsp pine nuts

3 tbsp blanched almonds

juice of 2 lemons

2 loaves of warm Arabic Bread (see
  page 217)

mint leaves, finely chopped,
  to sprinkle

sea salt and freshly ground black
  pepper

Traditionally, this quintessentially Bedouin dish is prepared using jmeed, which is a dried yogurt or buttermilk sometimes called rock cheese. Anwaar Younis gave me her recipe for Jordan's national dish, which I've tweaked a little. Mansaf is a communal dish and a great symbol of generosity that is often served on special occasions. Sometimes eaten with the right hand, the meat is torn apart and rolled into a ball, which is then dipped into the yogurt. Jmeed is not easy to source in the West, so I have used Greek yogurt instead.

1 Melt the butter in a heavy-based saucepan over a medium heat, add the lamb shank(s), carrots, onion, whole garlic cloves, cardamom pods, bay leaf and cinnamon stick and cook for 4–5 minutes, turning frequently, until the meat has browned. Season with salt to taste, then cover with 1.25l/44fl oz/5 cups water and bring to the boil. Reduce the heat to low, then cover and simmer for 1 hour or until the meat is tender and falling off the bone. Strain well, reserving the stock and the meat, but discarding the vegetables and spices.

2 Put the rice, 750ml/26fl oz/3 cups of the reserved stock and the turmeric in a separate heavy-based pan over a medium heat. Bring to the boil, then reduce the heat to low and simmer for 25 minutes or until the rice is cooked through and all the stock has been absorbed, adding a little more stock as needed and stirring every so often to achieve a creamy texture. Season to taste with salt and pepper.

3 Meanwhile, separate the meat from the bone, cut into smaller pieces and set aside. Put the yogurt in the pan the meat was cooked in and place over a medium heat, then add the egg and whisk well. Return the meat to the pan and bring the mixture to a gentle boil. Reduce the heat to low and simmer, stirring often so that the yogurt doesn't catch, for 15–20 minutes until the yogurt is thick and creamy. If the mixture is too runny, add the cornflour and mix until thickened.

4 Toast the pine nuts and almonds in a heavy-based pan over a medium heat for 1–2 minutes until golden, shaking the pan often.

5 Put the crushed garlic in a small bowl, add the lemon juice and mix. To serve, lay out the Arabic Bread on a large serving platter and pour the garlic mixture over it. Spoon over the rice, then spoon over a couple of tablespoons of the lamb and yogurt mixture. Scatter with the meat pieces and then sprinkle over the toasted nuts and mint. Serve the remaining cooked yogurt on the side.

meaty ratatouille

SERVES 4
PREPARATION TIME: 25 minutes
COOKING TIME: 30 minutes

3 tbsp olive oil

3 onions, thinly sliced

1 garlic bulb, cloves separated and crushed with the blade of a knife

250g/9oz minced lamb, beef or pork

¼ tsp ground cinnamon

½ tsp ground allspice

1 large courgette, roughly chopped

2 carrots, roughly chopped

1 large potato, roughly chopped

7 small tomatoes, quartered

2 thyme sprigs (optional)

2 heaped tbsp tomato purée

1 aubergine, roughly chopped

2 tbsp pine nuts, to sprinkle

sea salt

Vermicelli Rice (see page 215), to serve

Greek yogurt, to serve (optional)

Think of this as a Lebanese relative of ratatouille, if you like. It's about using fresh produce from the garden or market, as available, and layering them in a pot. You can go as chunky or as fine as you like. Just make sure the aubergine is cut into larger pieces, as they cook the fastest. The kind of tomatoes you use here are important so do taste and adjust, adding more or less tomato purée for colour and richness when needed.

1 Heat the oil in a large heavy-based saucepan over a medium heat, add the onions and garlic and let them sweat for 3–5 minutes until soft and translucent.

2 Add the minced lamb, cinnamon and allspice, and season with salt. Stir well, then cook for a further 2–3 minutes until browned.

3 Add the courgette, carrots, potato, tomatoes and thyme, if using. Dilute the tomato purée in about 750ml/26fl oz/3 cups water and pour into the pan and stir well. Cover and bring to the boil, then reduce the heat to low. Add the aubergine and simmer, covered, for 20 minutes until the vegetables are cooked but still have a slight bite to them.

4 Toast the pine nuts in a heavy-based pan over a medium heat for 1–2 minutes until golden and fragrant, shaking the pan often.

5 Sprinkle the toasted pine nuts over the ratatouille and serve with Vermicelli Rice and yogurt, if you like.

lamb & herb stew

SERVES 4
PREPARATION TIME: 30 minutes
  plus overnight soaking
COOKING TIME: 2–2 ½ hours

115g/4oz/heaped ½ cup dried red
  kidney beans, soaked overnight

2 tbsp sunflower oil

1 onion, finely chopped

1 leek, finely chopped

1 handful of chives, finely chopped

1 handful of fenugreek leaves or
  1 tbsp dried fenugreek

1 handful finely chopped dill leaves,
  plus extra for sprinkling

2 handfuls of parsley leaves

2 handfuls of coriander leaves

400g/14oz boneless lamb shoulder,
  cut into 2cm/¾in cubes

4 whole dried black limes (limu
  amani), pierced with the tip of
  a knife (optional)

juice of 2 lemons

sea salt and freshly ground black
  pepper

Chelow Rice (see page 214), to serve

Greek yogurt, to serve

Upon first sight, you may not be compelled to try one of Iran's most popular dishes, known locally as ghormeh-e sabzi. But don't be misled by first impressions. This dish is a splendid testimony to the Persian love of herbs and fragrance, and is a harmonious melange of texture and flavour. For an equally fulfilling vegetarian option, double the kidney bean portion to make up for the absent lamb.

1 Put the red kidney beans in a deep, heavy-based saucepan and cover with water. Bring to a rolling boil over a medium heat and continue to boil for 10–15 minutes, until the beans are tender but with a slight bite to them. Drain and set aside.

2 Meanwhile, heat the oil in a heavy-based saucepan or casserole dish over a medium heat. Add the onion and leek and fry for 5 minutes until soft and golden.

3 Add all the herbs and stir well, then cook for 10 minutes until fragrant, stirring often. Increase the heat to high, add the lamb and stir well to coat with the onion and leeks, then cook for about 2 minutes until the meat is browned on all sides.

4 Add the drained kidney beans to the pan, cover with water and bring to the boil. Reduce the heat to low, then cover with a lid and simmer for 1½–2 hours, or until the beans are soft, the meat is tender and the sauce reduced and well blended.

5 When the stew has been simmering for about an hour, add the dried limes, if using (any sooner and they will turn the stew bitter), pushing them down into the liquid. They will tend to pop back up, so try to cover them with a few pieces of meat to keep them submerged.

6 Just before serving, season the dish with lemon juice, and salt and pepper to taste and mix well. Serve with the Chelow Rice and yogurt.

baked spiced lamb tortellini

SERVES 4
PREPARATION TIME: 1 hour,
  plus resting and making the herb
  butter
COOKING TIME: 25 minutes

100g/3½oz/scant ⅔ cup flour, plus
  extra for seasoning

100g/3½oz/scant ⅔ cup semolina
  flour, plus extra to dust

1 tsp sea salt, plus extra for
  seasoning

3 eggs

½ tsp extra virgin olive oil

2 tbsp sunflower oil

1 onion, finely chopped

250g/9oz finely minced lamb or beef

½ tsp ground cinnamon

½ tsp ground allspice

½ tsp crushed chilli flakes

700ml/24fl oz/2¾ cups Greek
  yogurt

1 tbsp cornflour, if needed

60g/2¼oz/heaped ⅓ cup
  pine nuts

1 recipe quantity Herb Butter (see
  page 211)

sumac, to sprinkle

Vermicelli Rice (see page 215),
  to serve (optional)

Known as shish barak in Lebanon, Syria and Palestine, the Armenians and Turks have a variation called manti. I love making them with friends while sharing a bottle of wine.

1 Sift together the flours and salt onto the work surface. Create a well in the middle, add 2 of the eggs and the olive oil and mix gently with a fork, gradually incorporating the eggs, oil and flour.

2 When the dough begins to come together, start kneading it with both hands for about 10 minutes, gradually pouring in 1–2 teaspoons water, until you form a malleable and firm dough that is not sticky. Wrap the dough in cling film and leave to rest for about 20 minutes.

3 Meanwhile, heat the sunflower oil in a heavy-based pan over a medium heat. Add the onion, cover and sweat for 4–5 minutes until soft. Add the lamb, cinnamon, allspice, and the chilli flakes and a little salt and cook for 5 minutes until the meat has browned. Remove and set aside.

4 Preheat the oven to 200°C/400°F/Gas 6. Divide the dough in half. Working with one half at a time, flatten the dough on a lightly dusted work surface and roll it out to about 1mm/¹⁄₁₆in thick. Using a 10cm/4in pastry cutter, stamp out 24–30 circles.

5 Place one circle in the palm of your hand, then place a generous teaspoonful of the meat mixture in the centre. Fold the dough over the filling and seal the edges to form a half-circle, then bring together the two tips of the half circle and seal tightly, leaving a hole in the centre. Place, sealed edges facing downwards, on a lightly floured baking tray. Repeat with the remaining circles and meat mixture. Bake in the oven for 20 minutes or until lightly golden and crunchy.

6 Meanwhile, heat the yogurt in a heavy-based saucepan over a medium heat, then break in the remaining egg and mix well. Bring the mixture to a gentle boil, then reduce the heat to low and simmer for 3–4 minutes, stirring continuously. The texture should be thick and creamy. If the mixture is too runny, then dissolve the cornflour into it and mix well until thickened.

7 Toast the pine nuts in a heavy-based pan over a medium heat for 1–2 minutes until golden and fragrant, shaking the pan often. Ladle the yogurt sauce into bowls, top with the tortellini and drizzle some herb butter over them. Sprinkle with the sumac and toasted pine nuts and serve with Vermicelli Rice, if you like.

Quinces stuffed with veal & wheat berries

SERVES 4
PREPARATION TIME: 25 minutes
COOKING TIME: 2¼ hours

juice and zest of 1 lemon, reserving the squeezed lemon shells

4 large quinces of similar size

70g/2½oz/2 cups wheat berries or rice

2 tbsp vegetable oil, plus extra for greasing

1 onion, finely chopped

1 tbsp peeled and finely chopped root ginger

3 garlic cloves, crushed

150g/5½oz minced veal

¼ tsp ground allspice

¼ tsp ground cinnamon

¼ tsp ground nutmeg

7 tbsp verjuice, or lime juice to taste

7 tbsp clear honey

1 tsp orange blossom water (optional)

7 tbsp Greek yogurt

½ tsp Aleppo pepper flakes or crushed chilli flakes

2 tbsp almonds

chopped mint leaves, to sprinkle

sea salt and freshly ground black pepper

Undressed Herb Salad (see page 67), to serve

I have an infatuation with quince's hints of jasmine, guava and vanilla, which leave a lingering perfume on your fingers: aromas that intensify as the fruit cooks. You can use minced beef or lamb to make the stuffing if you prefer.

1 Pour plenty of water into a large mixing bowl and add the lemon juice and the squeezed lemon shells. Slice off and reserve the tops of the quinces, then scoop out and reserve the seeds and some pulp, leaving 1cm/½in of the rind. Add the rinds to the water.

2 Put the wheat berries in a heavy-based pan over a medium heat, cover with three times their volume in water and cook for 1 hour or until the berries have cooked through but still have a bite to them. Drain.

3 Preheat the oven to 180°C/350°F/Gas 4. Heat the oil in a heavy-based pan over a medium heat and sauté the onion for 3–5 minutes until translucent. Add the ginger and 2 of the crushed garlic cloves and cook until aromatic. Add the reserved quince pulp and seeds, veal, allspice, cinnamon and nutmeg and cook for another 2–3 minutes. Pour in 3 tablespoons of the verjuice, add the cooked wheat berries and season to taste with salt and pepper, then mix thoroughly. Fill the cored quinces with the wheat berry mixture, replace the tops and place in a 15–20cm/6–8in lightly greased round baking dish.

4 Put 250ml/9fl oz/1 cup water in a mixing bowl with the remaining verjuice and the lemon zest, honey and orange blossom water and season to taste with salt. Pour the mixture over the stuffed quinces, cover with foil and bake in the oven for 1 hour or until the quinces are soft, basting occasionally with the juices. Remove the quinces from the oven. If the juices have not reduced down to a thick pouring glaze, transfer the juices to a saucepan over a medium heat and simmer to reduce further.

5 Meanwhile, put the yogurt, Aleppo pepper, remaining garlic and salt in a blender and whizz the mixture for about 1 minute until it's frothy.

6 Toast the almonds in a heavy-based pan over a medium heat for 1–2 minutes until golden and fragrant, shaking the pan often.

7 Spoon 2 tablespoons of the yogurt into each of four shallow bowls, place a cooked quince on top, then drizzle over a few spoonfuls of the thickened juice. Sprinkle with mint and the toasted almonds and serve with the Undressed Herb Salad.

aubergine, veal & yogurt crumble

SERVES 4
PREPARATION TIME: 25 minutes
COOKING TIME: 50 minutes

4 tsp tahini

1 garlic bulb, cloves separated and finely chopped

3 tbsp lemon juice

400g/14oz/1 ½ cups Greek yogurt at room temperature

40g/1 ½oz salted butter

2 onions, finely chopped

4 tbsp pine nuts

400g/14oz minced veal

2 tsp ground allspice

2 tsp Aleppo pepper flakes or crushed chilli flakes

2 tsp dried mint

500g/1lb 2oz/2 cups chopped tomatoes

2 tbsp pomegranate molasses

4 aubergines, about 1 kg/2lb 4oz in total

125ml/4fl oz/½ cup olive oil

2 small loaves of stale Arabic Bread, roughly torn (see page 217)

chopped mint leaves, to sprinkle

pomegranate seeds (see page 216), to sprinkle

sea salt and freshly ground black pepper

This is a version of a dish known as fattet makdous. The word fatteh in Arabic means "tear or crumble" or "of crumbs", and traditionally stale bread is used as the base. If you prefer, you can use lamb or beef, or lentils for a vegetarian stuffing option.

1 Preheat the oven to 200°C/400°F/Gas 6. Meanwhile, put the tahini, 1 teaspoon of the garlic, the lemon juice and 1 tablespoon water into a bowl and mix well. Add the yogurt and mix until the mixture forms a smooth, creamy texture. Season to taste with salt and pepper, and set aside at room temperature to allow the flavours to develop.

2 Melt the butter in a heavy-based frying pan over a medium heat, add the onions and cook for about 4 minutes until soft and translucent. Add half the pine nuts and cook for 1–2 minutes, until slightly browned, then add the veal, allspice, Aleppo pepper flakes, dried mint and the remaining garlic, and season to taste with salt and pepper. Mix well. Reduce the heat to low and cook until the meat has browned. Pour in the tomatoes and stir well to combine, then reduce the heat to low and cook for 5–8 minutes. Remove from the heat and pour in the pomegranate molasses, mixing well to incorporate. Cover and set aside.

3 Cut the aubergines in half, lengthways, keeping the stalks intact, as they make moving the aubergines easier as well as being more aesthetically pleasing. Transfer the aubergines to a baking tray, skin-side down. Puncture the flesh of each aubergine a couple of times with a fork, taking care not to tear through the skin. Rub each aubergine half with 1 tablespoon of the oil and season to taste with salt and pepper. Bake in the oven for about 20 minutes or until the flesh is soft.

4 Remove the aubergines from the oven (keep the oven on) and, using a fork, gently press down the flesh to mash it. Transfer two of the aubergine halves to each of four plates. Put the Arabic Bread on a baking tray and bake in the oven for 2–3 minutes until golden, turning over halfway. Check on the bread every minute to make sure it colours and crisps up evenly.

5 Toast the remaining pine nuts in a heavy-based pan over a medium heat for 1–2 minutes until golden and fragrant, shaking the pan often.

6 Assemble the aubergines by spooning 2 tablespoons of the meat and tomato mixture into each cavity, and pouring over 2 tablespoons of the yogurt dressing. Crumble over the toasted Arabic Bread, sprinkle with mint and pomegranate seeds and serve with the toasted pine nuts.

Veal Shoulder with butter beans

SERVES 4
PREPARATION TIME: 10 minutes,
  plus overnight soaking
COOKING TIME: 1 hour 40 minutes

250g/9oz/1¾ cups dried butter
  beans, soaked overnight (see
  Cooking Chickpeas, page 215)

2 tbsp sunflower oil

1 onion, finely chopped

300g/10½oz boneless veal or lamb
  shoulder, cut into 4cm/1½in cubes

1 garlic bulb, cloves separated and
  crushed with the blade of a knife

2–3 marrow bones (optional)

1 tsp ground cinnamon

1 tsp ground allspice

140g/5oz tomato purée

sea salt and freshly ground black
  pepper

Vermicelli Rice (see page 215),
  to serve

warm Arabic Bread (see page 217),
  to serve

This stew conjures up memories of my grandmother, after-school dinners on a dark, winter's evening and fighting over the last bone, then pounding it heavily on the chopping board being careful not to let a single drop of marrow escape. I have listed the bones as optional, but for me, the highlight of this dish has always been "inhaling" the rich marrow, so pleasing in its texture and gentle nutty sweetness. If you do want to cook the meat on the bone, ask your butcher to chop the bones into smaller pieces, and then add them with the butter beans. When the dish is served, use a marrow spoon to extract the marrow.

1 Drain the soaked butter beans, rinse well and set aside.

2 Heat the oil in a saucepan and add the onion. Cover, then sweat over a medium heat for 4–5 minutes, stirring often until the onions are soft and translucent. Add the veal and sear for 3–5 minutes until browned on all sides.

3 Add the garlic, butter beans, marrow bones, if using, cinnamon and allspice and cover with 1.2l/40fl oz/4¾ cups water. Increase the heat to high and bring to the boil, then reduce the heat to medium-low, cover with a lid and leave to simmer for about 1 hour.

4 Add the tomato purée and season to taste with salt and pepper (don't add salt until this stage as it can extend the cooking time of the beans). Cover and cook for a further 30 minutes or until the butter beans are soft, the meat is tender and the sauce has reduced and thickened. Serve with Vermicelli Rice and warm Arabic Bread.

Oxtail with Oozing Okra

SERVES 4–6
PREPARATION TIME: 35 minutes,
  plus making the harissa and stock
  (optional)
COOKING TIME: 1 hour

800g/1lb 12oz tomatoes

350g/12oz oxtail

1 tsp paprika

½ tsp ground cinnamon

5 tbsp sunflower oil

1 large onion, thinly sliced

3 garlic cloves, finely chopped

5cm/2in piece of root ginger,
  peeled and grated

1 cardamom pod, crushed using
  a pestle and mortar

300g/10½oz small potatoes,
  cut in half

¼ tsp Harissa (see page 210)

4 ready-to-eat dried apricots,
  halved

700ml/24fl oz/2¾ cups Vegetable
  Stock (optional, see page 211)

350g/12oz baby okra

1 handful of coriander leaves, finely
  chopped

sea salt

Couscous (see page 216), to serve

There are variations of this dish across North Africa and the Middle East, as well as a multitude of other cuisines, and its health benefits are many. You can reduce the sliminess of okra by soaking it in a vinegar solution, or by frying it. When you wash okra, dry it and any surface it will touch, including the knife, and always trim it without puncturing. Try to use very small okra if you can find them. If you prefer to bake the dish, toss the okra in 2 tablespoons olive oil first and bake at 180°C/350°F/Gas 4 for about 10 minutes.

1 With a sharp knife, cut a cross in the skin of each tomato, then put them in a heatproof bowl and cover with boiling water. Leave to stand for 2–3 minutes or until the skin peels, then drain. Plunge into cold water to stop them cooking, then peel off the skins and discard. Slice in half and scoop out the seeds, then finely chop the flesh.

2 Rub the oxtail with sea salt, paprika and cinnamon. Heat 2 tablespoons of the oil in a heavy-based saucepan over a medium heat, then add the oxtail. Cook until browned, then remove, cover and set aside.

3 Add the onion to the pan, cover and sweat for 2–3 minutes until soft and translucent. Add the garlic, ginger and cardamom and cook for a further minute until aromatic. Add the potatoes, toss to cover and cook for 1 minute, then return the meat to the pot, add the prepared tomatoes, harissa and apricots and cover with vegetable stock or water. Bring to the boil over a high heat and simmer for 45 minutes or until the meat is tender and the potatoes are cooked. Alternatively, remove the meat from the pan, slice around the bone, chop the meat into rough cubes and return to the pan with the bones.

4 Meanwhile, wash the okra under running water to remove any grit and pat dry completely with kitchen paper. Prepare the okra using a paring knife to shave off the crown, diagonally, into a fine point, being sure not to break the okra open at any point, or you will have more of the mucilaginous substance released. Heat the remaining oil in a frying pan over medium heat, then, once the oil is hot, add the prepared okra and coriander and fry for 8–10 minutes until the okra is bright green and cooked, being sure not to brown them. Transfer to the stew and cook for a further 5 minutes. Serve with Couscous.

seafood

almond-crusted scallops

SERVES 4
PREPARATION TIME: 10 minutes,
 plus making the preserved lemon
COOKING TIME: 10 minutes

100g/3 ½oz/1 cup ground almonds

1 tsp ground mahlab (optional)

2 eggs

16 scallops, about 500g/1lb 2oz

4 tbsp sunflower oil

125ml/4fl oz/½ cup verjuice, or lime
 juice to taste

100g/3 ½oz cold salted butter, diced

2 wedges of Preserved Lemon (see
 page 212), rind rinsed and finely
 chopped

60g/2 ¼oz/⅓ cup dates, pitted and
 roughly chopped

sea salt

Couscous (see page 216), to serve

Fattoush Salad (see page 61),
 Undressed Herb Salad (see page
 67) or Shaved Beetroot, Radish &
 Grapefruit Salad (see page 62),
 to serve

These plump scallops are inspired by North African flavours, and their gentle sweetness is highlighted by the dates, nutty almonds and subtle fragrance of mahlab. The sharpness of the preserved lemons and verjuice works well to balance it out, and the buttery goodness is always welcome.

1 Put the ground almonds and mahlab, if using, in a large mixing bowl, mix well and season to taste with salt.

2 Break the eggs into another bowl and whisk well. Toss the scallops in the whisked egg to coat. Remove them from the egg, shaking them to remove any excess egg, then add them to the ground almond mixture. Toss again to coat.

3 Heat the oil in a frying pan over a medium heat (the oil should not be so hot that it's smoking) and sear the scallops for about 2 minutes on each side until golden brown and just cooked through (the flesh will be bouncy when pushed, and if you slice one open, it will be a soft pinky-white). A good scallop should be tender and juicy so it's important not to overcook them.

4 Remove the scallops from the pan and transfer them to a warmed plate and cover. Add the verjuice to the pan, scraping up the brown bits and simmering the mixture for 2–3 minutes to reduce it.

5 Reduce the heat to medium-low and add the butter one piece at a time, whisking to create a creamy consistency. Increase the heat to medium-high and let the butter foam as you continue to whisk. Once it starts to turn brown, quickly remove the pan from the heat before it begins to burn. Add the scallops, preserved lemon and dates and toss well to coat. Serve with Couscous and one or more of the salads.

mussels in arak

SERVES 4
PREPARATION TIME: 25 minutes
COOKING TIME: 12 minutes

2kg/4lb 8oz fresh mussels

50g/1¾oz salted butter

2 shallots, very finely chopped

200ml/7fl oz/scant 1 cup Arak or
   Pernod

200ml/7fl oz/scant 1 cup
   dry white wine

2 tomatoes, very finely chopped

4 garlic cloves, finely chopped

1 bay leaf

juice of 1½ lemons

3 tbsp tarragon leaves, finely
   chopped, plus extra for sprinkling

sea salt and freshly ground black
   pepper

warm Arabic Bread (see page 217)
   or Potato Matchsticks (see page
   218), to serve

Arak, very much the national drink in Lebanon, is nicknamed the "milk of lions", most probably because when mixed with water to serve, it turns a milky white, but also because it was drunk by men, sometimes in the mornings, to show off their strength and masculinity. Arak is not traditionally used for cooking, but it works wonderfully in this dish, which has a double hit of anise from the Arak (use Pernod if you prefer) and tarragon. The flavour mellows nicely, leaving behind only the slightest hint of anise.

1 Wash the mussels under cold running water, pulling off any beards from the shells (this should be done with a gentle pull in the direction of the "hinge"). Only do this just before cooking as this process can injure/ kill the mussel, which is why some may not open after cooking. Scrape off any barnacles using the back of a sharp knife and discard any open mussels that don't close when given a tap on the work surface.

2 Melt the butter in a large, deep, heavy-based pan over a medium–low heat, add the shallots and cover and sweat for about 3–4 minutes until soft and translucent. Pour in the Arak and wine and add the tomatoes, garlic, bay leaf, lemon juice, tarragon, and salt and pepper to taste, then stir and simmer for about 2 minutes until reduced by half. Taste and adjust the seasoning if needed.

3 Add 125ml/4fl oz/½ cup water if you find the broth too reduced, then add the mussels. Cover and cook for 3–4 minutes, shaking the pan gently until all the mussels have opened. Don't overcook mussels, as they turn dry and tough. Discard any mussels that have not opened. Sprinkle with extra tarragon and serve with warm Arabic Bread or Potato Matchsticks.

Slow-braised spiced squid

SERVES 4
PREPARATION TIME: 30 minutes,
  plus making the spice mixture
COOKING TIME: 2 hours

60g/2¼oz salted butter

1 onion, finely chopped

4 cleaned squid, about 1kg/2lb 4oz
  in total, tentacles reserved

1kg/2lb 4oz tomatoes

400g/14oz fennel bulbs

8 garlic cloves, finely chopped

1 small hot red chilli, deseeded and
  finely chopped

80g/2¾oz/½ cup coarse or extra
  coarse bulgur wheat (grade 3 or
  4), rinsed

3 tbsp finely chopped dill leaves plus
  extra for sprinkling

170ml/5½fl oz/⅔ cup Arak, Ouzo
  or Pernod

¼ tsp Lebanese Seven Spices (see
  page 211)

500ml/17fl oz/2 cups fish stock

juice of 1 lemon (optional)

2 tbsp olive oil

sumac, for dusting

sea salt and freshly ground black
  pepper

lemon wedges, to serve

Standing apart from much of the Levant and the rest of Palestine, the people of Gaza have an affection for heat, with chilli and dill forming one of the cuisine's sacred combinations. This squid recipe is another example of the Levant's flair for stuffing, and while the recipe calls for bulgur, rice can also be used. While not traditional, I have added fennel and a generous drizzle of Arak.

1 To make the stuffing, melt half the butter in a wide, heavy-based saucepan over a high heat. Add the onion, reduce the heat to medium-low and cook for about 5 minutes until soft and translucent.

2 Chop the tentacles into 2cm/¾in dice. Chop 250g/9oz of the tomatoes and one of the fennel bulbs.

3 Add the tentacles, garlic, chilli and chopped fennel to the pan, and cook for 1 minute until fragrant, stirring once. Mix in the chopped tomatoes, bulgur wheat, 4 tablespoons water, 2 tablespoons of the dill, 3 tablespoons of the Arak and the spice mixture and heat through, stirring. Season to taste with salt and pepper. Set aside until the mixture is cool enough to handle.

4 Meanwhile, cut the remaining tomatoes and fennel bulbs into quarters.

5 Stuff each squid cavity two-thirds full with a quarter of the squid and tomato stuffing and secure with wooden cocktail sticks.

6 Preheat the oven to 130°C/250°F/Gas ½. Put the remaining butter in a 30cm/12in diameter flameproof pan that is deep enough to hold the stock. Put the pan over a high heat, and when the butter has melted, add the stuffed squid and sear on each side for 1–2 minutes. Pour in 125ml/4fl oz/½ cup of the Arak and let the mixture simmer over a low heat for 5 minutes until reduced by half. Add the quartered tomatoes and fennel, pour in the fish stock and sprinkle in the remaining dill and any remaining stuffing. Cover with foil and cook in the oven for 1½ hours. Remove the foil for the last 30 minutes of cooking to reduce the liquid slightly. During the last 10 minutes of cooking, change the oven setting to grill (or heat a separate grill and move the pan into it), and grill for the last few minutes until the squid is soft and tender.

7 Add the remaining Arak, lemon juice, if using, and oil to the pan, season to taste with salt and pepper, then sprinkle with dill. Transfer the stuffed squid to plates, spoon over the Arak sauce and dust with sumac. Serve with lemon wedges for squeezing over.

prawn, spinach & bread crumble

SERVES 4
PREPARATION TIME: 25 minutes,
 plus making the bread
COOKING TIME: 25 minutes

2 loaves of stale Arabic Bread
 (see page 217), roughly crumbled

2 tbsp sumac

2 tbsp olive oil

100g/3 ½oz salted butter

1 large onion, finely chopped

1 garlic bulb, cloves separated and
 finely chopped or crushed

1 small hot red chilli, finely chopped
 (optional)

900g/2lb large raw prawns,
 peeled and deveined

200ml/7fl oz/scant 1 cup Arak or
 Pernod

6 tomatoes, finely chopped

2 handfuls of coriander leaves,
 finely chopped

3 handfuls of spinach leaves,
 finely chopped

juice of 1 lemon

sea salt and freshly ground black
 pepper

This dish resembles a Greek prawn saganaki or a prawn vindaloo, but it's really my take on a similar dish my father prepares. I've turned it into another crumble (like the Aubergine, Veal & Yogurt Crumble on page 119), by tossing in some crisped Arabic breadcrumbs to soak up the all-important juices. I've also added a lacing of Arak to give it a more intoxicating flavour.

1 Preheat the oven to 180°C/350°F/Gas 4. Put the bread pieces on a baking sheet. Sprinkle with sumac, drizzle over the oil and toss to combine. Bake in the oven for 10 minutes, shaking the sheet a couple of times, until they are crisp and golden.

2 Meanwhile, melt 55g/2oz of the butter in a heavy-based saucepan over a medium heat, add the onion, then cover and sweat for 5 minutes until soft and translucent. Add the garlic, chilli, if using, and prawns and toss to coat, then sear the prawns for about 2 minutes on each side until they are light pink. Remove the prawns, cover and set aside.

3 Add the Arak to the pan and leave to bubble and reduce for 2–3 minutes. Add the tomatoes and coriander and cook for 4–5 minutes until the tomatoes have softened. Add the spinach leaves, the prawns and the remaining butter, season to taste with salt and pepper and toss to combine, cooking for 3–4 minutes until the spinach has wilted and the prawns are just cooked through. Squeeze over the lemon juice. Remove from the heat and transfer to bowls. Sprinkle over the crisped Arabic Bread crumbs and serve.

spiced prawn & coconut rice

SERVES 4
PREPARATION TIME: 45 minutes,
  plus making the rice
COOKING TIME: 45 minutes

30g/1oz unsalted butter

1 onion, finely chopped

1 small hot red chilli, deseeded and
finely chopped

½ tsp ground cinnamon

3cm/1¼in piece of root ginger,
peeled and finely chopped

2 tsp tomato purée

1 tsp ground turmeric (optional)

1 tsp ground fenugreek (optional)

500g/1lb 2oz large raw prawns,
peeled and deveined

5 garlic cloves, crushed

2 small handfuls of coriander
leaves, finely chopped, plus extra
for sprinkling

250ml/9fl oz/1 cup coconut cream

zest and juice of 1 lime or 2 tsp
dried lime powder

6 tbsp sunflower oil

1 recipe quantity Parboiled Rice
(see page 214)

sea salt and freshly ground black
pepper

lime wedges, to serve

This rice dish packs a little more heat than one would expect from Persian cuisine. Hailing from Southern Iran, it's a great example of the Indian influences on the Persian Gulf, following a rich history of trade. This recipe strays from tradition with the addition of coconut cream.

1 Melt the butter in a frying pan over a medium heat, then add the onion and fry for 3–5 minutes until soft and translucent. Add the chilli, cinnamon, ginger and tomato purée, plus the turmeric and fenugreek, if using, and cook, stirring, for another 2–3 minutes.

2 Add the prawns, garlic and coriander, stirring briefly so that they are covered in the spice and herb mixture, and cook for 2 minutes. Remove the pan from the heat. Mix in the coconut cream and lime zest and juice. Season to taste with salt and pepper.

3 Heat the oil in a heavy-based saucepan over a medium heat until it's sizzling. Using a spoon, sprinkle 4–5 tablespoons of the rice across the bottom to cover the base. Add 2–3 tablespoons of the prawn and coconut mixture and continue creating alternate layers of prawn mixture and rice, building the mixture up into a dome shape. Finish with a layer of rice. (Tipping all the rice in at once will squash and compress it, and the end result will not be as light and fluffy.)

4 Using the handle of a wooden spoon, make three holes in the rice all the way to the bottom of the pan.

5 Wrap the saucepan lid in a clean kitchen towel and tie it into a tight knot at the handle, then use it to cover the pan as tightly as you can so that steam does not escape. (The kitchen towel will prevent the moisture from dripping into the rice, making it soggy.) Cook the rice over a medium heat for 2–3 minutes until the rice is steaming (you will see puffs of steam escaping at the edges of the lid), then reduce the heat to low and cook for 20–25 minutes, with the lid on all the time.

6 Serve the rice and tahdeeg (crispy bottom) following the instructions in steps 5–7 of Steamed Rice on page 214. Sprinkle with extra coriander and serve with lime wedges.

sea bass with spiced caramelized onion rice

SERVES 4
PREPARATION TIME: 20 minutes
COOKING TIME: 50 minutes

whole sea bass, about 500g/1lb 2oz,
 cleaned and scaled

125ml/4 floz/½ cup sunflower oil

4 onions, thinly sliced

2 tbsp ground cumin

1 tsp ground cinnamon

1 tsp ground allspice

200g/7oz/1 cup medium-grain rice

2 tbsp pine nuts

2 tbsp olive oil

3 tbsp finely chopped parsley leaves
 (optional)

sea salt and freshly ground black
 pepper

lemon wedges, to serve

Tarator (see page 220), to serve

This fragrant dish called seeyadeeyeh is a family favourite. It was handed down to my Aunt Amale by my grandmother, finally making its way into my repertoire. My grandmother grew up along the coast of Batroun where her family's picturesque restaurant, Jammal, still stands overlooking the water grottos where she once swam. This recipe is a homage to her sea-loving soul.

1 Cut off the fish head and season it with salt. Set aside the remaining fish. Heat the sunflower oil in a heavy-based frying pan over a medium heat. When the oil begins to sizzle, add the fish head and fry for about 5 minutes on each side. Remove the fish head and set aside.

2 Add the onions to the pan and fry for about 5 minutes until golden, stirring occasionally. Remove from the heat and transfer the onions to a plate lined with kitchen paper. Spread three-quarters of the drained onions evenly across the base of a heavy-based saucepan. Place the pan over a low heat, add the fish head and cover with 500ml/17fl oz/2 cups water. Add the cumin, cinnamon and allspice, and season to taste with salt. Cover, increase the heat to medium-high and bring to the boil, then remove the fish head and reserve.

3 Add the rice to the pan, reduce the heat to low and cook, covered, for about 30 minutes or until the rice is tender and the water has been absorbed.

4 Preheat the oven to 200°C/400°F/Gas 6. Meanwhile, toast the pine nuts in a heavy-based pan over a medium heat for 1–2 minutes until golden and fragrant, shaking the pan often.

5 Put the uncooked fish in a baking dish, season to taste with salt and pepper and drizzle with the olive oil. Bake for 20 minutes or until the fish flakes easily when pushed with a fork. Divide the fish into four equal portions.

6 Transfer the cooked rice to a dish, stand the fish head in the centre, if you like, and arrange the fish portions on top of the rice. Add the remaining caramelized onions and the toasted pine nuts to the dish. Sprinkle with parsley and serve the dish with the lemon wedges and Tarator.

Veiled sea bass with a spicy surprise

SERVES 4
PREPARATION TIME: 20 minutes,
  plus making the preserved lemon
COOKING TIME: 25 minutes

1 handful of parsley leaves

1 handful of coriander leaves

2 tbsp finely chopped dill leaves

1 tbsp peeled and roughly chopped root ginger

1 mild red chilli, deseeded and roughly chopped

1 wedge of Preserved Lemon (see page 212), rind rinsed and roughly chopped

8 garlic cloves, crushed with the blade of a knife

¼ tsp ground cumin

6 tbsp olive oil, plus extra for greasing

4 sea bass, about 1.3kg/3lb in total, scaled and gutted

12 large bottled vine leaves, rinsed

sea salt and freshly ground black pepper

Couscous (see page 216), to serve

lemon wedges, to serve

The inspiration for "veiling" these sea bass came from chef Greg Malouf, who "veils" quails using vine leaves. As I had an excess of bottled vine leaves, and a few sea bass defrosting, it seemed appropriate to marry them. The vine leaves lock the moisture in as the fish is steamed and they also lend a very subtle sweetness. If using fresh vine leaves, blanch them in boiling water for a minute, or until pliable.

1 Preheat the oven to 190°C/375°F/Gas 5 and lightly grease a baking tray with oil. Put the parsley, coriander, dill, ginger, chilli, preserved lemon, garlic and cumin in a blender and pulse several times until you've made a rough paste, stopping to scrape the sides down as needed. Pour in 4 tablespoons of the oil and pulse once more to combine. Spoon the mixture into the fish cavities.

2 Season the sea bass with salt and pepper and rub with the remaining oil. Wrap each sea bass with 3 vine leaves, starting at the head and working all the way down, but leaving the tail exposed. Put the fish, seam-side down, on the baking tray and bake for 20–25 minutes, depending on the size of the fish (the general rule is 7 minutes cooking time per 2.5cm/1in measured at the thickest part of the fish), until the fish is tender and cooked through. Serve with Couscous and lemon wedges.

Salmon with herby butter and barberries

SERVES 4
PREPARATION TIME: 30 minutes,
  plus making the saffron liquid
COOKING TIME: 30 minutes

60g/2¼oz salted butter, softened,
  plus extra for greasing

40g/1½oz/heaped ½ cup dried
  barberries or cranberries

3 handfuls of parsley leaves,
  finely chopped

3 handfuls of coriander leaves,
  finely chopped

2 handfuls of tarragon leaves,
  finely chopped

2 handfuls of dill leaves, finely
  chopped

6 garlic cloves, very finely chopped

40g/1½oz/⅓ cup walnut pieces,
  coarsely chopped

2 tbsp Saffron Liquid (see page 212)

2 tbsp pomegranate molasses

1 salmon, about 1.5kg/3lb 5oz,
  scaled, butterflied and skin scored

sea salt and freshly ground black
  pepper

Chelow Rice (see page 214), to serve

lemon or lime wedges, to serve

This is an ideal dish for a lavish dinner party, exuding buttery goodness with a balance of herbs, sweet and tangy barberries and a pleasant hint of nuttiness from the walnuts, all coming together to create a parade of flavours. If you would rather, you could use haddock, cod or sea bass.

1 Preheat the oven to 180°C/350°F/Gas 4 and grease a baking pan with some of the butter.

2 Put the barberries in a bowl and cover with water, then leave to soak for 5 minutes. Drain well and pat dry with kitchen paper.

3 In a bowl, mix the herbs, garlic, drained barberries, walnuts, saffron liquid, 40g/1½oz of the butter and the pomegranate molasses to create a paste. Season with salt and pepper to taste.

4 Rub the interior and exterior of the fish with some salt and stuff the fish with the butter and herb paste. Sew up the fish cavity using a needle and thread or secure with 3–4 wooden cocktail sticks.

5 Melt the remaining butter in a small saucepan over a medium heat. Baste the fish with the butter and season with pepper.

6 Bake, uncovered, for 25–30 minutes, depending on the size of the fish (the general rule is 7 minutes cooking time per 2.5cm/1in measured at the thickest part of the fish), until the fish is tender, cooked through, crisp and golden. Remove the fish from the oven and transfer it to a platter. Drizzle with the cooking juices and serve with Chelow Rice and lemon wedges.

tamarind & herb mackerel stew

SERVES 4
PREPARATION TIME: 30 minutes
COOKING TIME: 1 hour

250g/9oz tamarind pulp, from a block

4 tbsp sunflower oil

1 large onion, finely chopped

1 tsp ground turmeric

1 small hot red chilli, deseeded and finely chopped

1 tbsp dried fenugreek

4 handfuls of coriander leaves, finely chopped

1 handful of parsley leaves, finely chopped

1 garlic bulb, cloves separated and finely chopped or crushed

mackerel fillets, about 1kg/2lb 4oz in total, cut into 2.5cm/1in-thick pieces

sea salt and freshly ground black pepper

Chelow Rice (see page 214), to serve

I find tamarind to be quite underrated. It's a souring agent that lends a very distinctive flavour to curries and stews, such as this wonderfully rich and pungent dish from the Persian Gulf region of Iran. Tamarind is sold in several forms and can be found in major supermarkets as well as in Asian, Spanish and Middle Eastern grocers. I prefer to use it in block form rather than concentrate, since it's nearly identical to fresh pods but easier to use because you don't have to break it out of its shell. It's also more tart and flavourful. If you prefer, you could use cod, haddock or tuna.

1 Put the tamarind pulp in a large heatproof bowl, pour over 500ml/ 17fl oz/2 cups boiling water and leave to soak for about 10 minutes. With a fork or your hands, mash the tamarind until it "dissolves" and you are left with a light brown, thick, sauce-like paste. Strain through a fine sieve, discarding the seeds and tough fibres. (Tamarind can be prepared as above and stored in an airtight container in the refrigerator for 2 weeks.)

2 Heat half the oil in a large, heavy-based saucepan over a medium-low heat. Add the onion and fry for 3 minutes until translucent and lightly brown. Add the turmeric, chilli and fenugreek, and cook for a further 3–4 minutes, until aromatic. Add the coriander, parsley and garlic and cook for 2–3 minutes, until the herbs wilt and darken in colour, stirring often. Add the tamarind paste and simmer, partially covered, for 30 minutes.

3 Meanwhile, season the mackerel with salt and pepper. Heat a heavy-based frying pan over a medium-low heat, add the remaining oil and fry the fish for 4–5 minutes on each side until golden brown. Remove and set aside on a plate lined with kitchen paper.

4 Add the fish to the herb and tamarind mixture in the saucepan and cook over a low heat for about 20 minutes or until the liquid has reduced and thickened. The fish should flake easily when pushed with a fork. Season to taste with salt and pepper and serve with Chelow Rice.

Spicy Snapper in the Tripoli Manner

SERVES 4
PREPARATION TIME: 20 minutes,
 plus making the tarator
COOKING TIME: 40 minutes

whole red snapper, 2kg/4lb 8oz,
 cleaned and gutted

2 tbsp olive oil

1 onion, quartered

3 mild red chillies, tops sliced off

8 garlic cloves, crushed with the
 blade of a knife

1 tsp ground allspice

1 tsp ground cinnamon

1 tsp sea salt, plus extra for
 seasoning

3 handfuls of coriander leaves, plus
 extra to serve

50g/1¾oz/½ cup chopped walnuts

3 tomatoes, finely chopped

50g/1¾oz/⅓ cup pine nuts

1 recipe quantity Tarator (see page
 220)

freshly ground black pepper

Vermicelli Rice (see page 215),
 to serve

lemon wedges, to serve

Known as samkeh harra, this is a speciality of the port city of Tripoli in the north of Lebanon, where you'll even find the mixture turned into a paste and wrapped in Arabic bread as a sandwich. The colour contrast of the red snapper against the creamy tahini with flecks of herbs makes for a visually appealing dish.

1 Preheat the oven to 200°C/400°F/Gas 6. Put the fish on a baking tray, season to taste with salt and pepper and drizzle with the oil. Cover with foil and bake for 30–40 minutes, depending on the size of the fish (the general rule is 7 minutes cooking time per 2.5cm/1in measured at the thickest part of the fish), until the fish is golden and tender.

2 Meanwhile, put the onion, chillies, garlic, allspice, cinnamon and salt in a food processor and pulse for 1 minute. Add the coriander and pulse again for a further 1–2 minutes until a thick, cohesive paste develops. Transfer the paste to a heavy-based frying pan over a medium heat. Add the walnuts and tomatoes, stir well and cook for about 5 minutes until fragrant.

3 While the mixture is cooking, toast the pine nuts in a heavy-based pan over a medium heat for 1–2 minutes until golden and fragrant, shaking the pan often. Set aside.

4 Pour the tarator over the garlic and coriander paste, mix well to combine and cook for 1–2 minutes until warm.

5 Transfer the fish to a large serving dish, being careful to keep it in one piece, then pour about half the dressing over the cooked fish, reserving the rest for serving on the side. Sprinkle the fish with the toasted pine nuts and extra coriander leaves and serve with the Vermicelli Rice and lemon wedges.

blackened sea bream

SERVES 4
PREPARATION TIME: 10 minutes,
  plus marinating
COOKING TIME: 45 minutes

4 whole sea bream, pollock or
  haddock, about 1.25kg/2lb 12oz
  in total, cleaned and gutted, then
  butterflied (head and tail intact)

2 tbsp smoked sea salt flakes

1 tbsp tamarind paste or lemon
  juice

3 tbsp olive oil

1 tbsp ground dried lime (optional)

chopped coriander leaves,
  to sprinkle

sea salt and freshly ground black
  pepper

Chelow Rice (see page 214) or
  Vermicelli Rice (see page 215),
  to serve

Burnt Tomato & Chilli Jam (optional,
  see page 219), to serve

FOR THE GREEN MANGO
  CHUTNEY
2 green mangoes, sliced into
  1cm/½in cubes

3cm/1¼in piece of root ginger,
  peeled and finely chopped or
  grated

½ garlic clove, finely chopped
  or crushed

½ tsp turmeric

¼ tsp ground fenugreek

small pinch of crushed chilli flakes

4 tbsp cider vinegar

2 tbsp clear honey

a small pinch of sea salt

The infamous masqouf, as Iraq's national dish is known, is a much-revered dish for Iraqis, reserved for special occasions. Considered to be food for the mind as well as the body, this Baghdad speciality sprang up along the banks of the Tigris, where the day's catch would be served to Arak-sozzled patrons in cafés. It's traditionally prepared with freshwater fish, similar to carp, butterflied and hung on skewers over brushwood fires. Mango chutney was introduced via Indian traders, and Iraqis made it their own with the inclusion of spices such as fenugreek. You may need 2 large grilling baskets.

1 Put all the fish in a grill pan and season the interiors and exteriors generously with the smoked salt.

2 Put the tamarind paste in a mixing bowl, add 3 tablespoons water and mix well. Add the olive oil and dried lime, if using, and whisk well. Season to taste with black pepper. Baste each of the fish liberally all over with the tamarind marinade. Cover and set aside for 30 minutes.

3 Meanwhile, prepare the mango chutney. Put the mangoes, ginger, garlic, turmeric, fenugreek, chilli flakes, cider vinegar, honey, salt and 350ml/12fl oz/1½ cups water in a heavy-based saucepan over a medium heat. Cover and bring to the boil, then reduce the heat to low and simmer for 20–25 minutes until the mango is soft and most of the liquid has evaporated. The chutney should be slightly runny.

4 Depending on your choice, preheat a grill to high, preheat a charcoal barbecue until the charcoal is burning white or turn on a gas barbecue. Secure the fish by flattening them between the wire racks of large fish-grilling baskets, 2 fish per basket, then cook for 7 minutes on each side or until charred, crispy and flaky. Alternatively, preheat the oven to 180°C/350°F/Gas 4 and bake the fish on wire racks placed above baking trays for 10–15 minutes, depending on the size of the fish (the general rule is 7 minutes cooking time per 2.5cm/1in measured at the thickest part of the fish).

5 If using fillets, then heat a shallow, nonstick frying pan over a medium heat and sear the fish for 5 minutes on each side, carefully turning them.

6 Sprinkle coriander over the fish and serve with Chelow Rice, along with some of the green mango chutney and some Burnt Tomato and Chilli Jam, if you like.

monkfish tagine with chermoula

SERVES 4
PREPARATION TIME: 15 minutes,
  plus marinating, grinding the
  saffron and making the chermoula
  and preserved lemon
COOKING TIME: 1 ¼ hours

4 monkfish fillets, about 500g/
  1lb 2oz in total

1 recipe quantity Chermoula
  (see page 210)

2–3 tbsp olive oil

1 onion, thinly sliced

250g/9oz tomatoes, sliced

300g/10½oz large waxy potatoes,
  thinly sliced

50g/1¾oz pitted prunes, thinly
  sliced

a pinch of ground saffron (see page
  212)

2 wedges of Preserved Lemon, rind
  rinsed (see page 212)

1 bay leaf

Couscous (see page 216), to serve

This is very loosely based on a recipe by Claudia Roden. You can use any kind of meaty fish that can withstand the lengthy cooking time, which renders the fish soft and moist. I use a tagine pot to cook this, but if you don't have one, use a heavy-based ovenproof dish.

1 Put the monkfish in a bowl and spread half the chermoula over the top. Cover and leave to marinate in the fridge for 2 hours.

2 When you are ready to cook, preheat the oven to 150°C/300°F/Gas 2. If you are using a tagine dish, season it first by rubbing 1 tablespoon of the oil over the inside.

3 Lay half the onion, tomato, potato and prune slices over the base, then lay the marinated monkfish fillets on top. Season with the saffron, add the preserved lemon wedges and the bay leaf, then repeat the layer of sliced vegetables and prunes. Cover with 250ml/9fl oz/1 cup water, put the lid on and bake in the oven for 1 hour.

4 Remove the dish from the oven. Put the remaining oil and one-third of the remaining chermoula in a bowl and mix well. Drizzle this mixture over the tagine. Return to the oven and cook, uncovered, for a further 15 minutes. Serve hot, with the remaining chermoula either drizzled over the tagine or served on the side, accompanied by Couscous.

vegetarian

pan-fried squares

SERVES 4
PREPARATION TIME: 40 minutes
COOKING TIME: 35 minutes

100g/3½oz/heaped ¾ cup plain flour, sifted

100g/3½oz/ heaped ¾ cup fine semolina

½ tsp caster sugar

½ tsp sea salt, plus extra for seasoning

¼ tsp dried active yeast

6 tbsp olive oil, plus extra for greasing

1 red onion, thinly sliced

1 yellow pepper, deseeded and thinly sliced

1 apple

juice of ½ lemon

6 sundried tomatoes in oil, drained and thinly sliced

125g/4½oz soft goat's cheese

30g/1oz salted butter

freshly ground black pepper

Undressed Herb Salad (see page 67), to serve (optional)

Pomegranate & Cucumber Salad (see page 64), to serve

These crêpe-like semolina squares are prepared using dough patiently stretched to paper-thin thickness, stuffed, then folded into squares. The apple lends moisture and gentle sweetness. The cheese quantity may be increased to taste.

1 Put the flour, semolina, sugar and salt in a mixing bowl and combine with a fork. Put 125ml/4fl oz/ ½ cup warm water in a small bowl, sprinkle over the yeast and mix well, then gradually pour the liquid over the flour mixture as you mix it into a dough.

2 Knead the dough for 15 minutes until you achieve a very smooth, elastic and malleable dough that is soft but not sticky. Shape the dough into a ball, drizzle 1 tablespoon of the oil over your hands and then grease the dough ball. Return the dough to the bowl, cover with a damp kitchen towel and leave to rest for about 10 minutes.

3 Meanwhile, prepare the filling. Heat 2 tablespoons of the oil in a frying pan over a medium heat, add the red onion and cook for 5 minutes until slightly golden. Add the pepper and cook for 3–4 minutes until softened but with a slight bite to it. Core and slice the apple into thin wedges, then sprinkle it with the lemon juice to stop it discolouring. Add the apple to the pan with the sundried tomatoes. Toss everything together and cook for a further 1 minute. Remove the pan from the heat and leave to cool, then crumble over the goat's cheese and season to taste with salt and pepper.

4 Lightly grease a baking sheet with more of the oil and divide the dough into four equal portions about the size of a golf ball. Using your fingers, begin to spread one of the dough balls outwards into a very thin, almost transparent circle about 25–30cm/10–12in in diameter, using a little bit of the remaining oil as required, and then dot with one-quarter of the butter.

5 Divide the filling into four equal portions. Spoon one-quarter of the prepared filling into the centre of the circle. Fold one-third of the circle into the middle and repeat the same with the opposing side. Now fold each open end into the middle to achieve a square with the filling secure between the layers. Transfer the prepared square to the prepared baking sheet. Repeat steps 4 and 5 with the remaining dough balls and filling.

6 Put a heavy-based, nonstick frying pan over a medium heat. Add the squares one at a time, flattening each one with the palm of your hand, and cook for 4–5 minutes on each side until crispy and golden. Serve with the salads, if you like.

falafel & tarator wraps

SERVES 4–6
PREPARATION TIME: 30 minutes,
  plus soaking and draining the
  chickpeas, and making the bread
  and tarator
COOKING TIME: 10 minutes

250g/9oz/1 heaped cup dried
  chickpeas, soaked overnight (see
  page 215)

1 onion, quartered

2 garlic cloves, crushed with the
  blade of a knife

½ green pepper, deseeded

1 handful of mint leaves

1 handful of parsley leaves

1 handful of coriander leaves

1 tsp sea salt, plus extra for
  seasoning

1 tsp ground allspice

½ tsp ground cumin

½ tsp bicarbonate of soda

1 tbsp plain flour, if needed

sunflower oil, for deep-frying

4–6 small loaves of Arabic Bread
  (see page 217)

shredded lettuce

Tarator (see page 220)

1 onion, thinly sliced (optional)

1 tomato, thinly sliced (optional)

pickles, banana peppers, turnips
  and beets, thinly sliced (optional)

1 handful of parsley leaves, finely
  chopped

freshly ground black pepper

*It's commonly believed that falafel originated millennia ago
in Egypt, where they are prepared using a mixture of broad
beans and chickpeas. I prefer to stick with chickpeas, but don't
be tempted to use the tinned variety, as they will fall apart.*

1 Drain the chickpeas well and leave in a colander for 2 hours to
remove as much moisture as possible, shaking the colander every once
in a while. Alternatively, a faster approach would be to use a salad
spinner, if you have one: add the chickpeas, close and spin 2–3 times to
remove the excess moisture. Set aside.

2 Put the onion, garlic, pepper, herbs, salt and spices into a food
processor and whizz for 1–2 minutes until blended into a rough paste
(it should not be too smooth or the batter will fall apart during cooking).
Squeeze out any excess water and discard it. Return the paste to the
food processor and add the drained chickpeas and pulse a few times to
incorporate until you have a smooth paste. The consistency of the paste
should be grainy with a shade of pistachio green. Taste and adjust the
seasoning, if needed, then add the bicarbonate of soda. Add the flour
if you think the mixture needs help with binding. Mix well to combine.
Using a tablespoon, form the chickpea mixture into 2.5cm/1in patties,
handling the mixture as little as possible. You should make 20–24 patties.
Place on a baking sheet and set aside to firm up.

3 Preheat the oven to low. Pour the oil into a wide, deep pan or wok
and place over a medium heat. Alternatively, use a deep-fat fryer,
in which case you'll need more oil. The oil is ready when it begins to
bubble or reaches 180°C/350°F. If you don't have a thermometer, check
the readiness of the oil by dropping a small piece of the falafel mixture
into the oil: if it browns within 1 minute, the oil is ready.

4 Gently transfer the patties into the hot oil in 2–3 batches and deep-fry
for 1–2 minutes on each side until golden brown (or for 3–4 minutes
in total if deep-frying). Using a slotted spoon, transfer the patties to a
plate lined with kitchen paper. Place in the oven while deep-frying the
remaining patties. Once cooked, cut the patties in half, if you like. Add
the Arabic Bread to the oven and warm for 1 minute.

5 Lay a loaf of bread on a plate. Sprinkle a little lettuce in the centre
of the loaf. Put some of the falafel patties on the lettuce, drizzle with
some tarator, top with some accompaniments and sprinkle with parsley.
Tightly roll up the bread, tucking in one end. Repeat with the remaining
ingredients. Serve using kitchen paper or napkins to soak up the juices.

Sabich Salad

SERVES 4
PREPARATION TIME: 15 minutes,
  plus making the bread and
  hummus
COOKING TIME: 20 minutes

8 eggs

2 Earl Grey tea bags

skins of 2 small yellow onions

1–2 tsp sea salt, plus extra for
seasoning

2 aubergines, sliced lengthways into
  1cm/½in-thick slices

5 tbsp olive oil

4 tbsp tahini

1 garlic clove, finely chopped
  or crushed

a pinch of crushed chilli flakes

juice of 1½ lemons

4 loaves of Arabic Bread, unpeeled
  (see page 217)

1 small cucumber, finely chopped

1 small red onion, finely chopped

1 tomato, finely chopped

4 tbsp Hummus (see page 27)

chopped parsley and coriander
  leaves, to sprinkle

freshly ground black pepper

Green Mango Chutney (see page
  143), to serve

This rowdy salad is based on the sabich sandwich, a very popular breakfast fare in and around Jerusalem. The eggs are traditionally boiled gently for 6 hours over a low heat. However, in an effort to remain sane, I prefer to bring them to boiling point, then remove them from the heat and leave them to wait in the hot water while I prepare the salad.

1 Put the eggs, tea bags, onion skins and salt in a saucepan and cover with water. Bring to the boil, then remove from the heat and leave to sit while you prepare the rest of the salad.

2 Brush the aubergine slices with 1½ teaspoons of the oil on each side, then season with salt and pepper on both sides.

3 Place a griddle pan over a high heat until hot, then cook the aubergines (you may need to do this in batches) for 2–3 minutes on each side until soft and cooked through, with golden grill marks.

4 Put the tahini in a mixing bowl, add the garlic, chilli flakes, juice of 1 lemon and 3 tablespoons water and mix well. Season with salt and pepper.

5 Preheat the grill to high and grill the bread for about 2 minutes on each side until crispy and golden brown.

6 Meanwhile, to make the salsa, put the cucumber, red onion and tomato in a serving bowl and mix well. Drizzle over the remaining oil and a squeeze of lemon juice. Season to taste with salt and pepper.

7 Before serving, run the eggs under cold water for just long enough so that you can handle them, then peel the eggs and slice thinly.

8 Place the crisped Arabic Bread rounds on four plates. Spread each with some hummus, then add a few aubergine slices and some egg slices. Drizzle over the tomato and cucumber salsa and some of the tahini dressing. Sprinkle with the herbs and serve with a dollop of Green Mango Chutney.

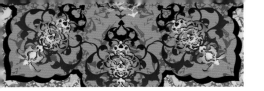

koshari

SERVES 4
PREPARATION TIME: 25 minutes
COOKING TIME: 30 minutes

5 tbsp olive oil

2 small mild red chillies (or more to taste), deseeded and finely chopped

6 garlic cloves, finely chopped

1 tsp ground cumin

400g/14oz tomatoes, finely chopped, or tinned chopped tomatoes

150g/5 ½oz/heaped ¾ cup brown lentils, rinsed

3 tbsp sunflower oil

400g/14oz onions, thinly sliced

150g/5 ½oz spaghetti, tagliatelle or reshteh

150g/5 ½oz/1 cup elbow macaroni

50g/1 ¾oz/1 heaped cup coarse or extra coarse bulgur wheat (grade 3 or 4)

20g/¾oz salted butter

50g/1 ¾oz/½ cup vermicelli broken into 4cm/½in lengths (or bought ready broken from a Middle Eastern store)

mint leaves, to sprinkle

sea salt and freshly ground black pepper

Undressed Herb Salad (see page 67), to serve

lime wedges, to serve

While koshari may be Egypt's glorious answer to street food, the word is not Arabic but rather derived from the Hindi word khichri, meaning a dish of rice and lentils. It's an import, brought to Egypt by the British Army.

1 Heat 2 tablespoons of the olive oil in a heavy-based saucepan over a medium heat, add the chillies, garlic and cumin and cook for about 1 minute until aromatic. Add the tomatoes and bring to the boil, then reduce the heat to low and leave to simmer, covered, for 20 minutes, stirring often, until the mixture is thick and sauce-like. Season to taste with salt and pepper.

2 At the same time, heat a heavy-based saucepan of water over a high heat and add the lentils. Bring to the boil, then reduce the heat to low; cover and simmer for 20–30 minutes until soft. Drain, then cover to keep warm.

3 Meanwhile, heat the sunflower oil in a frying pan over a medium heat, add the onions and fry for about 15 minutes, stirring often, until caramelized and golden brown. Transfer to a plate lined with kitchen paper. Set the empty pan to one side.

4 Heat another large saucepan of water over a high heat, season with salt and add another tablespoon of olive oil. Bring to the boil, then add the spaghetti and macaroni at the same time and cook for 10 minutes or according to the packet instructions. The macaroni may take a bit longer to cook, in which case add it first.

5 Put the bulgur in a small heatproof bowl, cover with double its volume of boiling water and leave to soak until all the water is absorbed and the bulgur is tender, about 10–15 minutes.

6 Heat the frying pan used for the onions over a medium heat, add the butter and fry the vermicelli for 3–5 minutes until golden and crispy, stirring often. Transfer to a plate lined with kitchen paper and set aside.

7 When the pasta has finished cooking, drain, then return to the pan and toss with the remaining olive oil. Cover and keep warm.

8 Place a layer of pasta on each of four plates, sprinkle over the bulgur, then add the vermicelli, lentils and tomato sauce. Sprinkle with the caramelized onions and mint. Serve with an Undressed Herb Salad, and with lime wedges for squeezing over.

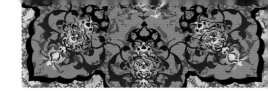

lentil, bulgur & tamarind pilaf

SERVES 4
PREPARATION TIME: 20 minutes,
 plus soaking
COOKING TIME: 35 minutes

1½ tbsp tamarind paste or juice of
1 lemon

250g/9oz/1¼ cups brown lentils

120g/4¼oz/½ cup coarse or extra
 coarse bulgur wheat (grade 3 or 4)

2 tbsp sunflower oil

3 red onions, thinly sliced

1 garlic bulb, cloves separated and
 finely chopped

3 handfuls of coriander leaves,
 roughly chopped

4 tbsp olive oil

½ tsp ground cumin

¼ tsp Aleppo pepper flakes or
 crushed chilli flakes

sea salt and freshly ground black
 pepper

Courgette & Sumac Fritters (see
 page 50), to serve

White Cabbage Salad (see page
 220), to serve – you may like to
 omit the garlic from this recipe
 as the pilaf also contains garlic

This is my interpretation of a savoury dish whose native name translates as "burnt his fingers". Traditionally, the dish is prepared with reshteh, or noodles similar to tagliatelle. I have also encountered the dish without the reshteh, and topped with fried Arabic breadcrumbs instead.

1 Put the tamarind paste, if using, in a small mixing bowl, add 3 tablespoons hot water and leave to soak for about 10 minutes. With a fork or your hands, mash the tamarind until it dissolves and you are left with a light brown, thick, sauce-like paste. Strain through a fine sieve, discarding the seeds and tough fibres.

2 Put the lentils in a heavy-based saucepan and cover with 1l/35fl oz/ 4 cups water. Cover and bring to the boil over a high heat, then reduce the heat to low and simmer for about 20 minutes or until the lentils are slightly tender. Add the bulgur wheat, season to taste with salt and cook for a further 10–15 minutes until the bulgur is soft and the lentils are tender but still intact.

3 Meanwhile, heat the sunflower oil in a heavy-based frying pan over a medium heat, add the red onions and fry for 4–5 minutes or until lightly coloured. Add the garlic and coriander and stir well, cooking for 1–2 minutes until the mixture is aromatic and the coriander wilts.

4 Add the lentils and bulgur wheat to the pan, pour in the olive oil and tamarind paste or lemon juice, then add the cumin and Aleppo pepper flakes and stir well. Season to taste with salt and pepper. Serve with Courgette and Sumac Fritters and White Cabbage Salad.

Upside-down cauliflower rice cake

SERVES 4
PREPARATION TIME: 30 minutes,
plus making the rice, harissa and
vegetable stock, and resting
COOKING TIME: 1 hour 5 minutes

400g/14oz/2 cups rice, soaked (see steps 1 and 2 of Parboiled Rice, page 214)

1 garlic bulb, cloves separated and finely chopped

1 cardamom pod, crushed

¼ tsp ground cinnamon

¼ tsp ground allspice

½ tsp dried lime powder

½ tsp Harissa (see page 210)

800ml/28fl oz/3¼ cups Vegetable Stock (see page 211)

7 tbsp olive oil

2 small red onions

250g/9oz parsnips, thinly sliced lengthways

300g/10½oz cauliflower florets

400g/14oz aubergines, partially skinned to leave strips of skin about 2.5cm/1in wide, then cut lengthways into 2cm/¾in slices

75g/2½oz/⅓ cup tinned chestnuts, drained, rinsed and thinly sliced, or cooked fresh chestnuts, thinly sliced

250g/9oz small tomatoes, thinly sliced

butter, for greasing

40g/1½oz/¼ cup almonds

2 tbsp pine nuts

mint leaves, to sprinkle

pomegranate seeds, to sprinkle

sea salt

Greek yogurt, to serve

The Arabic title of this Jordanian-Palestinian dish literally means "flipped over". The recipe is traditionally served warm and includes meat, but I like it better cold and have opted to keep it vegetarian. Adjust the harissa to taste.

1 Put the soaked rice in a heavy-based saucepan over a medium heat and add the garlic, cardamom, cinnamon, allspice, dried lime powder, harissa and vegetable stock. Heat over a medium heat, cover and bring to the boil, then reduce the heat and simmer for 15 minutes or until the liquid has been absorbed. The rice will still have a little bite to it but will steam further in the oven later on.

2 Preheat the oven to 200°C/400°F/Gas 6. Put 2 tablespoons of the oil in a deep frying pan over a medium heat. Fry the red onions for about 5 minutes until they are translucent and slightly golden. Transfer to a plate lined with kitchen paper and set aside.

3 Put the parsnips in a thin layer on a baking sheet and brush both sides with some of the oil. Put the cauliflower on another baking sheet and toss with a little oil. Repeat with the aubergines.

4 Bake the vegetables in the oven until the parsnips are just tender (about 10 minutes), the cauliflower is tender but still with a little bite (about 15 minutes) and the aubergines are golden and pliable (10–15 minutes). Alternatively, you can fry all these vegetables: start by frying the parsnips for 3–4 minutes or until golden and crisp. Repeat with the cauliflower, frying for about 3 minutes until golden, then fry the aubergines for about 4 minutes, first sprinkling the slices with salt.

5 Reduce the oven temperature to 180°C/350°F/Gas 4. Grease a bundt tin and line the base and sides with aubergine slices, with the wide ends at the base, and then the parsnips with the wide ends at the top (laid in opposite directions to create a full layer of vegetables). Layer in one-third of the rice, half the cauliflower, half the red onions, half the chestnuts and half the tomato slices. Repeat and finish off with a layer of rice, pressing down gently. Cover very tightly with foil and bake in the oven for 30 minutes or until the rice has cooked through. Remove from the oven and leave to rest for 20 minutes before gently flipping the cake over onto a serving plate. If it falls apart a bit, gently reconstruct it.

6 Toast the almonds and pine nuts in a heavy-based pan over a medium heat for 1–2 minutes until golden and fragrant, shaking the pan often. Sprinkle the toasted nuts, mint and pomegranate seeds over the rice cake and serve hot or cold, with yogurt on the side.

courgettes stuffed with herbed rice

SERVES 4
PREPARATION TIME: 1 hour
COOKING TIME: 1 hour 10 minutes

1kg/2lb 4oz courgettes or marrows

625g/1lb 6oz tomatoes

2 small onions

100g/3½oz/½ cup short-grain rice

½ tsp ground allspice

1 handful of parsley leaves, finely
  chopped

3 tbsp finely chopped mint leaves

4 tbsp olive oil

juice of 2 lemons

1 tbsp pine nuts

1 heaped tbsp tomato purée

5 garlic cloves

sea salt and freshly ground black
  pepper

Greek yogurt, to serve

warm Arabic Bread (see page 217),
  to serve

Reserve the courgette cores to make succulent fritters (see page 50). The stuffing is essentially a tabbouleh salad mixture mixed with rice – it's a great way to use up leftover tabbouleh.

1 Rinse the courgettes and trim off the stem ends, leaving the wide base intact. Using a vegetable corer, scrape out the flesh and seeds, being sure to remove as much of it as you can without breaking through the courgette skin. If you do accidentally cut too hard and crack the courgettes, you can still stuff them but you will need to be gentle with them. Set the hollowed-out courgettes aside.

2 Finely chop 1 of the tomatoes and 1 of the onions and put in a mixing bowl. Add the rice, half the allspice, the parsley, 1 tablespoon of the mint, half the oil and half the lemon juice. Mix well and season to taste with salt and pepper. Toast the pine nuts in a heavy-based pan over a medium heat for 1–2 minutes until golden and fragrant, shaking the pan often. Add them to the mixture.

3 Thinly slice the remaining tomatoes and onion. Drizzle a heavy-based pan with the remaining oil, then arrange layers of tomato and onion rings over the bottom. Add the remaining allspice and some salt.

4 Stuff the courgettes by gently packing enough of the rice mixture to fill them three-quarters full, so leaving room for the rice to expand. Put the stuffed courgettes on top of the tomato and onion layers in the pan.

5 Mix the tomato purée with 250ml/9fl oz/1 cup water and pour the mixture over the courgettes in the pan. Season to taste with salt and pepper. Lay a heatproof plate that fits inside the pan on top of the courgettes to keep them compressed and minimize any movement. Pour in about 250ml/9fl oz/1 cup water or enough liquid to ensure the courgettes are immersed, though not necessarily the plate too.

6 Heat the pan over a high heat and bring to the boil, then reduce the heat to medium-low and leave to simmer, covered, for 45–60 minutes or until the courgettes are tender. To check if they are ready, pierce gently with a fork: the flesh should be soft and the rice cooked.

7 Meanwhile, grind the garlic and a pinch of salt using a pestle and mortar to make a paste. Add the remaining mint and pound for another minute, then mix in the remaining lemon juice. Drizzle the garlic and lemon mixture over the courgettes. Leave to simmer for a further 5 minutes so that the flavours seep in. Serve warm or at room temperature with yogurt and warm Arabic Bread.

vine leaves with bulgur, figs and nuts

SERVES 4
PREPARATION TIME: 1 hour,
  plus resting
COOKING TIME: 1 hour 40
  minutes–2 hours 10 minutes

150g/5½oz bottled vine leaves
  or 24 fresh vine leaves

juice of 2 lemons

150ml/5fl oz/scant ⅔ cup olive oil

1 small red onion, thinly sliced

2 garlic cloves, finely chopped

80g/2¾oz/½ cup coarse
  bulgur wheat (grade 3), short-grain
  rice or risotto rice

2 ripe fresh figs or 2 ready-to-eat
  dried figs, finely chopped

30g/1oz/¼ cup walnuts, finely
  chopped

2 tbsp finely chopped parsley leaves

2 tbsp finely chopped mint leaves

2 tbsp finely chopped coriander
  leaves

1 tsp ground allspice

1 tsp Aleppo pepper or crushed
  chilli flakes

1 large tomato, cut into 1cm/½in
  slices

1 onion, cut into 1cm/½in slices

1 potato, cut into 1cm/½in slices

sea salt and freshly ground black
  pepper

Greek yogurt, to serve

Usually known by their Turkish name "dolma", which means "to be stuffed", the word encompasses a whole family of stuffed vegetables. To create a hearty main course, add a layer of lamb chops between the tomatoes and potatoes.

1 If using packaged vine leaves, fill a bowl with warm water. Remove the vine leaves from the packaging or brine and separate the leaves, one by one, transferring them to the bowl of water. Leave to soak for about 10 minutes. Change the water and soak the leaves again.

2 If using fresh vine leaves, pour boiling water into a heatproof bowl, add the juice of half a lemon, then immerse the fresh vine leaves in the boiling water for 3–4 minutes until softened. Drain, then rinse under cold water. Shake off the excess water and transfer the leaves to a chopping board. Cut the hard stems out and set aside.

3 Heat 2 tablespoons of the oil in a heavy-based frying pan over a medium heat, and fry the red onion for 4–5 minutes until softened. Add the garlic and fry for 1 minute until aromatic, stirring often, then mix in the bulgur wheat, figs, walnuts, herbs, spices and 2 more tablespoons of the oil. Season to taste with salt and pepper and set aside.

4 Lightly grease a deep, heavy-based saucepan with another 2 tablespoons of the oil and lay the tomato slices over the base, followed by the onion slices and then the potato slices. Sprinkle with salt.

5 Working with one vine leaf at a time, place the vine leaf, wider-base facing you with the shiny side down and the protruding stem exposed. Place 1 teaspoon of the stuffing 1cm/½in from the base. Fold over the leaf and then the sides and begin rolling it into a tight cylindrical shape with the seam-side down. Repeat with the remaining vine leaves and stuffing, layering the leaves over the potato layer as you finish rolling them. Make sure the vine leaves fit snugly inside the pan, then cover with water and weigh them down with a heatproof plate.

6 Cover the pot with a tight-fitting lid and bring to the boil over a medium heat. Reduce the heat to low and simmer gently for 1½–2 hours or until the vine leaves are meltingly smooth and the sauce has thickened. If too much water has evaporated and the vine leaves seem to be tough, add a little more water and continue cooking. Once finished cooking, pour over the remaining oil and lemon juice and leave to rest for 10–15 minutes before serving warm or cool, with yogurt.

broad beans with yogurt tahdeeg

SERVES 4
PREPARATION TIME: 45 minutes,
  plus making the rice and advieh
COOKING TIME: 50 minutes

800g/1lb 12oz fresh broad beans in
  the pod or 400g/14oz frozen broad
  beans

6 tbsp sunflower oil

1 recipe quantity Parboiled Rice
  (see page 214)

3 tbsp Greek yogurt, plus extra
  to serve

1 tsp orange blossom water

1 handful of dill leaves, finely
  chopped, plus extra for sprinkling

1 tsp Advieh 1 (see page 211)

zest and juice of 1 orange

6 garlic cloves, crushed

55g/2oz unsalted butter

sea salt and freshly ground black
  pepper

This is a vibrant vegetarian rice dish that can be made with either fresh or frozen broad beans.

1 Shell the fresh broad beans, if using, then blanch and skin them as follows. Put the beans in a saucepan of boiling water and leave to boil for a maximum of 2 minutes. Drain, then transfer the beans to a bowl of iced water to stop them cooking further. Slip the skins off. If using frozen beans, thaw them, then slip them out of their skins.

2 Pour the oil into a heavy-based saucepan and heat over a medium heat until the oil is sizzling.

3 Put 4–5 tablespoons of the rice in a bowl with the yogurt and orange blossom water and mix well. Spread it gently across the bottom of the saucepan to cover the base. This will form the tahdeeg.

4 Mix the remaining rice with the broad beans, dill, advieh, orange zest and juice and garlic, and season to taste with salt and pepper. Sprinkle the rice lightly into the saucepan, building the mixture up into a dome shape. Using the handle of a wooden spoon, make three holes down into the rice, being careful not to puncture the tahdeeg.

5 Melt the butter in a small saucepan over a low heat. Add 2 tablespoons water, mix well, then pour the mixture over the rice.

6 Wrap the saucepan lid in a clean kitchen towel and tie it into a tight knot at the handle, then use it to cover the pan as tightly as you can so that steam does not escape. (The kitchen towel will prevent the moisture from dripping into the rice, making it soggy.)

7 Cook the rice over a medium heat for 2–3 minutes until the rice is steaming (you will see puffs of steam escaping at the edges of the lid), then reduce the heat to low and cook for about 45 minutes, with the lid on all the time. Serve the rice and tahdeeg following the instructions in steps 5–7 of Steamed Rice on page 214. Sprinkle the rice with dill and serve with extra yogurt.

mixed bean & herb noodle soup

SERVES 4
PREPARATION TIME: 30 minutes
  plus overnight soaking and
  making the stock
COOKING TIME: 1 hour 40 minutes,
  plus cooking the kidney beans
  (optional) and chickpeas until just
  tender

4 tbsp sunflower oil

3 large onions, thinly sliced

½ tsp turmeric

100g/3 ½oz/ ½ cup dried kidney
  beans, soaked overnight and
  cooked until just tender (following
  the instructions for chickpeas on
  page 215), or 200g/7oz/1 cup
  tinned kidney beans, drained and
  rinsed

50g/2oz/ ¼ cup dried chickpeas,
  soaked overnight with 1 tsp
  bicarbonate of soda added to the
  water, then cooked until tender
  (see page 215)

1.5l/52fl oz/6 cups Vegetable Stock
  (see page 211)

50g/2oz/ ¼ cup brown lentils,
  rinsed

55g/2oz reshteh

1 small handful of finely chopped
  dill leaves

1 small handful of finely chopped
  parsley leaves

1 small handful of finely chopped
  coriander leaves

85g/3oz spinach leaves

juice of 1 lemon

sea salt and freshly ground pepper

TO SERVE
100ml/3 ½fl oz/scant ½ cup soured
  cream or liquid kashk

warm Thin Flatbread (see page 218)

lemon wedges

Mint & Butter Drizzle (see page 220)

This hearty soup is a quintessential part of the Norouz (Persian New Year). The fine noodles, or reshteh, are associated with new beginnings and good fortune. You could substitute the reshteh with thin egg noodles, linguini, or angel hair pasta broken into shorter lengths. If you use tinned kidney beans, they should be added at the same time as the lentils.

1 Heat half the oil in a large, heavy-based saucepan over a low heat, add one of the onions and cook for 3–5 minutes until soft and translucent. Stir in the turmeric and fry for another 1 minute.

2 Add the kidney beans and chickpeas to the onion and pour in the stock. Increase the heat to high and bring to the boil, then lower the heat to medium-low and simmer for 1 hour or until the beans are tender.

3 Add the lentils to the pan and simmer for a further 30 minutes until soft and tender, adding some water if the lentils are too dry.

4 Meanwhile, heat the remaining oil in a heavy-based frying pan over a medium heat and fry the remaining onions until crispy and golden.

5 Add the reshteh, herbs, spinach and lemon juice to the beans and cook for about 5 minutes until the noodles are cooked but still have a little bite to them and the spinach has wilted. Season to taste with salt and pepper.

6 Sprinkle the golden onions over the top of the soup and serve with sour cream, Thin Flatbread, lemon wedges and Mint and Butter Drizzle.

broad beans, peas & fennel tagine

SERVES 4
PREPARATION TIME: 15 minutes,
plus making the preserved lemon
and vegetable stock
COOKING TIME: 40 minutes

20g/¾oz salted butter

1 leek, thinly sliced

5 garlic cloves, finely chopped

1 wedge of Preserved Lemon (see
page 212), rind rinsed and finely
chopped

5cm/2in piece of root ginger,
peeled and finely chopped

250ml/9fl oz/1 cup dry, citrusy
white wine

400g/14oz fennel bulb, cut into
8 wedges

4 tinned artichoke hearts in brine,
drained and quartered

1 handful of fresh or frozen,
defrosted broad beans, skins
removed

2 tbsp finely chopped tarragon
leaves

500ml/17fl oz/2 cups Vegetable
Stock (see page 211)

a pinch of ground saffron or
turmeric (see page 212)

1 handful of fresh, shelled or frozen,
defrosted peas

125g/4½oz soft goat's cheese,
crumbled (optional)

sea salt and freshly ground black
pepper

Couscous (see page 216), to serve

*This is a really simple but flavourful light and brothy stew
that makes use of splendid spring vegetables. It's worked well
to convert a few fennel-haters from the dark side. It's rustic
in nature, so adjust the size of the vegetables, making them
smaller, if you like.*

1 Melt the butter in a heavy-based pan over a medium heat and add
the leeks. Cover and sweat for 1–2 minutes until the leeks have softened
slightly. Add the garlic, half the preserved lemon, and the ginger, then
cover and cook for 1 minute until the mixture is aromatic.

2 Pour in the wine and bubble for 4–5 minutes until reduced by half.
Add the fennel, artichoke hearts, broad beans and half the tarragon,
and toss well.

3 Meanwhile, heat the stock in a saucepan over a medium heat,
then add the saffron and pour the mixture over the vegetables. Cover
and bring to the boil, then reduce the heat to low and simmer for
20–25 minutes or until the vegetables are cooked through.

4 Add the peas, the remaining tarragon and the remaining preserved
lemon, season to taste with salt and pepper and cook for a further
5 minutes. Transfer to bowls, crumble over some the goat's cheese,
if using, and serve with couscous.

slow-cooked broad bean & tomato stew

SERVES 4
PREPARATION TIME: 30 minutes,
  plus soaking the broad beans and
  preparing the onion (optional)
COOKING TIME: 10 minutes, plus
  cooking the broad beans

400g/14oz/2⅔ cups dried broad
  beans, soaked for 48 hours and
  cooked for around 3 hours until
  soft, following the instructions for
  chickpeas on page 215

1 onion, trimmed and quartered
  (optional)

10g/¼ oz salted butter

5 garlic cloves, finely chopped

2 tomatoes, finely chopped

4 tbsp finely chopped coriander
  leaves

1 tbsp tahini

2 tsp ground cumin

juice of 2 lemons

4 tbsp olive oil

sea salt and freshly ground black
  pepper

warm Arabic Bread (see page 217),
  to serve

4 hard-boiled eggs, halved, to serve
  (optional)

This wonderfully wholesome, cheap and filling stew is a staple of the Egyptian diet, where it's regularly enjoyed for breakfast topped with hard-boiled eggs. (See Sabich Salad on page 152 for another way of preparing the eggs.) The Arabic name for this dish is fool mudammas – the word mudammas originates from the Coptic word for "buried" and was probably applied to this dish following the ancient cooking method of burying a covered pot filled with beans and water under hot coals. Dried broad beans, which are brown in colour, are very easy to find at Middle Eastern grocers.

1 Strain the cooked broad beans, reserving the cooking liquid.

2 Soak the onion quarters, if using, in a bowl of iced water for 30 minutes to make the flavour milder and to keep the onion crisp.

3 Melt the butter in the empty pan from the broad beans over a medium heat, then add the garlic and cook for 1 minute until aromatic. Add the tomatoes and half the coriander and cook for a further 2 minutes.

4 Add the broad beans, 125ml/4fl oz/½ cup of the reserved cooking liquid, the tahini, 1½ teaspoons of the cumin, the lemon juice (it's best to taste the mixture as you add this to make sure it isn't too sour) and half the oil to the tomato mixture, then heat through. Season to taste with salt and pepper and stir well to combine. If the broad beans are still quite firm, move some into a bowl, mash them with a potato masher and then return them to the pan.

5 Transfer the stew to a large serving bowl, drizzle with the remaining oil and sprinkle the remaining cumin and coriander over the top. Serve with Arabic Bread and with onion and hard-boiled eggs, if you like.

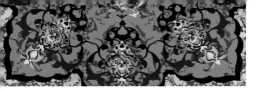

smokey aubergine & split pea stew

SERVES 4
PREPARATION TIME: *30 minutes,*
  plus making the advieh
COOKING TIME: *1 ½ hours*

2 tbsp sunflower oil

1 large onion, thinly sliced

250g/9oz/1 cup yellow or green split
  peas

1 tsp Advieh 1 (see page 211)

3 garlic cloves, crushed

1 tomato, roughly chopped

55g/2oz tomato purée

2–3 whole dried black limes (limu
  amani), pierced with the tip of a
  knife (optional)

1 tbsp pomegranate molasses

600g/1lb 5oz aubergines, cut into
  2cm/¾in slices

4 tbsp olive oil, or to taste

sea salt and freshly ground black
  pepper

TO SERVE
Chelow Rice (optional, see page 214)

Potato Matchsticks (see page 218)

Greek yogurt

Gheimeh is traditionally a lamb stew served with fried potatoes or aubergine, but I prefer this vegetarian version. Here I have added chargrilled aubergines for an extra layer of smokiness. I serve this comforting stew with potato matchsticks rather than chunky fries.

1 Heat the sunflower oil in a large, shallow saucepan over a medium–low heat. Add the onion and fry until light golden.

2 Rinse the split peas and add them to the pan with the advieh, garlic and tomato. Cover with about 1l/35fl oz/4 cups water and mix well, then bring the mixture to the boil. Reduce the heat to low and simmer for 15 minutes, then add the tomato purée and dried limes, if using, and cook for a further 15 minutes until the split peas are cooked but still have a little bite to them.

3 Add a little more water, if needed, keeping in mind that the stew is meant to be thick and simmer for another 30 minutes. Season with pomegranate molasses, salt and pepper.

4 Meanwhile, preheat the grill to medium–high or heat a griddle pan over a medium-high heat. Rub the aubergine slices with salt and the olive oil, then grill or griddle for approximately 10 minutes, turning occasionally, until softened and lightly browned.

5 Add the aubergine slices to the stew in one or two layers, pushing them down gently so that they are just covered with the stew juices, then cover and simmer for a further 20 minutes. The aubergine should have a melt-in-your-mouth texture, while the peas should be tender but not disintegrating. Serve the stew with the Chelow Rice, if you like, and Potato Matchsticks, with yogurt on the side.

Note: you will only need half a batch of the fries if serving the stew with the rice.

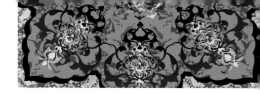

mess of pottage

SERVES 4
PREPARATION TIME: 20 minutes
COOKING TIME: 1 hour 20 minutes

300g/10½oz/1½ cups brown lentils, picked of any impurities and rinsed

4 tbsp sunflower oil

1 onion, finely chopped

2 tbsp coarse bulgur wheat (grade 3), rinsed

1 tsp ground allspice

2 red onions, sliced into thin rings

2 tbsp olive oil

sea salt

White Cabbage Salad (see page 220, to serve)

warm Arabic Bread (see page 217, to serve)

These days, mujadarah holds a very special place in my heart. Just as Esau, according to the Book of Genesis, traded his birthright away to his brother Jacob for what many believe to have been a form of this "Mess of Pottage", when I'm stressed and missing home there's not much I wouldn't give up for a comforting bowl of this warming lentil stew.

1 Put the lentils in a heavy-based saucepan, cover with about 1l/35fl oz/4 cups water and bring to the boil over a medium-high heat. Reduce the heat to low and simmer for about 1 hour or until the lentils are soft.

2 Meanwhile, heat half the sunflower oil in a frying pan over a medium heat, add the onion and fry for about 5 minutes until softened and lightly golden.

3 Use a slotted spoon to remove the onions from the pan and add them to the cooked lentil mixture. Add 250ml/9fl oz/1 cup water, the bulgur and allspice. Season to taste with salt and simmer for a further 20 minutes.

4 At the same time, heat the remaining sunflower oil in the frying pan over a medium heat and fry the red onion rings for 10–15 minutes until softened and lightly browned. Remove from the heat and transfer to a plate lined with kitchen paper using a slotted spoon.

5 Once the lentil mixture has finished cooking (the consistency should be that of a thick, moist porridge), pour in the olive oil and mix well. Adjust the seasoning, if required, then transfer to a large serving dish or individual bowls and leave to cool to room temperature. Top with the caramelized red onion rings and serve with a White Cabbage Salad and Arabic Bread.

teta's smokey musaqa'a

SERVES 4
PREPARATION TIME: 30 minutes,
  plus soaking the chickpeas
  (optional)
COOKING TIME: 1 hour 5 minutes,
  plus cooking the chickpeas until
  they are just tender (optional)

1kg/2lb 4oz aubergines

125ml/4fl oz/½ cup olive oil

1kg/2lb 4oz beefsteak tomatoes

2 tbsp sunflower oil

1 onion, thinly sliced into rings

3 garlic cloves, crushed with the
  blade of a knife

125g/4½oz/heaped ½ cup dried
  chickpeas, soaked overnight and
  cooked until tender (see page 215),
  or 250g/9oz/heaped 1 cup tinned
  chickpeas, drained and rinsed

½ tsp ground allspice

1 tbsp tomato purée (optional)

sea salt and freshly ground black
  pepper

TO SERVE
Greek yogurt

mint leaves (optional)

Arabic Bread (optional, see page
  217)

Vermicelli Rice (optional, see page
  215)

The word moussaka, applied to the famous Greek dish, doesn't actually have any meaning in the Greek language. Instead, it's thought the dish came to Greece by way of the Phoenicians and then took on French influences (hence the béchamel sauce). Meaning "cold" or "chilled" in Arabic, musaqa'a is a humble vegetarian stew that is best served at room temperature.

1 Preheat the oven to 200°C/400°C/Gas 6. Partially skin the aubergines, leaving strips of skin about 2.5cm/1in wide, then cut them lengthways into 2cm/¾in slices. Brush the slices on both sides with 6 tablespoons of the olive oil (or more or less, as preferred) and place in a 20 x 15cm/ 8 x 6in baking dish, overlapping as necessary. Sprinkle with a little salt and bake in the oven for about 20 minutes or until soft. Alternatively, preheat the grill to medium-high and grill the prepared slices for about 5 minutes on each side or until softened and lightly browned. Transfer to a plate and set aside.

2 Core the tomatoes and score the bottoms with a sharp knife. Put them in a heatproof bowl. Pour over enough boiling water to cover and leave for 1 minute or until the skins begin to peel. Drain the tomatoes and plunge into cold water to stop them cooking, then peel off the skins and discard. Cut the tomatoes in half, scoop out and discard the seeds, then slice the tomatoes into 5mm/¼in thick slices.

3 Heat the sunflower oil in a heavy-based saucepan over a medium heat. Add the onion and garlic, then cover and sweat for 4–5 minutes, stirring often, until translucent. Add the tomato slices and chickpeas in layers, seasoning each layer with a pinch of allspice, salt and pepper. Cover with about 250ml/9fl oz/1 cup water. If the tomatoes are not a rich red colour, then add the tomato purée for more depth of flavour and colour. Cover the pan and bring to the boil, then reduce the heat to low and leave to simmer for 20 minutes.

4 Add the cooked aubergine slices on top of the stew in layers, overlapping if necessary. Gently press them down just enough so that they are lightly covered by the tomato broth. Cover and cook for another 20 minutes. Remove from the heat, uncover and leave to cool down to room temperature. Serve with the yogurt and with mint for sprinkling, Arabic Bread and Vermicelli Rice, if you like.

desserts

semolina pancakes

SERVES 4
PREPARATION TIME: 25 minutes,
  plus rising
COOKING TIME: about 30 minutes

125ml/4fl oz/½ cup milk

1 tsp dried active yeast

¼ tsp caster sugar

100g/3½oz/scant ⅔ cup semolina
  flour (also known as fine semolina)

50g/1¾oz/scant ½ cup self-raising
  flour

1 tsp baking powder

a pinch of fine sea salt

100g/3½oz/¾ cup blanched
  almonds

4 tbsp argan oil

2 tbsp clear honey

250g/9oz ricotta or 1 recipe quantity
  Clotted Cream (see page 215)

30g/1oz honeycomb, roughly
  chopped

These semolina pancakes are known as beghrir, which means "1000 holes". The name refers to the multitude of holes that develop on the surface as they cook.

1 Warm the milk in a saucepan over a low heat. Mix the yeast and sugar with 3 tablespoons of the warmed milk, then pour this mixture into a large mixing bowl and set aside. Reserve the remaining warm milk.

2 Sift the flours, the baking powder and salt into a mixing bowl.

3 Add the remaining milk to the yeast mixture along with 125ml/4fl oz/½ cup warm water, and whisk well. Add the flour mixture a little at a time, whisking vigorously until it is well incorporated and the mixture is smooth.

4 Cover the bowl with a kitchen towel and set aside in a warm place for at least 1 hour or until the mixture is frothy and has doubled in size. If you are not making the pancakes until the next day, leave the mixture covered overnight in the fridge after it has risen.

5 Meanwhile, preheat the oven to 150°C/300°F/Gas 2. Spread the almonds on a baking sheet and bake for 5–7 minutes until golden, shaking the pan to toss them around halfway through the cooking time. Transfer to a pestle and mortar or a small blender and grind for about 5 minutes until you get a very smooth, wet paste, stopping to scrape down the sides every once in a while. Transfer to a serving bowl and mix in the argan oil and honey. Taste and add more oil and/or honey, if you like. Leave the oven on.

6 When you're ready to cook the pancakes, whisk the batter. It should be the texture of double cream (thin with a little water, if necessary). Place a non-stick pan over a medium-low heat. Working in batches, pour 1 tablespoon of the batter into the pan to create a thin, round pancake, about 7cm/3in in diameter, tilting the pan if necessary, then repeat, spacing the pancakes slightly apart. Cook on one side for 1–2 minutes until plenty of holes have developed, the tops have set and the bottoms are golden. Stack the first batch of pancakes between sheets of parchment paper on an ovenproof plate and keep warm in the oven. Repeat with the remaining batter to make about 24 pancakes in total.

7 To create half-moon shapes, seal the edges of the pancakes together by pinching them together only halfway along. Spoon a little ricotta into each pancake, then drizzle some of the almond butter over the top, sprinkle with honeycomb and serve.

fruit cocktail with clotted cream & nuts

SERVES 4
PREPARATION TIME: 15 minutes,
  plus making the clotted cream

8 strawberries

1 small pineapple

1 avocado

2 kiwi

1 small mango

4 tbsp shelled pistachios

250ml/9fl oz/1 cup banana and
  strawberry smoothie

1 recipe quantity Lebanese Clotted
  Cream (see page 215)

4 tbsp blanched almonds, roughly
  chopped

4 tbsp clear honey

Refreshingly satisfying fruit cocktail concoctions are popular across the Levant and are enjoyed throughout the day. They are a great way to make use of whatever seasonal fruits are available.

1 Prepare the fruits as necessary, then chop into cubes or pieces, depending on the fruits' shape, measuring roughly 2cm/¾in.

2 Put the pistachios in a heatproof bowl and pour over boiling water to cover. Leave for 1–2 minutes to allow the skins to loosen. Strain and then rub them dry, in batches if needed, using a kitchen towel. Discard the loose skins, and rinse the pistachios well once under cold running water to remove any remaining skin. Dust off the skins from the kitchen towel used earlier and pat the pistachios dry once more. Roughly chop.

3 Pour the banana and strawberry smoothie equally into four tall cocktail glasses, add the fruit in layers and then spoon over the clotted cream. Sprinkle with the pistachios and almonds and drizzle with the honey. Serve immediately.

Lebanese Clotted Cream
with Dulche de Leche & Caramelized Bananas

SERVES 4
PREPARATION TIME: 5 minutes,
  plus cooling and making the
  clotted cream
COOKING TIME: 1 hour 5 minutes

300ml/10½fl oz/1¼ cups
  sweetened condensed milk

1–2 pinches sea salt flakes, plus
  extra to serve

15g/½oz butter

3 bananas, thinly sliced

2 tbsp dark rum or pineapple juice

2 recipe quantities Lebanese Clotted
  Cream (see page 215)

Growing up, we lived on a dairy farm for a while, where we made our own clotted cream. This creamy treat, loosely based on a popular dessert known as layali Lubnan (or Lebanese nights), uses a version made by adding cornflour, which is easier to prepare. If preferred, you can make the dulce de leche in advance and warm it through gently before using in the recipe (see step 5).

1 Preheat the oven to 220°C/425°F/Gas 7. To make the dulche de leche, pour the sweetened condensed milk into a shallow baking dish and sprinkle over a pinch of the salt flakes. Stir well.

2 Cover the baking dish with foil and place it in a deep roasting tin. Pour enough hot water into the tin so that it reaches halfway up the sides of the dish, creating a bain marie.

3 Place the bain marie and baking dish in the oven and bake for about 1 hour or until the mixture has browned and caramelized, checking on the mixture occasionally to make sure it isn't burning and adding more hot water as necessary to keep the correct level. Remove from the oven and set aside.

4 Melt the butter in a heavy-based frying pan over a medium heat and add the bananas and rum. Flambé the ingredients for a few seconds, if you like, or bubble for 1–2 minutes until the alcohol has reduced a little. Remove the pan from the heat and toss to combine so that the banana slices are covered with the buttery juices.

5 If the dulce de leche has been resting in the fridge or has cooled, warm it gently by resting the bowl over a little hot water and stirring until it has returned to a thick pouring consistency.

6 Divide the clotted cream among four bowls, add a drizzle of the dulce de leche and then top with some of the caramelized banana slices. Sprinkle with some more sea salt, if you like, and serve.

pomegranate & rose quark summer cake

SERVES 8
PREPARATION TIME: 45 minutes,
  plus cooling and chilling
COOKING TIME: 40 minutes

5 eggs, at room temperature

200g/7oz/1 cup caster sugar

zest of ½ lemon

100g/3 ½oz/scant 1 cup self-raising
  flour

small piece of cold unsalted butter

100ml/3 ½fl oz/scant ½ cup
  whipping or double cream

8 gelatine leaves or 2 sachets
  powdered gelatine

500g/1lb 2oz quark

juice of 1 lemon

¼ tsp rosewater or vanilla extract
  (optional)

seeds from 175g/6oz pomegranates
  (see page 216), plus extra to
  decorate

icing sugar, to dust

chopped mint leaves, to sprinkle

It's a bold statement, but it's safe to say that this marvellous cake falls into my "top five favourite cakes" category. The following Middle Easternized version is based on my friend Sascha Minn's quark summer cake rather than a classic dessert from the region. It's an elegant cake: summery, zesty, light and fluffy. The quark cheese keeps the fat content to a minimum, and Greek yogurt can be substituted if you're unable to find quark. If you're averse to raw eggs, you can omit them, although it will affect the filling's texture. Either way, wash a slice of this cake down with a glass of bubbly and forget your worries.

1 Separate two of the eggs; put the egg whites in a glass mixing bowl and the egg yolks into a large mixing bowl. (If you have time, chill the glass bowl first, as this will improve the texture of the egg whites.)

2 Whisk the egg whites vigorously for 2 minutes until you achieve soft peaks, keeping the mixer or whisk moving around the edges and the centre at all times to ensure that all the egg white is mixed thoroughly. Set aside.

3 Add a whole egg to the egg yolks in the large mixing bowl along with 100g/3 ½oz/½ cup of the sugar and 1 tablespoon water. Beat for about 1 minute until you achieve a creamy consistency.

4 Add the lemon zest to the bowl, and sift in the flour. Beat for about 1 minute to incorporate. Next, add in the whisked egg whites and fold in thoroughly with a large metal spoon, making sure to remove any lumps. Try not to tap the bowl with the spoon as you'll lose the air, which will reduce the general fluffiness of the cake.

5 Preheat the oven to 170°C/325°F/Gas 3. Put the butter in the centre of a deep, springform 20cm/8in cake tin and line with parchment paper, cutting around the edges closely so it fits the base. (The butter will help the parchment paper to stick to the tin.) Pour the mixture into the prepared cake tin and level it with the back of a spoon.

6 Bake in the oven for 35–40 minutes on the top shelf or until the cake is lightly golden and a skewer inserted into the centre comes out clean.

7 Leave the cake to cool for about 20 minutes before releasing the base and carefully peeling off the parchment paper. Using a serrated knife, carefully slice the cake horizontally into two layers, turning it as you go to help keep the knife level. Transfer the two cake layers to a wire rack to cool.

8 Put the cream in a medium bowl and whip for about 2 minutes until soft peaks form. Be careful not to over-whip. Set aside.

9 Cut up the leaf gelatine, if using, into smaller pieces using kitchen scissors. Put in a small bowl, cover with cold water and leave to soak for 2 minutes, then drain well. Return to the bowl and pour over 4 tablespoons hot water as you whisk vigorously, making sure all the gelatine dissolves and there are no lumps remaining. Alternatively, follow the packet instructions if using the powdered gelatine.

10 Separate the two remaining eggs. Whisk the egg whites as in step 2. Put the yolks and remaining sugar in a large mixing bowl and beat vigorously for 1–2 minutes, then pour in the gelatine and continue beating vigorously.

11 Add the quark, whipped cream, lemon juice and rosewater, if using, and fold into the mixture with a large metal spoon. Add the whisked egg whites and fold in gently, just enough to incorporate with no remaining lumps. Add the pomegranate seeds and gently fold in.

12 Place the cake tin, base removed, on a serving plate, add the base layer of the sponge cake, cut-side up, and lock the tin. Pour in the filling, gently spread it to level and then cover with the other sponge cake layer. Transfer to the fridge and leave to chill for at least 1 hour until the filling sets. Dust with icing sugar and sprinkle with extra pomegranate seeds and mint and serve.

evaporated milk pudding
with Crushed Arabic Coffee

SERVES 4
PREPARATION TIME: 10 minutes,
  plus cooling and setting
COOKING TIME: 15 minutes

200ml/7fl oz/heaped ¾ cup whole
  milk

200ml/7fl oz/heaped ¾ cup
  evaporated milk or unsweetened
  condensed milk

40g/1½oz/heaped ⅓ cup caster
  sugar

3 tbsp cornflour

a large pinch of ground cardamom

a few drops of rosewater

1 tbsp Arabic coffee or espresso
  beans or dark chocolate, finely
  chopped, to decorate

1 tbsp pistachios, finely chopped,
  to decorate

Based on the classic Middle Eastern milk flan known as muhallabiah, this dessert also draws inspiration from Arabic coffee. The milk mixture is infused with cardamom, a spice with which Arabic coffee is commonly brewed. The creamy sweetness is contrasted splendidly with the bitter coffee beans. It's an incredibly simple and rapid way to satiate a sweet craving with very minimal mess. Adjust the rosewater to taste. Note that evaporated milk is also sometimes known as unsweetened condensed milk. Be careful not to use sweetened condensed milk by mistake.

1 Put the milk, evaporated milk, sugar, cornflour and cardamom into a heavy-based pan and whisk well to combine. When the mixture is smooth, put the pan over a medium-low heat and bring it to the boil, whisking continuously until thickened, and making sure it does not boil over. Once the mixture coats the back of a spoon without running off, remove the pan from the heat.

2 Pour the mixture through a fine sieve secured over a pouring jug. Add the rosewater and leave to cool slightly for 10–15 minutes.

3 Pour the mixture into glasses or dessert bowls, cover tightly with cling film and place in the fridge for about 2–3 hours until really cold and set.

4 When the puddings are cold and set, remove from the fridge and sprinkle with Arabic coffee beans and pistachios and serve.

middle eastern cheesecake

SERVES 8
PREPARATION TIME: 15 minutes
COOKING TIME: 1 ½ hours

125g/4½oz/ heaped ½ cup caster
sugar

1 tsp lemon juice

1 tsp orange blossom water

125g/4½oz butter, melted, plus
extra for greasing

a pinch of ground saffron or
turmeric (see page 212)

250g/9oz frozen shredded filo pastry
(kataifi), defrosted, or sheets of
filo pastry

500g/1lb 2oz Nabulsi cheese or
mozzarella

500g/1lb 2oz mascarpone

½ tsp ground mahlab (optional)

30g/1oz/¼ cup shelled pistachios

This Palestinian sweet, known as knafeh Nabulsieh, is a speciality of the city of Nablus in the West Bank, and is made using Nabulsi cheese – a semi-soft white brined cheese that becomes soft and stretchy when heated. You need to soak the Nabulsi overnight to reduce its saltiness. Alternatively, you can use mozzarella and mascarpone as a substitute. The cheesecake can be made with semolina ("fine knafeh"), shredded filo ("coarse knafeh") or a combination of both ("wavering knafeh").

1 Dissolve the sugar in 125ml/4fl oz/½ cup water in a heavy-based saucepan. Add the lemon juice and heat over a medium-high heat until the sugar has dissolved. Bring it to the boil, stirring occasionally, then reduce the heat to low and let it simmer for about 15 minutes until it reaches a syrupy consistency. Remove the pan from the heat and stir in the orange blossom water. Set the syrup aside to cool.

2 Put the melted butter and the saffron in a bowl and leave to steep for a few minutes, stirring just to incorporate.

3 If not using kataifi, use kitchen scissors to shred the filo into the smallest-size strings possible. Put the shredded pastry into a mixing bowl. Pour in the saffron butter and use your fingers to rub the butter all over the pastry strings.

4 Preheat the oven to 180°C/350°F/Gas 4. Shred the Nabulsi into another mixing bowl, add the mascarpone and mahlab, if using, and use your hands to mix it together.

5 Generously grease a round 23cm/9in cake tin with butter and spread about half of the buttered filo strings across the bottom. Spread the cheese mixture across the pastry layer evenly, then cover by spreading the remaining layer of filo strings evenly over the top.

6 Bake in the oven for 1–1¼ hours until the cheese is bubbling and the pastry is golden. A good way of testing readiness is to wiggle the pan gently – the cheesecake should come away from the edges.

7 Finally, place under a hot grill for 1–2 minutes to achieve an evenly golden top layer. Pour the cooled sugar syrup over the top before serving, or serve with the syrup on the side, if preferred. Grind the pistachios into a powder using a pestle and mortar, then sprinkle the powder over the cheesecake. Slice into squares and serve.

fritter threads with Mulberry Swirl Ice Cream

SERVES 4
PREPARATION TIME: 40 minutes
  plus freezing
COOKING TIME: 30 minutes

250g/9oz/1 heaped cup granulated
  sugar

500ml/17fl oz/2 cups whole milk

1 tsp salep flour or cornflour

4 tbsp mulberry or blackberry syrup

180g/6¼oz/1½ cups self-raising
  flour, sifted

3 tbsp Greek yogurt

zest of 1 lime

a pinch of salt

1 tsp bicarbonate of soda

oil, for deep frying

sifted icing sugar, for dusting

50g/1¾oz/⅓ cup shelled pistachios,
  coarsely chopped

Salep flour (see page 194 and 209) is the powdered bulb of a wild orchid and it lends a playful elastic texture to the ice cream. Somewhat expensive and hard to find, it can be substituted with 2 teaspoons cornflour or some ground mastic gum.

1 Place a freezer-proof bowl in the freezer to chill. Alternatively, if using an ice cream maker, follow the manufacturer's instructions.

2 Meanwhile, put the sugar, milk and salep flour in a small bowl and stir until the sugar and salep have dissolved.

3 Pour the mixture into the chilled bowl and beat well, then put in the freezer for 45 minutes. Remove the bowl from the freezer and beat well, making sure to break up all the ice crystals, so you get a creamy end result. Return to the freezer for 30 minutes, then remove and repeat the process again, breaking up all the ice crystals that have developed. Repeat 2–3 more times.

4 When the ice cream mixture is softly firm, about 3–4 hours after the ice cream mixture was first placed in the freezer in step 3, transfer half the ice cream mixture into a separate bowl. Drizzle half of the mulberry syrup over the ice cream in the freezer-proof bowl, then add the remaining ice cream followed by the remaining syrup. Insert a knife or bamboo skewer deep into the bowl and draw "S" shapes into the ice cream mixture. Freeze for approximately 8 hours until firm.

5 When the ice cream is ready, put the self-raising flour, yogurt, lime zest, salt and bicarbonate of soda in a mixing bowl. Add 250ml/9fl oz/1 cup tepid water and stir until the mixture forms a thin, smooth batter. Leave to stand for 30 minutes.

6 Heat the oil in a large saucepan until it reaches 180°C/350°F or until a teaspoonful of the batter sizzles and floats to the surface immediately after it has been dropped in. Using a tablespoon, spoon the batter straight into the hot oil, working from the centre outwards in a spiral, trying to create fun effects. Cook the fritter threads for 1–2 minutes, moving them around only when the batter has set in the oil, and flipping them over so that they turn an even golden colour. Lift out of the oil using a slotted spoon and drain on kitchen paper. Repeat with the remaining batter. Serve the fritter threads alongside 1–2 scoops of the swirled ice cream, then dust with icing sugar and sprinkle with chopped pistachios.

Saffron Rice Pudding

SERVES 4
PREPARATION TIME: 15 minutes,
 plus making the saffron liquid and
 chilling
COOKING TIME: 1 hour 10 minutes

4 ready-to-eat dried figs

150ml/5fl oz/scant ⅔ cup clear
 honey

1 tbsp rosewater

1l/35fl oz/4 cups whole milk

30g/1oz unsalted butter

1 tsp ground cardamom

1 tsp ground cinnamon, plus extra
 for sprinkling

1 tsp Saffron Liquid (see page 212)

100g/3 ½oz/scant ½ cup short-
 grain pudding rice

150ml/5fl oz/scant ⅔ cup double
 cream

2 tbsp flaked almonds, to sprinkle

Nearly every culture has an adaptation of this ancient rice dish. This delicate and creamy version is inspired by two different Persian rice puddings: shir berenj and shollehzard. The former has a topping of honey or jam; the latter incorporates saffron. In Iran, a person will serve this dish to give thanks for their good fortune or to honour the departed.

1 Preheat the oven to 180°C/350°F/Gas 4. Slice the figs lengthways into sixths and place in a baking dish.

2 Bake in the oven for 10–15 minutes until tender. Meanwhile, mix 6 tablespoons of the honey with the rosewater. Remove the figs from the oven and pour the rose and honey mixture over them. Set aside to cool.

3 Put the milk, the remaining honey, the butter, cardamom, cinnamon and saffron liquid in a large heavy-based saucepan and bring the mixture to the boil over a medium heat. Meanwhile, rinse the rice several times under cold running water.

4 Stir the mixture well, then reduce the heat to low. Add the rice and bring just to the boil, then simmer for 50 minutes or more, stirring occasionally, until the rice is very soft and begins to disintegrate. The mixture should thicken into a pudding. Remove from the heat and set aside to cool.

5 Pour the cream into a bowl and whip until it forms stiff peaks. Gently fold it into the cooked rice. Pour the pudding into four dishes and leave to cool, then cover with cling film and put in the fridge to chill for several hours.

6 Meanwhile, toast the flaked almonds in a heavy-based pan over a medium heat for 1–2 minutes until golden and fragrant, shaking the pan often.

7 Before serving, sprinkle each pudding with a pinch of cinnamon, add the honeyed figs and sprinkle with the toasted almonds.

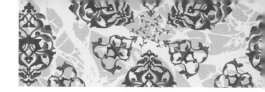

cardamom-scented profiteroles

MAKES 10
PREPARATION TIME: 30 minutes,
 plus cooling
COOKING TIME: 30 minutes

125ml/4fl oz/½ cup milk

115g/4oz butter

125g/4½oz/1 cup plain flour

a pinch of salt

4 eggs

zest of 1 lime

1 tsp ground cardamom

500ml/17fl oz/2 cups double cream

100g/3½oz/heaped ⅔ cup caster
 sugar

2 tbsp rosewater

50g/1¾oz/scant ½ cup shelled
 pistachios, finely chopped

4 tbsp pomegranate molasses

icing sugar, for dusting

dried edible rose petals, to decorate
 (optional)

*Although profiteroles may look and sound daunting, they
are in fact super-easy to make and don't take that much time
either. Here is my twist on Iran's popular cream-filled pastries.*

1 Preheat the oven to 180°C/350°F/Gas 4. Line a large baking sheet
with parchment paper. To make the choux pastry, put the milk, butter
and 125ml/4fl oz/½ cup water in a heavy-based saucepan over a
medium heat until the butter melts, then bring to the boil. Reduce the
heat to low and add the flour and salt, then beat vigorously with a
wooden spoon until the mixture forms a smooth paste and starts to pull
away from the sides of the pan.

2 Remove the pan from the heat and leave to cool for 2–3 minutes to
prevent the eggs curdling. Beat in the eggs, one at a time, ensuring
that each is thoroughly incorporated before you add the next. Continue
beating until the mixture forms a smooth, thick paste. Sprinkle over half
the lime zest and the cardamom and gently stir until just combined.

3 Spoon a heaped tablespoon of the choux pastry dough onto the
prepared baking sheet, sliding it off with your finger if needed. Repeat
with the rest of the mixture, leaving about 5cm/2in between each one to
allow for expansion during cooking, making about ten profiteroles.

4 Bake in the oven for 20–25 minutes or until the profiteroles have
puffed up and are golden brown. Turn off the oven, leaving the
profiteroles inside with the door slightly ajar for about 15 minutes.
If you tap the base of one of the profiteroles, it should make a hollow
sound. Pierce the side of each profiterole to release any hot air, which
helps to prevent them going soggy.

5 Put the cream and sugar in a mixing bowl and use an electric whisk
to beat the mixture until it forms stiff peaks. Add the rosewater, the
remaining lime zest and the pistachios and fold in gently. Put in the
fridge to firm up.

6 Once the profiteroles have cooled, cut each one in half horizontally,
but not all the way through. Remove the chilled cream from the fridge
and use a wooden cocktail stick to gently swirl in the pomegranate
molasses.

7 Spoon 2 tablespoons of the cream into the cavity of each profiterole.
Dust with icing sugar and decorate with dried rose petals, if you like.

tahini & chocolate brioche

SERVES 4
PREPARATION TIME: 45 minutes,
 plus rising
COOKING TIME: 50 minutes

4 tbsp milk

7g/¼oz dried active yeast

250g/9oz/2 cups plain flour,
 plus extra for dusting

a pinch of fine sea salt

3 tbsp caster sugar, plus an extra
 pinch

2 eggs, plus 1 egg yolk

125g/4½oz butter at room
 temperature, cut into cubes

1 tsp sunflower oil

1 tbsp plus 2 tsp tahini

40g/1½oz/heaped ¼ cup chocolate
 chips

Armenian communities across the Middle East have contributed much to the cuisine across the region, and this brioche is inspired by their tahinov hatz, a type of sweet bread roll spread with sugar and cinnamon.

1 Warm the milk in a small saucepan until tepid. Sprinkle in the yeast and stir well.

2 Sift the flour and salt into a mixing bowl, add the sugar, yeasty milk mixture and both eggs and mix thoroughly by hand. Knead in the butter, one piece at a time. The result should be a soft and elastic dough with a sticky consistency.

3 Dust the work surface with flour. Lightly grease your hands with a few drops of the oil, then remove the dough from the bowl and shape it into a tight, smooth ball. Lightly grease the mixing bowl and return the dough ball to the bowl. Cover with a kitchen towel and leave in a warm place to rise for 1–2 hours until it has doubled in size.

4 Tip the dough out onto a lightly floured surface and knock it back to deflate it, then knead it for 5 minutes, during which time it should become less sticky and more silky. Grease the bowl again and return the dough to the bowl. Cover and leave to rise in a warm place for another 1 hour or until it doubles in size again.

5 Lightly dust the work surface with flour again. Remove the dough from the mixing bowl and cut it into eight even-sized pieces, then roll each one into a ball. Working with one ball at time, and covering the others with a damp cloth while you work, flatten each ball and brush each one with ½ teaspoon of the tahini, then sprinkle about 5g/⅛oz of the chocolate chips in the centre. Working with one ball at a time, gather the edges of the dough over the tahini and chocolate, pinching them together into pouches to seal the filling in tightly. Transfer to a non-stick 900g/2lb loaf tin and repeat with the remaining balls. Cover and set aside for 1 hour or until they have doubled in size.

6 Shortly before the balls have fully risen, preheat the oven to 180°C/350°F/Gas 4. In a mixing bowl, whisk the egg yolk with 1 tablespoon water and the pinch of sugar to create an egg wash, then brush this over the top of the dough balls.

7 Bake in the oven for 35–45 minutes until the top is golden brown and a skewer inserted into the middle comes out clean. Remove the brioche from the oven and leave it to stand for 5 minutes before turning it out onto a wire rack to cool. When completely cold, cut into slices.

egyptian spiced bread pudding

SERVES 4
PREPARATION TIME: 15 minutes
COOKING TIME: 30 minutes

4 all-butter croissants

2 tbsp raisins or dried mixed berries

2 tbsp flaked almonds, plus extra
to sprinkle

2 tbsp pine nuts, plus extra for
sprinkling

2 tbsp roughly chopped shelled
pistachios

250ml/9fl oz/1 cup milk

5 tbsp caster sugar

¼ tsp ground cinnamon

2 tsp orange blossom water

250ml/9fl oz/1 cup whipping cream

4 tbsp desiccated coconut

1 small egg, beaten

This dessert, known as Um Ali Bread Pudding, is named after the mother um Ali. The tales of both the mother and the dessert are many and intriguing. This dessert is a quick and easy way to win legions of hearts. It's also a mouth-watering way to use up stale croissants – or a great reason to go and buy some!

1 Preheat the oven to 180°C/350°F/Gas 4 and line a baking sheet with parchment paper.

2 Tear up the croissants into bite-size pieces, place on the baking sheet and bake in the oven for 10 minutes until crisp and golden.

3 Spread the baked croissant pieces across the base of a baking dish, about 28cm/11¼in square. Sprinkle over the raisins, almonds, pine nuts and pistachios, making sure they are spread evenly.

4 Heat the milk in a heavy-based saucepan over a medium heat, add 3 tablespoons of the sugar and mix well to dissolve. Reduce the heat to low, add the cinnamon and orange blossom water and heat through at a gentle simmer for 3–4 minutes. Remove the pan from the heat and leave it to cool so that the egg will not scramble when it's added to it.

5 Meanwhile, put the cream and the remaining sugar in a mixing bowl and whisk until the mixture forms soft peaks. Sprinkle in the coconut and gently fold to incorporate.

6 Add the egg to the cool milk mixture and whisk to combine. Ladle the mixture into the baking dish and spread the whipped cream over the top.

7 Bake in the oven for 15 minutes until everything is bubbling and the top is golden, if necessary placing it under a hot grill for the last 1–2 minutes to brown the top. Remove from the oven and leave to stand for a couple of minutes. Serve warm.

Wild Orchid ice cream in filo cups

SERVES 6
PREPARATION TIME: 40 minutes,
  plus freezing
COOKING TIME: 15 minutes

700ml/24fl oz/2¾ cups whole milk

2 tsp salep flour or cornflour

¼ tsp mastic powder or about
  2 small mastic tears ground using
  a pestle and mortar, or xanthan
  gum

175g/6oz/¾ cup caster sugar

1 tsp rosewater

2 tbsp roughly chopped pistachios,
  plus extra for sprinkling

3 sheets of filo pastry

40g/1½oz butter

dried edible rose petals, to decorate
  (optional)

Salep flour, which gives this ice cream its light and elastic consistency, is milled from the dried tubers of a species of wild orchid found in the Anatolian plateau. These tubers apparently resemble the testicles of a fox, and this gave the flour its name! It's widely thought to be an aphrodisiac.

1 Pour 350ml/12fl oz/1½ cups of the milk into a small mixing bowl, add the salep flour and mastic powder and stir to dissolve.

2 Place a large pan over a medium heat, add the remaining milk and the sugar and whisk well to dissolve. Bring the mixture to the boil, then gradually pour the salep and milk mixture into the hot milk as you continue to whisk vigorously, gently simmering the mixture over a low heat for 5 minutes. Make sure the mixture does not rise up in the pan and then overflow.

3 Remove the pan from the heat and mix in the rosewater and pistachios. Transfer to a freezer-safe mixing bowl and leave to cool completely, then chill in the fridge.

4 Once the mixture has chilled, transfer to the freezer for 45 minutes, then remove and whisk well to break up all the ice crystals while incorporating as much air as possible to yield a creamier, fluffier end result. Return to the freezer for 30 minutes, then remove and repeat the process again, breaking up all the ice crystals that have developed. Repeat two or three more times until completely frozen. This should take about 8 hours. You may find that your whisk can no longer do the job as the ice cream hardens, in which case a spatula is a good substitute.

5 Preheat the oven to 180°C/350°F/Gas 4. Remove the sheets of filo from their packaging and cover them with a damp kitchen towel.

6 Melt the butter in a small saucepan and lightly brush six cups of a muffin pan with some of it. Brush one filo sheet with more melted butter, add another layer on top, brush that one with butter and then repeat with the final layer. Slice the stack into six 15 x 13cm/6 x 5in rectangles, then gently press these rectangles into the greased muffin pan so that they form cup shapes.

7 Bake in the oven for 6–8 minutes or until golden brown. Lift the filo cups out of the pan and leave to cool. Fill each cup with a scoop of ice cream and sprinkle with pistachios and dried rose petals, if you like.

ginger & molasses semolina marble cake

SERVES 4
PREPARATION TIME: 25 minutes
COOKING TIME: 50 minutes

125g/4½oz butter

250g/9oz/2 cups fine semolina

55g/2oz/heaped ¾ cup caster sugar

1 tsp bicarbonate of soda

325ml/11fl oz/scant 1⅓ cups natural yogurt

8cm/3¼in piece of root ginger, peeled and grated

zest of 1 lemon

2 tsp date or carob molasses

50g/1¾oz/⅓ cup blanched almonds

FOR THE SYRUP (OPTIONAL)

125g/4½oz/heaped ¼ cup caster sugar

1 tsp lemon juice

1 tsp orange blossom water

I've broken with tradition by adding molasses and ginger to this classic egg-free cake, and reducing the amount of syrup. Don't use Greek yogurt in this recipe, as it's too thick.

1 Preheat the oven to 180°C/350°F/Gas 4. Grease a 22cm/8½in square baking tin with a little butter and line the base with parchment paper. Melt the remaining butter in a small saucepan, then set aside to cool.

2 Put the semolina, sugar and the bicarbonate of soda in a large mixing bowl. Pour in the melted butter and rub well with your fingers to combine.

3 Pour the yogurt into a large jug, add the ginger and lemon zest and mix well. Pour the mixture over the semolina mixture and mix again.

4 Put the date molasses in a ramekin and dilute it with a few drops of water, so that it will be easier to drizzle off the teaspoon.

5 Spoon one-third of the semolina mixture into the prepared baking tin and shake gently to even out the surface, then drizzle one-third of the diluted molasses over the top. Repeat with another third of the semolina mixture and molasses. Top with the remaining mixture and molasses.

6 Using a skewer or fork, gently swirl the mixture around the tin a few times to create a marbled effect. Don't over-mix. Smooth the surface, then, using a sharp knife, score the surface into diamond or square patterns (you'll have to slice again after baking but this is to help ensure that the almonds are not randomly placed), then place an almond in the centre of each diamond or square. Bake in the oven for 30–45 minutes, or until a skewer inserted into the middle comes out clean.

7 Meanwhile, if making the syrup, put 4 tablespoons water, the sugar, lemon juice and orange blossom water in a heavy-based saucepan over a medium heat, and stir well. Bring to the boil and keep at a rolling boil for about 5 minutes, stirring often until well incorporated, thickened and syrupy. Stir well and set aside.

8 Remove the cake from the oven, leave to cool for a few minutes, then turn out onto a plate. Gently peel off the parchment paper. Slice into diamonds or squares, as marked earlier. Taste a small piece, adding syrup if you like.

baklawa

SERVES 8
PREPARATION TIME: 30 minutes,
  plus resting
COOKING TIME: 30 minutes

125g/4½oz/heaped ½ cup caster
  sugar
juice of ½ lemon
300g/10½oz/2 cups blanched
  almonds
300g/10½oz/2 cups shelled
  pistachios
1 tsp ground cinnamon
1 tsp orange blossom water
125g/4½oz unsalted butter
14 sheets of filo pastry

*Baklawa refer to a whole host of sweets prepared using filo
pastry and which come in differing shapes.*

1 Put the sugar, 125ml/4fl oz/½ cup water and the lemon juice in a
heavy-based saucepan and heat over a medium heat. Stir well, then
bring to the boil and keep at a rolling boil for about 5 minutes, stirring
often, until thickened and syrupy. Stir well and set aside to cool.

2 Toast the almonds in a heavy-based pan over a medium heat for
1–2 minutes until golden and fragrant, shaking the pan often.

3 Put the pistachios in a heatproof bowl and pour over boiling water.
Leave for 1–2 minutes to allow the skins to loosen. Strain and then rub
them dry with a kitchen towel. Discard the skins, then rinse the pistachios
under cold running water. Pat the pistachios dry with a clean towel.

4 Put the toasted almonds and pistachios in a small food processor and
blitz until they are roughly chopped, then tip into a mixing bowl. Add
half of the syrup and the cinnamon, and mix well to combine. Add the
orange blossom water to the remaining syrup.

5 Preheat the oven to 180°C/350°F/Gas 4. Grease a 38 x 25cm/15 x 10in
baking tray with a little butter. Melt the rest of the butter in a small pan.

6 Remove the sheets of filo from their plastic packaging and cover them
quickly with a damp kitchen towel to stop them drying out, uncovering
each one only when it's needed.

7 Place one sheet in the baking tray (trimming to fit, if necessary) and
brush with some of the melted butter. Repeat until you have finished a
first layer of 6 sheets of filo. Spread the nut mixture evenly over the top.
Layer the rest of the pastry sheets on top of the filling as before. (It's
customary to have fewer sheets on the bottom layer.) Brush more butter
on top of the last sheet and pour in any remaining butter.

8 With a sharp knife, cut the pastry into elongated diamonds with sides
of 3cm/1¼in or into rectangles of the same dimensions.

9 Bake in the oven for 20 minutes until the top is lightly golden and
crispy. Remove from the oven and pour as much of the remaining syrup
as you like over the top; or if you have a very sweet tooth, you could use
it all. Leave it to sit, uncovered, for a couple of hours before serving. You
can store it in an airtight container for up to 2 weeks.

ma'amoul shortbread cookies

MAKES 26
PREPARATION TIME: 45 minutes,
  plus chilling and resting
COOKING TIME: 15 minutes

140g/5oz/scant 1 cup semolina,
  plus extra for dusting

35g/1¼oz/¼ cup farina (potato
  starch)

2 tbsp caster sugar

¼ tsp ground mahlab or ground
  almonds

75g/2½oz butter, melted

1 tbsp orange blossom water

icing sugar, to dust

PISTACHIO FILLING
35g/1¼oz/¼ cup pistachios

1 tbsp caster sugar

¼ tsp orange blossom water

WALNUT FILLING
35g/1¼oz/⅓ cup walnut pieces

15g/½oz caster sugar

¼ tsp orange blossom water

DATE & WALNUT FILLING
40g/1½oz/¼ cup pitted dates

4–5 walnuts

a pinch of ground nutmeg

5g/¼oz butter, melted

These cookies are traditionally created using three beautiful wooden moulds, each engraved to identify their fillings.

1 Put the semolina, farina, sugar and mahlab in a mixing bowl. Add the melted butter along with the orange blossom water and beat well. Knead the mixture for 3–4 minutes, working it into a pliable dough. Cover with cling film and chill in the fridge for 2 hours.

2 Meanwhile, prepare the fillings. For the pistachio filling, put the pistachios, sugar and orange blossom water in a small food processor or blender. Whizz for 1 minute to form a rough paste, then transfer to a bowl and wash the food processor.

3 For the walnut filling, put the walnuts, sugar and orange blossom water in the washed food processor or blender. Whizz for 1 minute to form a rough paste. Transfer to a bowl and wash the food processor.

4 For the date and walnut filling, put the dates, walnuts and nutmeg in the washed food processor or blender. Melt the butter and add to the mixture, then whizz for 1 minute to form a rough paste.

5 Remove the dough from the fridge and leave to rest at room temperature for about 20 minutes before kneading it for 2 minutes.

6 Divide the dough into three even-sized amounts and roll out each piece into a long, thin, rod-like shape. Pinch off small lumps of the dough (about 2.5cm/1in pieces), and flatten them with your palms, making sure it's quite thin but not so thin that it will tear.

7 Dust the ma'amoul mould cavities with semolina and then invert and tap gently to remove the excess. Gently flatten the dough into each mould cavity and add the relevant filling. Bring the edges together and seal well, then flatten the surface to create a level base for the cookie to sit on, pinching off any excess dough. Gently release by tapping the mould on the work surface. Repeat until you have about eight pistachio cookies, eight walnut cookies and ten date and walnut cookies (which are smaller). Each of your cookies should be clearly stamped with its design.

8 Preheat the oven to 200°C/400°F/Gas 6. Dust a baking sheet with semolina and place the cookies on it. Bake for 10–15 minutes for the larger cookies and about 8–10 minutes for the smaller ones until the sides are slightly golden in colour. Leave to cool, then dust with icing sugar.

Note: I like to add the filling using the mould because I find it yields more consistent results. Alternatively, flatten the dough in the palm of your hand while making a hole in it, then stuff it with the filling, seal the edges, roll it into a ball, then finally press it into a mould.

date fudge

SERVES 4
PREPARATION TIME: 45 minutes,
 plus setting and cooling
COOKING TIME: 20 minutes

100g/3½oz/1 cup walnut halves,
 plus 55g/2oz/½ cup walnuts,
 roughly chopped

500g/1lb 2oz/scant 3 cups dried
 pitted dates

300g/10½oz unsalted butter

300g/10½oz/scant 2½ cups plain
 flour

50g/2oz/scant ½ cup icing sugar

1 tsp ground cinnamon

½ tsp ground cardamom

a pinch of salt

55g/2oz/⅓ cup pistachios

55g/2oz/⅓ cup almonds

This delicate confection tends to crumble between your fingers, so make sure you have a plate or a napkin on hand to put it on. It's so moreish that you will want to chase every last crumb.

1 Toast the walnut halves in a heavy-based pan over a medium heat for 2–3 minutes until golden brown and fragrant, shaking the pan often.

2 Stuff a toasted walnut into each date and then pack them tightly in a 20cm/8in baking tin, 3cm/1¼in deep.

3 Melt the butter in a deep heavy-based saucepan over a medium–low heat, then add the flour, icing sugar, cinnamon, cardamom and salt and stir constantly for 10–15 minutes, until the mixture resembles a smooth golden caramel.

4 Pour the mixture over the dates and smooth out with the back of a metal spoon. Leave to set for 20 minutes.

5 Grind the walnut pieces, pistachios and almonds separately using a pestle and mortar. Sprinkle a thin layer of pistachios over the top of the fudge, then one of walnuts and finally almonds, then repeat until all the nuts have been used. Press the nuts down with your hands so that they stick to the fudge. Leave to cool completely, then, using a sharp knife, cut into small squares or diamonds to serve.

date & tahini truffles

SERVES 4
PREPARATION TIME: 20 minutes
COOKING TIME: 1 minute

12 pitted dates

2 tbsp tahini

1/8 tsp ground cardamom

2 tsp macadamias

2 tsp sesame seeds

2 tsp desiccated coconut

1/2 tsp ground coffee

Known as both an aphrodisiac and the poor man's food, there are more than 400 varieties of dates available in Iraq. These include soft and semi-soft, or dry dates, also known as bread dates. The tahini is a wonderful nutty addition to this recipe. The truffles are suitable for gluten- and dairy-free eaters. Listed below are just some ideas for coatings, which you can, of course, adapt to your taste.

1 Put the dates, tahini and cardamom in a food processor and whizz for 1–2 minutes to create an oily paste. Put in the fridge for 10 minutes to help the mixture firm up.

2 Meanwhile, blend the macadamias to a powder using either a mini blender or a pestle and mortar.

3 Toast the sesame seeds in a heavy-based pan over a medium heat for 1 minute until golden and fragrant, shaking the pan often.

4 Mould the date paste into 12 round balls (about 2cm/¾in in diameter). Put four small, shallow bowls on the work surface and put a different coating in each one: toasted sesame seeds, desiccated coconut, ground macadamia and ground coffee. Roll three truffle balls in each of the flavourings until they are well coated. You may find that you need to apply gentle pressure to get the coconut to stick. Transfer to a plate and serve.

Note: If you're not planning on eating the truffles shortly after making them, transfer to a rigid plastic container lined with parchment paper and store in the fridge for up to 1 week.

turkish delight

SERVES 4
PREPARATION TIME: *40 minutes*
COOKING TIME: *1 ½ hours*

5cm/2in piece of root ginger, peeled and grated

820g/1lb 13oz/4 cups caster sugar

juice of 1 lemon

200g/7oz/scant 1⅔ cups cornflour

1 tsp cream of tartar

50g/1¾oz ready-to-eat dried apricots, finely chopped

1 tbsp lime juice

2 tbsp desiccated coconut

1 tsp rosewater

3 tbsp shelled pistachios, roughly chopped

dried edible rose petals (optional)

75g/2¾oz/scant ⅔ cup icing sugar

This recipe is more zesty and a lot less sickly than the Turkish delight you may be used to, with a texture that is very jelly-like and melt-in-the-mouth. It's best to make sure all your flavourings are prepared and easily accessible. You don't want to be rushing around looking for these later on while your Turkish delight mixture solidifies in the saucepan...

1 You will need up to three heavy-based saucepans and up to three 20cm/8in square silicone or rigid plastic containers, depending on the number of flavours you want to make. Line the containers with parchment paper and have the saucepans to hand.

2 Put the grated ginger in a ramekin, add 2 tablespoons boiling water and set aside to steep.

3 Meanwhile, to make the sugar syrup, put the sugar, 375ml/13fl oz/1½ cups water and the lemon juice in a heavy-based saucepan and heat over a medium heat. Put a sugar thermometer in the liquid and bring it to the boil, stirring often, until the temperature reaches 110°C/230°F (soft-ball stage). Remove the pan from the heat and set aside to cool.

4 Put 125g/4½oz/½ cup of the cornflour, the cream of tartar and 750ml/26fl oz/3 cups water into another heavy-based saucepan and stir it very gently over a low heat for about 15 minutes. The mixture will initially develop into a gooey ball. Be gentle when you stir it, because it has resistant characteristics; with patience the mixture will dissolve and become milky with no lumps.

5 Now, increase the heat to medium and stir the mixture constantly, concentrating fully on the job at hand, as you bring it to a gentle simmer until it reaches a creamy consistency with no lumps. Don't let it boil or it will turn into a thick, rubbery paste. (If this happens, you will need to make the cornflour mixture again.)

6 As soon as you feel it starting to stick to the bottom of the pan, remove it from the heat. Quickly pour it into the sugar syrup, stirring as you do so until the mixtures are well combined. At first the mixture will be rather milky-white, but as you continue to stir it, it should become clear. Place the pan over a medium heat and bring the mixture to the boil, stirring constantly but gently as you continue to remove any

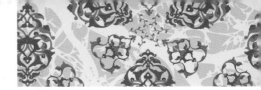

lumps, and making sure that the mixture is well combined and does not collect and harden around the edge of the pan.

7 After a while, the mixture should start becoming clearer and then eventually (after 40 minutes or so of stirring) it will develop a yellowish hue and a thicker texture. To test for readiness, scoop out a little with a spoon and leave it to cool on a cold plate: after a few minutes, it should wrinkle when you run a finger over it.

8 If you are making only one flavour, then remove the pan from the heat, and stir in the chosen ingredients to combine (see below), then pour the flavoured mixture into a lined container. If you are using several flavour combinations, then you will need to divide the mixture up between the required number of saucepans.

9 Place the pans over a medium heat and, once they have heated through, divide the mixture evenly amongst them and then mix in the flavourings accordingly (see below). The reason for the preheating is that the cold temperature of the pan would shock the mixture, quickly hardening it and making mixing anything into it difficult.

10 For ginger and apricot: drizzle over 1 tablespoon of the ginger liquid (or more to taste) and sprinkle over the chopped apricot. Stir to combine, then spread out to form a flat layer in one of the lined containers.

11 For lime and coconut: drizzle over the lime juice and sprinkle over the desiccated coconut. Stir to combine, then spread out to form a flat layer in the second lined container.

12 For rose and pistachio: drizzle over the rosewater and sprinkle over the chopped pistachios and dried rose petals, if using. Stir to combine, then spread out to form a flat layer in the third container. Leave them all to cool, uncovered, overnight at room temperature.

13 The following day, sift the icing sugar in with the remaining cornflour to create some dusting mixture. Generously dust a work surface and then tip out one portion of the Turkish delight on to it. Sprinkle over enough dusting mixture until the Turkish delight is no longer sticky to handle. Powder the edge of a very sharp knife with some of the dusting mixture and cut the Turkish delight into cubes. Repeat with the other flavours.

14 Put the Turkish delight cubes into paper bags, separated into flavours. Sprinkle in a little of the dusting mixture, then toss the Turkish delight pieces so that all the exposed sides are covered.

Note: Don't store the Turkish delight in an airtight container because it will release moisture, making the sweets sticky. Store for up to 2 weeks.

mint & gunpowder tea

SERVES 4
PREPARATION TIME: 5 minutes

1 teabag of gunpowder tea or
  green tea
8 mint sprigs
about 3 tbsp caster sugar, to taste

Mint tea is so popular in Morocco that it's served after every meal and has been coined "Berber whisky" because it's served at every social gathering. There is an art form that comes with pouring the tea: the higher the pour the better, so that a light foam develops on the surface.

1 Pour 1l/35fl oz/4 cups boiling water into a teapot, add the teabag and the mint sprigs and leave the tea to brew for 2–3 minutes.

2 Pour the tea into individual Moroccan tea glasses or mugs and serve with sugar to taste.

café blanc

SERVES 4
PREPARATION TIME: 2 minutes

4 tsp orange blossom water
1 tbsp clear honey (optional)

This is not coffee as you know it, but rather a soothing and digestive herbal tea, popular in Lebanon and Syria, made from hot water subtly scented with orange blossom essence and sweetened with honey. Try it just before bedtime. I prefer it unsweetened.

1 Pour 1l/35fl oz/4 cups boiling water into a teapot, add the orange blossom water and honey, if using, and mix well to combine.

2 Pour the liquid into individual glasses or mugs and serve.

middle eastern & north african pantry

Aleppo pepper closely resembling the Ancho in flavor, hails from Aleppo, Syria. They are a bright red, mildly spicy pepper, with a high oil content and a hint of fruity sweetness with earthy, smoky tones. Aleppo pepper paste is difficult to find in the West though varying qualities of crushed flakes can be found in most Middle Eastern stores and sourced online.

Allspice (the dried unripe berries of the *Pimenta dioica* plant), is indispensable in Lebanese cuisine. It's used to flavour a variety of stews and dishes and is frequently the only spice used.

Arak is Lebanon's national drink – a clear, colourless, unsweetened, aniseed-flavoured alcohol distilled from grapes.

Argan oil is a nutty-tasting oil that comes from the fruit of the argan tree. It has been used by the Berber people for centuries for its medicinal properties and to enhance their dishes. It's used in Morocco in tagines and couscous. It's also mixed with honey and eaten with bread or pancakes.

Barberries are beautiful, red, jewel-like dried fruits that are bursting with tartness. If you cannot find them, cranberries are a suitable substitute.

Black limes/dried limes (*limu amani*), are dried in the sun until they become very hard and turn black. They are used to lend a unique sharp, astringent flavour to fishy stews, soups and dishes rich in pulses and meats. They may be punctured, broken open or ground to a powder before being used in a recipe.

Bulgur wheat, also known as *burghul*, is a cereal food made from different wheat species, usually durum wheat. It's sold parboiled, dried and with the bran partially removed. It's available in four grinds or sizes: fine (1), medium (2), coarse (3) and extra-coarse (4). The bulgur you see labelled in most chain supermarkets in the UK as "fine" is, in fact, close to "medium" (grade 2). So if the grade is important, it's best to source your bulgur from a Middle Eastern/ ethnic store, which will usually carry an assortment of grades. Bulgur is considered more nutritious than white rice and couscous because of its high fibre, vitamin and mineral content. It's one of the ingredients used in tabbouleh (though only sparingly). The coarser varieties are preferred in stuffings and pilafs.

Couscous can be bought in instant and pre-cooked versions, but ignore them as these will turn into mush when cooked. Instead, choose non-instant couscous (available at most Middle Eastern grocers). It will take longer to cook and is traditionally steamed in a couscoussière, which houses the necessary mesh-steamer inside a pot in which a flavourful broth or stew is simmered. If you cannot find a couscoussière, use a regular steamer and line the steamer basket or colander with a muslin cloth or kitchen towel. Couscous is traditionally served alongside a tagine or stew.

Dried edible rose petals have a delicate sweet fragrance and usually come in pink, lilac or red. They are best kept in an airtight container as they lose their aroma quite quickly.

Freekeh is an ancient grain and cereal food made from green wheat native to many parts of the Middle East and North Africa. It has a nutty undertone and a smoky aroma. It's high in fibre, protein, vitamins and minerals. It can be purchased cracked and whole, and might require careful cleaning to rid it of any stones. Freekeh has wonderful smoky, earthy tones, and so some brands are preferable for certain dishes that require more subtle flavours.

Gram flour can be made from split peas (*channa dal*) or chickpeas. Here I use the chickpea variety. Most gram flours on sale in the UK are made from chickpeas, but it's worth checking.

Kishk is a fine, powdery cereal that is a mixture of bulgur wheat that has been fermented, usually with yogurt. To many people it's a treasured acquired taste, with its musky, cheese-like, soured tones. It can be found at only some Middle Eastern grocers.

Mahlab is a spice derived from the sour cherry stones of the Saint Lucia tree (*Prunus mahaleb*). The kernels from these cherries are ground to an aromatic powder. The flavour is a combination of bitter almond and cherry. Mahlab is used for its unique taste, ground or whole, to flavour different dishes around the Middle East. If the recipe calls for actual sour cherries (such as the Venison & Sour Cherry Nests on page 30), use morello cherries.

Mastic is a gum and an aromatic resin that is cultivated from the bark of the Mediterranean mastic tree. It's crushed and used in powder form in many desserts in parts of the Mediterranean and across the Middle East. Use mastic tears (drop-shaped pieces of the resin) or powder sparingly because the flavour the gum imparts can become overpowering.

Moghrabieh, a form of rolled semolina, like couscous, but much larger, cooks unevenly because the grains are rolled into inconsistently sized balls. These starchy balls swell and become soft and chewy when cooked and are fantastic at absorbing the flavours of the dish they are cooked in. If you're unable to find moghrabieh, then fregola may be substituted. I like to steam the moghrabieh when I cook it, which helps to keep the grains distinct.

Orange blossom water is a clear, fragrant water distilled from macerated blossom flowers of the Seville orange. It's believed that a spoon of orange blossom water diluted with water and some sugar or honey, otherwise known as Café Blanc (see page 207), can increase your heart rate. It's a traditional ingredient in Middle Eastern desserts.

Pomegranate molasses is a syrup made by boiling down the juice of pomegranates until it's reduced to a thick, crimson-brown liquid. It's used in meats, stews, salads and as a condiment. The flavour is both sweet and tart.

Rosewater is a clear, fragrant water distilled from macerated fresh wild roses. It's a traditional ingredient in Middle Eastern desserts and is used alone or in combination with orange blossom water in many desserts.

Salep flour is milled from the dried tubers of a wild orchid species found in the Anatolian plateau. It's prominently used in both a popular milk and spice beverage of the same name and also a light ice cream. Salep can be quite hard to find and rather expensive, but you could substitute it with cornflour or even some ground mastic gum.

Smen (or *samneh*, *semneh*) is an oil made from clarified butter that is aged and sometimes buried underground. It has a very distinctive rancid aroma and pungent flavour. As the aroma becomes stronger with age, the more prized the smen becomes as a reflection of a family's wealth. Still considered a delicacy in Morocco, it's an intricate part of traditional tagines and other dishes.

Sumac is a tangy, deep red or burgundy spice derived from the dried berries of the sumac bush. It's used along with lemon or in place of lemon to add a tart flavour to dishes such as Spinach & Sumac Turnovers (see page 37), as well as meats, fried eggs and dips. It can also be added to other spices, like the Wild Thyme Mixture (see page 220).

Tahini, a paste of ground sesame seeds, is one of the main ingredients used in hummus b tahini and other Middle Eastern dishes. It can be made into a sauce called Tarator (see page 220) by thinning it down with water and flavouring it with lemon juice, salt and garlic. It's a popular condiment in many Middle Eastern dishes.

Tamarind is a souring agent that lends a very distinctive flavour to curries and stews. It's sold in several forms and can be found in major supermarkets as well as in Asian, Spanish and Middle Eastern grocers. I prefer to use block rather than concentrate tamarind, since it's nearly identical to fresh pods but easier to use because you don't have to break it out of its shell. It's also more tart and flavoursome.

Verjuice, the unfermented sour juice extracted from semi-ripe grapes, adds a wonderfully delicate, sweet-tangy tone to dishes, salads and reductions. It's available in some supermarkets and Middle Eastern delicatessens.

Wheat berries (whole unprocessed wheat kernels) are high in fibre with a chewy texture, and although they take time to cook, they don't need to be soaked.

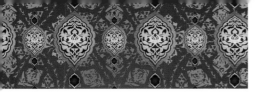

basic recipes & methods

BASIC RECIPES

CHERMOULA

I've had an unremitting crush on chermoula for decades. While the name points to the North African condiment, my father has been making a version of this scrumptious sauce to stuff his infamous Coriander-stuffed Trout for years. If you like coriander and love garlic, then you'll quickly find chermoula creeping into plenty of your dishes. It's very versatile, lending itself equally well to tagines (see page 144) and marinades.

Serves 4
Preparation time: 10 minutes
Cooking time: 2 minutes

¼ tsp cumin seeds
2 handfuls of coriander leaves (or a combination of coriander and parsley leaves)
2 tbsp dill leaves
5cm/2in piece of root ginger, peeled and roughly chopped
2 chillies, deseeded and roughly chopped
2 wedges of Preserved Lemon (see page 212), flesh removed, roughly chopped
8 garlic cloves, crushed with the blade of a knife
4 tbsp olive oil, plus extra for storing
sea salt

1 Toast the cumin seeds in a heavy-based pan over a medium heat for 1–2 minutes until fragrant, shaking the pan often.

2 Put all the ingredients except for the oil into a food processor and pulse to combine into a rough paste. Pour in the oil and pulse once more to combine. Season to taste with salt. Use as required.

3 Transfer any unused chermoula to an airtight container and pour a thin layer of olive oil over the top. Seal and store in the fridge for up to 10 days.

HARISSA

Another North African condiment, this fiery sauce may be served separately but also makes its way into many North African dishes. This recipe is merely a guideline, and I recommend that you adjust the ingredients to give the flavour that best suits your taste, and then use it in proportion to your personal heat scale, depending on the recipe. Harissa will keep for up to 3 weeks.

Serves 4
Preparation time: 15 minutes, plus soaking and macerating
Cooking time: 2 minutes

15g/½oz whole hot, dried chillies (about 15)
4 tbsp olive oil, plus extra for storing
¼ tsp coriander seeds
¼ tsp caraway seeds
¼ tsp cumin seeds
8 garlic cloves, crushed
1 tbsp tomato purée

1 Put the dried chillies in a small heatproof bowl, cover with boiling water and leave to soak for about 20 minutes. Drain the chillies and pat dry on kitchen paper. Slice of the stems, then remove the seeds, if you like, and finely chop. Transfer to a small bowl, pour over the oil and leave to macerate for 1 hour.

2 Toast the coriander, caraway and cumin seeds in a heavy-based pan over a medium heat for 1–2 minutes until fragrant, shaking the pan often.

3 Put all the ingredients except for the tomato purée in a mini blender and purée to a fine paste, stopping occasionally to scrape down the edges. Stir in the tomato purée, then transfer to a small, sterilized glass jar. Cover with a thin layer of oil and seal.

4 Keep in the fridge for up to 3 weeks, topping up with more oil after each use.

ADVIEH

There are two variations of this spice mix.

ADVIEH 1

Makes: 1 tbsp
Preparation time: 2 minutes
Cooking time: 2 minutes

seeds from 4 cardamom pods
1 tsp cumin seeds
1 tsp turmeric seeds
½ tsp caraway seeds
1 tsp ground cinnamon

1 Toast the cardamom, cumin and turmeric seeds in a heavy-based pan over a medium heat for 1–2 minutes until fragrant, shaking the pan often.

2 Grind the spices and caraway seeds using a pestle and mortar. Combine with the cinnamon. Store in an airtight container in a cool, dark place for up to 3 months.

ADVIEH 2

Makes: about 4 tbsp
Preparation time: 2 minutes

1 tbsp ground pistachios
½ tsp ground dried edible rose petals
½ tsp saffron threads
1 tsp ground cardamom
1 tsp ground cinnamon

1 Mix together all of the ingredients until combined. Use as directed or store in an airtight container in a cool, dark place for up to 3 months.

LEBANESE SEVEN SPICES

This is a popular spice mixture in Lebanon. It works wonderfully as a rub on lamb and beef.

Makes: 2 tbsp
Preparation time: 2 minutes

1 tsp ground cloves
1 tsp ground allspice
1 tsp ground fenugreek
1 tsp grated nutmeg
1 tsp ground ginger
1 tsp ground cinnamon
1 tsp freshly ground black pepper

1 Mix all the ingredients together and use as directed. Store in a cool dark place for up to 3 months.

HERB BUTTER

A flavour-packed finishing touch for main dishes.

Serves 4
Preparation time: 5 minutes
Cooking time: 10 minutes

100g/3 ½oz butter
5 garlic cloves, finely chopped
1 handful of coriander leaves, finely chopped
1 handful of mint leaves, finely chopped
sea salt and freshly ground black pepper

1 Melt the butter in a heavy-based frying pan over a medium heat until it sizzles. Add the garlic and cook for 1 minute until aromatic.

2 Add the herbs, mix well and cook for about 5 minutes until fragrant. Season to taste with salt and pepper.

VEGETABLE STOCK

Home-made stock is easy to make and a great way to use up vegetables that are past their best. Sweating rather than browning the veg gives the best result, I find.

Makes: about 1.5l/52fl oz/6 cups
Preparation time: 15 minutes
Cooking time: 45 minutes

1 tbsp olive oil
5 white mushrooms, wiped clean and roughly chopped
4 garlic cloves, crushed with the blade of a knife
3 celery sticks, roughly chopped and leaves reserved
2 carrots, roughly chopped
1 fennel bulb, roughly chopped
1 leek, roughly chopped
1 onion, roughly chopped
1 bay leaf
1 handful of parsley leaves
sprig of thyme (optional)
sprig of rosemary (optional)
a pinch of ground allspice
a pinch of sea salt

1 Put the oil in a large stock pan over a medium heat. Add all the ingredients, then cover and sweat for 2–3 minutes. Pour in 2l/70fl oz/8 cups water. Cover and bring to the boil, then reduce the heat to low and simmer for 35 minutes. Strain, discarding the solids. Use as called for in a recipe or cool and freeze any remaining stock.

PRESERVED LEMONS

I suggest you prepare these as soon as possible, because they are very important to the North African kitchen and are called for in several recipes. Once you've tried cooking with them, you'll want to include them in your cooking forever. Follow the 3-week recipe for the best results, but if time is short, opt for the 5-day version instead, and if time is really short, use good-quality bought preserved lemons. You may occasionally notice a white substance forming on the top of the lemons. Although this substance is harmless, it's best to rinse it off before using.

PRESERVED LEMONS IN 3 WEEKS

Serves 4
Preparation time: 10 minutes, plus 3 weeks preserving

1.3kg/3lb lemons (around 16)
8 tbsp sea salt

1 Wash 8 of the lemons well and pat dry thoroughly. Soften them by rolling them back and forth on a work surface. (I recommend doing this whenever you use a lemon, as it encourages the juices to run freely.) Using a sharp knife, slice off any protruding stems and then slice the lemons vertically, almost into quarters, stopping before you reach the bottom. The lemon quarters will still be attached at the base by about 2.5cm/1in rind.

2 Gently ease the lemon quarters apart without tearing them at the base, then stuff the middle of each lemon generously with 1 tbsp of the sea salt.

3 Pack the lemons tightly into a sterilized 1l/35fl oz/4-cup preserving jar, squashing them down so that any juices are released.

4 Juice the remaining 8 lemons, then pour the juice over the lemon wedges to cover, adding more lemon juice if necessary to keep them submerged. Leave about 1cm/½in air space.

5 Seal the jar tightly and store at room temperature. Each day for the first 3 days, turn the jar upside down occasionally. After that, leave for 3 weeks before using, so that the lemon rinds have had time to soften. Once opened, they can be stored in the fridge for 6–12 months.

6 To use, remove a lemon or just detach a wedge, depending on the recipe, and rinse thoroughly in water to remove the excess salt. Most of the recipes in this book will call for the rind only, but the pulp is fine to use for its taste, if you like.

PRESERVED LEMONS IN 5 DAYS

Serves 4
Preparation time: 10 minutes, plus 5 days preserving
Cooking time: 30 minutes

650g/1lb 7oz lemons (around 8)
6 tbsp sea salt

1 Prepare the lemons following steps 1 and 2 of the 3-week version.

2 Put 1l/35fl oz/4 cups water in a large stainless steel pan over a medium heat. Add the lemons (and a small heatproof plate, if needed, to keep them submerged). Bring to the boil, then simmer for about 30 minutes, until softened. Remove from the heat and leave to cool.

3 Once cooled, transfer the lemons to a sterilized 1l/35fl oz/4-cup preserving jar and pour over some of the cooking juices to cover.

4 Seal the jar tightly and store at room temperature for 5 days. Each day, turn the jar upside down occasionally. Once opened, they can be stored in the fridge for 6–12 months. Use as specified in the 3-week version.

SAFFRON LIQUID

Saffron is an essential ingredient in the Persian kitchen. Although it is a delicately aromatic and mildly pungent spice, using too much will yield an overpowering medicinal taste, so use it sparingly. The deeper the colour of the threads, the better the quality. Ready-ground saffron can easily be adulterated, so I recommend using saffron threads. Store the saffron threads in an airtight jar in a cool, dark place. Increase the quantities based on requirement, and store any extra saffron liquid in an airtight container, in the fridge, for up to a week.

Makes 1 tbsp
Preparation time: 5 minutes, plus infusing
Cooking time: 30 seconds

10 saffron threads

1 Toast the saffron threads in a heavy-based pan over a medium heat for 30 seconds until fragrant, shaking the pan often.

2 Transfer the saffron to a mortar and leave to cool for 1–2 minutes, before grinding them into a powder.

3 Mix the ground saffron with 1 tablespoon boiling water and set aside to infuse for at least 1 hour (until a rich orange hue appears) before using. The colour and flavour will continue to develop for about 12 hours.

PANEER CHEESE

Paneer is a fresh cheese with a creamy taste and texture that is set with acid rather than rennet, making it completely vegetarian. It's somewhat similar to ricotta cheese, and salt is not traditionally added. Because it's a non-melting cheese, it can be fried. Note that you do need to allow two days for the yogurt to sour.

Makes 250ml/9fl oz/1 cup
Preparation time: 15 minutes, plus up to 2 days souring, 1 hour resting and up to 2½ hours straining
Cooking time: 10–15 minutes

375ml/13fl oz/1 ½ cups plain yogurt
2l/70fl oz/8 cups whole milk
½ tsp sea salt

1 Put the yogurt in a bowl and cover with a kitchen towel. Leave at room temperature for 24–48 hours, or until a sample tastes sour.

2 Once the yogurt has soured, pour the milk into a heavy-based saucepan and bring to a gentle boil over a medium heat, watching it carefully to make sure the milk does not boil over or catch on the base of the pan (in which case it would have to be discarded).

3 Whisk the soured yogurt well and pour it into the milk, then stir for at least 5–10 minutes until the milk solids curdle and separate from the whey. Remove the pan from the heat and leave to rest for up to 1 hour, during which time the milk will continue to curdle.

4 Meanwhile, line a colander with muslin cloth or cheesecloth and secure it over a large bowl. Pour in the curdled milk, collecting the curd in the mesh and the whey in the bowl. If you like, you can also reserve the whey, which can be used to make ricotta, dilute yogurt drinks (see page 221), cook rice and make breads or pancakes, and can also be added to soups.

5 Gather the edges of the muslin cloth and tie it in a tight bundle. For a soft paneer, leave the bundle to hang from the sink tap for about 30 minutes. For a firmer paneer, rest the bundle in a colander that has been secured over a bowl, adding weight to it, such as a pot containing a bag of beans, and leave to strain for a further 2 hours. Transfer to a bowl, cover and store in the fridge for up to one week. Serve with a mixed herb salad.

Note: For a much quicker preparation time, you can simply squeeze the juice of 1 lemon into the milk and stir often for up to 5 minutes until the milk curdles. However, this method does not yield as much curdling or creaminess as the yogurt method.

SAVOURY PASTRY DOUGH

This is the basic dough recipe for the savoury pastries that grace an authentic Lebanese dinner party, buffet or mezze. Use it in recipes such as the Spinach & Sumac Turnovers (see page 37) and the Minced Lamb & Onion Crescents (see page 24).

Serves 4
Preparation time: 20 minutes, plus resting
Cooking time: 1 minute

150g/5 ½oz/1 cup plain flour, plus extra for dusting
½ tsp sea salt flakes
1 tsp caster sugar
4 tbsp olive oil, plus extra for greasing
6 tbsp milk
½ tsp dried active yeast

1 Sift the flour, salt and sugar into a mound on a clean work surface and create a well in the middle. Add the oil to the centre of the well and, using your hands, begin to combine with the flour until all is incorporated.

2 Heat the milk until tepid, then pour it into a small bowl. Sprinkle the yeast into the milk and mix thoroughly. Add to the flour and oil mixture and knead for about 5 minutes, dusting the work surface with flour as necessary, or until smooth and elastic and a ball has formed.

3 Place the dough in a large bowl greased with a little oil, and score the top with a knife to loosen the surface tension. Cover with a damp, clean kitchen towel and place it in a warm, draught-free place for about 1 hour.

CHELOW RICE

Some of the recipes in this book follow a two-stage Persian technique of cooking rice, in which the rice is first parboiled and then steamed. The resulting chelow (plain) rice can be eaten as it is or it can have further ingredients added, which are layered up with the rice in the pan before the rice is steamed. These dishes are known as polow, or mixed rice.

The key to preparing this light and fluffy rice is to wash the loose starch out so that each grain of rice remains distinct after its cooked. Then soak the rice for 30 minutes before parboiling it. Buy the best basmati rice you can afford. Although the amount of salt used might seem surprisingly large, it will be rinsed off, so the rice will not taste salty.

PARBOILED RICE (STAGE 1)

Serves 4
Preparation time: 5 minutes plus soaking the rice
Cooking time: 5 minutes

400g/14oz/2 cups basmati rice
3 tbsp sea salt

1 Pick over the rice to remove any dirt or discoloured grains. Wash the rice thoroughly in five or six changes of water, until it runs clear, which signals that all the loose starch has been removed.

2 Pour 1l/35fl oz/4 cups warm water into a large bowl and add 1 tablespoon of the salt. Add the rice and leave to soak for no more than 30 minutes, running your fingers through it every so often to help loosen the grains. Strain the rice and rinse under warm water.

3 Pour 1.25l/44fl oz/5 cups water into a large saucepan and add the remaining salt. Bring to the boil over a high heat and stir in the well-strained rice, then bring back to the boil and cook, uncovered, for 3 minutes over a high heat, until the grains are soft on the outside but still firm in the centre. Do not stir the rice again, as this could break the grains.

4 Drain the parboiled rice in a sieve and rinse with tepid water, tossing the rice gently to remove the excess moisture and to separate the grains. At this point you can set the rice aside until you are ready to cook your chosen recipe, if you like. This means that you can parboil the rice the day before you want it, then continue with the recipe the following day. (Once it has cooled, it needs to be stored in the fridge, where it can be kept safely for up to 3 days. Return to room temperature before using.)

STEAMED RICE (STAGE 2)

The oil added at this stage forms the *tahdeeg* ("base of the pot") layer. If you want to make the dish healthier, use less oil than suggested, for a thinner tahdeeg.

Serves 4
Preparation time: 15 minutes
Cooking time: 45 minutes

3–6 tbsp sunflower oil
1 recipe quantity Parboiled Rice (see left)
55g/2oz unsalted butter

1 Heat the oil in a heavy-based saucepan over a medium heat until the oil is sizzling. Using a spoon, sprinkle 4–5 tablespoons of the parboiled rice across the bottom of the pan. Continue sprinkling the remaining rice, building it up into a dome shape. (Tipping it all in at once will compress the rice, and the end result will not be a light and fluffy dish.)

2 Use the handle of a wooden spoon to make three holes in the rice to the bottom of the pan. Melt the butter in a small saucepan over a low heat, then pour over the rice.

3 Wrap the saucepan lid in a clean kitchen towel and tie it into a tight knot at the handle, then cover the saucepan with the lid as tightly as you can so that any steam does not escape. (The kitchen towel will prevent the moisture from dripping into the rice and making it soggy.)

4 Reduce the heat to low and cook, covered, for another 20–40 minutes. If you cook for just 20 minutes, the rice will be light and fluffy and the tahdeeg will be golden, although quite loose; if you cook for the full 40 minutes, the rice will remain tender and fluffy but the tahdeeg will be firmer and darker, which is how it would be eaten in the Middle East. The choice is yours.

5 When the rice is cooked, place the saucepan in 5cm/2in cold water in the kitchen sink and leave for 1–2 minutes. This helps to shock the rice and loosen the tahdeeg.

6 Gently spoon the rice out (making sure not to disturb the tahdeeg), and sprinkle it lightly onto a dish, shaping it into a dome. Alternatively, gently tip the pan out onto the dish, allowing the rice to spill out into a mound.

7 Remove the tahdeeg by inverting the saucepan onto a plate, using a spatula to loosen it if necessary. Serve the tahdeeg separately on a plate or on top of the rice.

VERMICELLI RICE

Rice cooked with vermicelli is a popular side dish in the Middle East. If you buy the vermicelli from a Middle Eastern store, they will most likely come already broken up, otherwise vermicelli nests can be broken up. Egyptian rice, which is short or medium grain, is traditionally used to make this dish, but basmati may be substituted. In keeping with the Persian method of preparation, it's best to rinse the rice well to remove any starch. The quantity of water needed will depend on the quality of rice used.

Serves 4
Preparation time: 10 minutes
Cooking time: 30 minutes

200g/7oz/1 cup short- or medium-grain rice
30g/1oz butter
30g/1oz vermicelli
sea salt and freshly ground black pepper

1 Rinse the rice under cold running water until the water runs clear. Strain well and set aside.

2 Melt the butter in a heavy-based saucepan over a medium heat. Break the vermicelli into shorter lengths of about 2cm/¾in and cook for 2–3 minutes until golden, stirring often.

3 Add the rice to the cooked vermicelli, tossing until it is well incorporated, then pour over 500ml/17fl oz/2 cups boiling water. Increase the heat to high, then cover and bring to the boil. Reduce the heat to low and cook for 15–20 minutes until all the water has been absorbed and the rice is soft. Season to taste with salt and pepper before serving with other dishes.

SOAKING & COOKING CHICKPEAS

The ideal method for cooking chickpeas is to use a pressure cooker. Alternatively, follow the steps below.

Serves 4
Preparation time: 15 minutes, plus overnight soaking
Cooking time: 30 minutes–1 ½ hours

1 Put the dried chickpeas in a large bowl (they will double in size), cover with two times their volume in cold water and leave to soak overnight.

2 Rinse the soaked chickpeas well under cold running water and put in a heavy-based saucepan. Cover with water and then again by a half.

3 Bring to the boil over a medium-high heat, then reduce the heat to low, partially cover the pan and cook for 30 minutes. Then cover the pan fully and cook further depending on the results you want or what a recipe states: 30 minutes for al dente, 1 hour for tender or 1 ½ hours for mushy, skimming off any scum that forms with a slotted spoon. Keep an eye on the pan to make sure it does not overflow. Drain, then use as required, reserving the cooking liquid if necessary.

Note If you cannot use cooked chickpeas and have to resort to the tinned variety, be sure to soak them in water for 10–15 minutes and then rinse them well under running water to remove as much "tin" flavour as possible.

LEBANESE CLOTTED CREAM

Ashta (to skim) is the Lebanese clotted cream and adds a delicious finish to many desserts.

Serves 4
Preparation time: 5 minutes
Cooking time: 5 minutes

1 tbsp cornflour
250ml/9fl oz/1 cup single or whipping cream

1 Put the cornflour in a small bowl, add 1 tablespoon water and stir until completely smooth.

2 Pour the cream into a heavy-based saucepan and heat over a medium heat until warm. Whisk in the cornflour mixture, stirring vigorously for 3–5 minutes until it thickens to the consistency of clotted cream, then remove from the heat and leave to cool.

3 Transfer the clotted cream to a bowl, cover and put in the fridge to chill until ready to use.

ROASTED VEGETABLES

Vegetables that have been roasted or chargrilled have an intense flavour and a crispy yet juicy texture. Choose the cooking method (gas stove, charcoal barbecue, gas barbecue or oven) that suits the recipe and the situation.

Serves 4
Preparation time: 10 minutes, plus resting
Cooking time: 20 minutes

aubergines and/or peppers, as required

1 Turn a gas burner to a high heat and lean the aubergines and/or peppers, stem still on, directly over the burner, turning each one occasionally with tongs until all the sides are charred and the aubergines or peppers are soft. This should take about 5 minutes per side or 15–20 minutes in total. Use as many burners as necessary.

2 Alternatively, preheat a charcoal barbecue until the charcoal is burning white, turn on a gas barbecue or preheat the oven to 200°C/400°F/Gas 6. Cook the aubergines or peppers (poke aubergines a few times if grilling in the oven, to avoid them bursting) until all the sides are charred and the flesh is soft.

3 Remove from the heat and transfer to a sealable plastic bag, then seal and leave to rest for 10 minutes.

4 Holding the stem of one aubergine or pepper at a time, use the bag to peel off the skin and any charred edges.

OPENING POMEGRANATES

Pomegranates can be one of the messiest fruits to open, making your walls look like a toddler's canvas. The following method is efficient and makes capturing the seeds – its scarlet jewels – a more relaxed process.

1 Use the palm of your hand to roll the pomegranate on the work surface, which loosens the seeds, then cut off the pomegranate crown with a sharp knife. Score the fruit into segments, not cutting through all the way, but making sure to score just enough so that you can easily peel the skin.

2 Fill a large bowl with water, put the pomegranate in the water and begin to peel apart the scored segments. Discard the skin. Gently pry the seeds apart. All the white pith will float to the top, where you can sift it off with a sieve, and the seeds will sink to the bottom.

ACCOMPANIMENTS

COUSCOUS

The Moroccan way of preparing couscous is to steam it in a couscoussière. If you cannot find a couscoussière, a very suitable alternative is to use a regular steamer and line the steamer basket with a muslin cloth or kitchen towel. Instant couscous, which is readily available in the UK, is more convenient because it involves only a matter of rehydrating it in boiled or simmering water. Unfortunately, though, instant couscous cannot be steamed because the long cooking time will render it a mush. So, if you've gone to the trouble of cooking a stew, then you might as well steam the couscous at the same time. You can find non-instant couscous at most Middle Eastern grocers. You'll need to start cooking the couscous about 40 minutes before the stew is ready.

Serves 4
Preparation time: 20 minutes
Cooking time: 35 minutes

750ml/26fl oz/3 cups Vegetable Stock (see page 211)
375g/13oz/2 cups couscous
4 tbsp olive oil or 20g/¾oz butter, softened
sea salt

1 Heat the vegetable stock until warmed through. Meanwhile, place the couscous in a mixing bowl, add the olive oil and rub it in with your hands to distribute the fat evenly. Add 125ml/4fl oz/½ cup of the stock and stir with a fork until the couscous has absorbed the stock and plumped up. Season the couscous with salt to taste and break up any lumps with your fingers.

2 Pour the remaining stock into the bottom of a large steamer and place it over a medium heat. Line the steamer basket or a colander with a damp kitchen towel or muslin cloth and add the couscous. Fold the towel loosely over the couscous, ensuring it is not compressed. Alternatively, if you're cooking a stew at the same time, place the steamer basket on top of the stew pot. Cover and seal any open edges by wrapping a kitchen towel or foil around it to minimize the escape of steam. Simmer for 15 minutes.

3 Remove the couscous parcel from the steamer and toss the grains with a fork for 1 minute. Leave to cool for about 5 minutes. Gather the cloth into a parcel again and return to the steamer basket, cover and steam for a further 15 minutes, or until the grains are soft. Serve with a stew, if using.

ARABIC BREAD

Arabic bread is a pivotal part of the Middle Eastern eating experience, where it is used interchangeably with utensils to create delicate bites, wraps or sandwiches and to help mop up prized stew juices. It's in quite a separate league to the thick, heavy pitta breads sold in the West. Making Arabic bread at home is rewarding, and watching the air pockets develop is quite exciting. Sure, it's not the exact texture of commercial-grade Arabic bread, but that's precisely the point. Baking this beautiful bread is, in fact, not as hard as one may imagine: just be sure to have a well-heated oven ready before popping the dough in. Arabic bread has many uses. As well as being served alongside stews and other dishes with sauces, it can also be used in different ways. For example, you can also spread Wild Thyme Mixture (see page 220) and olive oil over the dough before popping it into the oven for a pizza-style snack (see also Spiced Lamb Flatbread Pizzas, page 107). Triangles of Arabic bread can be toasted and then used to dip into hummus, or added to Fattoush Salad (see page 61). Alternatively, the toasted bread can be crushed into large breadcrumbs and then used in a dish such as Aubergine, Veal & Yogurt Crumble (see page 119).

Serves 4
Preparation time: 25 minutes, plus rising
Cooking time: 3 minutes

300g/10½oz/2½ cups strong white bread flour,
  plus extra for dusting
½ tsp sea salt
1 tsp caster sugar
4 tbsp olive oil
2 tsp dried active yeast

1 Sift the flour into a mixing bowl, add the salt and sugar and pour in the oil, then mix well with your hands.

2 Add the yeast to 150ml/5fl oz/scant ⅔ cup lukewarm water and stir until dissolved. Pour the water and yeast mixture into the flour and oil mixture, little by little, combining it with your hands as you go, until a ball is formed. Depending on the age and brand of flour, you may find that you need more or less water.

3 Transfer the dough to a well-floured work surface and continue kneading it until it is smooth and elastic. Return the dough ball to the mixing bowl, then score the top with a knife to loosen the surface tension. Cover with a damp, clean kitchen towel and place it in a warm, draught-free place for about 1 hour or until it doubles in size.

4 Once the dough has doubled in size, turn it out on to a lightly floured work surface and knock it back, then knead gently before rolling it into a log. Divide the log into four balls of equal size, each weighing about 125g/4½oz. Lightly flour the work surface once more and use a rolling pin to roll out each ball, re-flouring the surface as necessary. For small loaves, roll out each ball of dough into a circle about 20cm/8in in diameter. For large loaves, roll out each ball of dough into a circle about 30cm/12in in diameter. Cover the loaves with a kitchen towel and leave to rest for a further 10 minutes.

5 Meanwhile, preheat the oven to 230°C/450°F/Gas 8 and place a baking sheet in the oven to warm up. Baking one loaf at a time, spray a loaf lightly with water and bake for 2 minutes until the top and edges are lightly golden and a pocket of air has formed (the cooking time depends on the heat of the oven and the thickness of the bread). Do not cook them for longer than 1 minute after the air pocket has formed, or they will turn out more brittle than pliable. Repeat with the remaining loaves. Leaving the breads to cool uncovered will also make them brittle, so if you are not serving them immediately, cover with a damp tea towel and store in a sealed plastic bag.

6 The breads can be kept, wrapped, in a fridge for up to 2–3 days or in a freezer for up to 1–2 months. Allow 20–30 minutes defrosting time. Alternatively, microwave briefly or bake in a hot oven for a couple of minutes.

THIN FLATBREAD

Nan-e taftoon as this bread is known in Iran, is traditionally baked in hot, deep ovens called tannours. It's also a great accompaniment to many of the dishes you'll find in this book. You can enjoy a simple but very satisfying meal by pairing freshly baked flatbreads with a good white cheese and an Undressed Herb Salad (see page 67).

Makes 6
Preparation time: 30 minutes, plus rising and resting
Cooking time: 25 minutes

1 tsp dried active yeast
750g/1lb 10oz strong white bread flour, plus extra
1 tsp sea salt
oil, for greasing

1 Dissolve the yeast in 55ml/1¾fl oz/scant ¼ cup warm water in a bowl and set aside for 5 minutes.

2 Meanwhile, mix the flour and salt on a clean work surface, then create a well in the centre. Add 400ml/14fl oz/1⅔ cups warm water to the yeast water and pour it into the well, then gradually work the liquid into the flour, mixing and kneading with your hands, until it forms a soft dough.

3 Knead the dough for 10–15 minutes until it is very smooth and elastic and comes away from the work surface. Transfer to a lightly oiled bowl, cover with a slightly damp kitchen towel and leave in a warm, draught-free place for 2 hours or until it has doubled in size.

4 When the dough has doubled, remove it from the bowl, place on a lightly floured work surface and knock back, kneading until it is soft and elastic. Roll the dough into a log, then divide it into six equal balls and space these out on the work surface. Score the top of each ball with a knife to loosen the surface tension. Cover with a damp, clean kitchen towel and leave to rest for 20 minutes.

5 Once the dough has rested, preheat the oven to 240°C/475°F/Gas 9 and place a large baking sheet in the oven to warm up. Working with one piece of dough at a time, knock it back on the floured work surface and then roll it out as thinly as possible into a 33 x 23 x 5mm/13 x 9 x ¼in rectangular shape to fit the baking sheet.

6 Remove the baking sheet from the oven and scatter some flour over it, then quickly but carefully transfer one of the thin sheets of dough to the baking sheet, stretching it just a little more, if needed, to fit the baking sheet (but being careful not to tear it and not to burn your hand on the baking sheet). Gently prick the surface with a fork to minimize large air pockets developing.

7 Bake for 2–4 minutes until the dough has blistered and is a very light, golden colour. The aim is for the bread to be soft with golden hints. While the first bread is baking, prepare the next one.

8 Remove the bread from the oven and place on a wire rack to cool (you will need at least 2 racks to cope with how fast the breads cook). The bread might be slightly crisp when it first comes out of the oven, but it will soften and become pliable as it cools. Serve warm or cold.

9 Once cold, wrap in a damp kitchen towel and refrigerate; alternatively, place in a sealable plastic bag and freeze for 1–2 months. When wanted, sprinkle the chilled or frozen breads with water. Microwave chilled breads for 30 seconds and frozen breads for 2 minutes. Alternatively, you can heat chilled bread in a non-stick frying pan over a medium heat for 45 seconds on each side.

POTATO MATCHSTICKS

Crispy, golden matchstick-sized chips are the perfect accompaniment for many of the dishes in this book. For consistently thin results, use a mandolin on the finest julienne setting. Alternatively, use a thin sharp knife. I like to cut the chips rather thin and long. You can keep them in iced water if you are making ahead, rather than just rinsing them, and then pat dry before frying.

Serves 4
Preparation time: 20 minutes
Cooking time: 10 minutes

500g/1lb 2oz potatoes, peeled
sunflower oil, for deep-frying
½ tsp sea salt

1 Slice the potatoes into thin matchsticks and rinse under cold running water to rid them of excess starch. Dry thoroughly on a clean kitchen towel or using a salad spinner.

2 Heat a large, deep frying pan to a high heat and pour in enough oil for deep-frying. Bring the temperature of the oil to 200°C/400°F. To test if the oil is hot enough, add a potato matchstick to the oil: if it sizzles and floats, the oil is ready.

3 Cook in batches, as necessary, for 4–5 minutes or until crisp and light golden. Remove from the oil and transfer to a plate lined with kitchen paper to drain. Season with salt before serving.

BURNT TOMATO & CHILLI JAM

Here's my take on this sweet and savoury speciality from the city of Marrakesh, which makes for a very versatile accompaniment to plenty of dishes, including Shipwrecked Potato Boats (see page 41) and Artichokes with Couscous (see page 33), along with cheese and an array of tagines, flatbreads, fries and so on. I make it in big batches because it's great to have extra on hand; I've witnessed, in bewilderment, a friend shovel it down by the spoonful.

Makes about 455ml/16fl oz/2 cups
Preparation time: 20 minutes
Cooking time: 1 hour

1kg/2lb 4oz tomatoes, quartered
½ tsp coriander seeds
¼ tsp ground cinnamon
1 small red onion, sliced into 5mm/¼in rings
2 red chillies, deseeded (optional) and thinly sliced
5 fat garlic cloves, crushed with the blade of a knife
5cm/2in piece of root ginger, peeled and roughly chopped
2 tbsp olive oil
1 tbsp clear honey
sea salt and freshly ground black pepper

1 Preheat the oven to 190°C/375°F/Gas 5.

2 Mix all the ingredients, except for the honey and the salt and pepper, together, then transfer to a baking tray and bake for 1 hour. Note that the tomatoes at the outer edges will burn, adding the characteristic depth of flavour to the dish; just be sure to shake the tray every so often and to stir the jam so that it does not stick to the tray.

3 Once everything has softened and the mixture begins to dry out, remove the tray from the oven. Transfer all the ingredients to a mixing bowl and pulverize with a hand blender to the desired texture; I prefer it a little on the chunky side. Mix in the honey and season to taste with salt and pepper. Serve immediately. Alternatively, transfer to a sterilized glass jar, cover with a thin layer of oil and seal. Keep the jar in the fridge for up to 2 weeks, topping up with more oil after each use.

GARLIC GONE WILD

This feisty dip is prepared in several ways in Lebanon, where it's known as *toum*. Usually, at home, pounded garlic is emulsified with olive oil and finished with a squeeze of lemon. In the north of the country, mint may be added. The garlic dip served in restaurants resembles more of an aioli, except that egg whites rather than a whole egg are used, as in this recipe. This garlic sauce is not at all for the faint-hearted: a little goes a long way. It is wonderful paired with raw *kebbeh* (a version of steak tartare eaten as a mezze) and chicken, such as in the Wild Thyme Chicken (see page 79), as well as spread onto warm, thick heirloom tomato slices, sprinkled with a little sumac and drizzled with olive oil. I prefer to prepare it with a good-quality vegetable oil instead of olive oil, as the olive oil tends to give a bitter taste and discolouration. I also find that using a pestle and mortar first to create a garlic paste yields better results.

Makes about 185ml/6fl oz/¾ cup
Preparation time: 10 minutes

1 garlic bulb, separated into cloves
1 tsp sea salt
1 egg white
250ml/9fl oz/1 cup sunflower oil
juice of ½ lemon, or more to taste
2 tsp finely chopped mint leaves (optional)

1 Pound the garlic cloves and salt using a pestle and mortar or small food processor until a paste forms. If using the pestle and mortar, transfer the garlic paste to the food processor, add the egg white and process for 1–2 minutes or until well incorporated, frothy and smooth.

2 While the blade is running (if your machine has a funnel), add the oil a little at a time (start with adding 1 teaspoon at a time for a few times and then gradually move up to 1 tbsp at a time) until the mixture reaches a creamy consistency. As the mixture emulsifies it will turn a pure white colour and will have a fluffy, creamy texture. Alternatively, you can add a little oil at a time intermittently (start with 1 teaspoon at a time for a few times and then increase to 1 tablespoon at a time) and running the blade for about 30 seconds at a time, repeating until the mixture has emulsified.

3 Finally, add the lemon juice and pulse for a further 20 seconds. Mix in the chopped mint, if using, then taste and adjust the seasoning as required.

WHITE CABBAGE SALAD

This salad is a wonderful accompaniment to mujadarah – a comforting Mess of Pottage (see page 169), among other dishes. You can substitute the lemon juice with cider vinegar for an equally delightful dressing.

Serves 4
Preparation time: 15 minutes

600g/1lb 5oz white cabbage, cut into long thin slivers
2 tomatoes, finely chopped
juice of 1 lemon
1 garlic clove, finely chopped
4 tbsp olive oil
sea salt and freshly ground black pepper

1 Toss all the ingredients together. Season to taste with salt and pepper. Leave to stand for 5 minutes before serving.

TARATOR

One of my ultimate dressings or dips, this wonderfully versatile mixture is traditionally paired with falafel (see Falafel & Tarator Wraps, page 150) and baked fish (see Spicy Snapper in the Tripoli Manner, page 141).

Serves 4
Preparation time: 10 minutes

200ml/7fl oz/heaped ¾ cup tahini
2 garlic cloves, crushed
juice of 2 lemons
1 tbsp finely chopped parsley leaves or other herb of your choice (optional)
sea salt

1 Put the tahini and garlic in a bowl, then gradually whisk in 200ml/7fl oz/generous ¾ cup water, alternating with the lemon juice. The tahini will initially thicken a bit before it dilutes to a yogurt-like consistency. Be sure to whisk until no lumps remain. You may not require all the lemon juice.

2 Season to taste with salt, and add more lemon juice if you require a little more acidity. Sprinkle in the parsley, if using, and serve.

MINT & BUTTER DRIZZLE

Mint is used extensively in Persian cuisine, and this drizzle is used with soups and other dishes.

Serves 4
Preparation time: 2 minutes
Cooking time: 4 minutes

30g/1oz unsalted butter or 2 tbsp sunflower oil
1 tsp dried mint

1 Melt the butter or heat the sunflower oil in a small, heavy-based saucepan.

2 Add the mint and fry for 1–2 minutes until cooked and fragrant.

WILD THYME MIXTURE

Za'atar is the Arabic word used to describe a wild, shrubby plant native to the Mediterranean. *Za'atar* belongs to the labiate family, sharing characteristics with wild oregano, marjoram and thyme, although it is most commonly referred to as wild thyme in the West. It can be eaten fresh in salads and used to stuff pastries, or the leaves can be dried and mixed with sumac, salt and toasted sesame seeds to create the wildly popular pungent blend made below. This blend is then mixed with olive oil for bread dipping or spreading across bread dough, and possibly garnished with cheese before being baked. *Za'atar* is extremely versatile and can be used to season a variety of vegetables, salads, fish and meat. The following blend will make several servings and keeps for up to 1 year in an airtight container.

Makes about 60g/2¼oz/1 heaped cup
Preparation time: 10 minutes
Cooking time: 1 minute

30g/1oz/¼ cup sesame seeds
30g/1oz/1 cup ground thyme, marjoram or oregano or a combination of all three
1 tbsp sumac
1 tsp fine sea salt

1 Toast the sesame seeds in a heavy-based pan over a medium heat for 1 minute until golden and fragrant, shaking the pan often.

2 Combine all the ingredients and use as required. Store the remainder in an airtight container away from sunlight for up to one year.

LABNEH DIP

Known as *labneh*, strained yogurt frequents the Levantine table. It can be served as part of a mezze with pounded garlic and chopped mint, preserved in some form, or simply spread onto Arabic bread with slivers of cucumber, a dusting of herbs and a drizzle of oil, or rolled into golf-sized balls and preserved in olive oil. The health benefits are numerous, and importantly it is also suitable for people who are lactose intolerant. The yogurt you see labelled as "Greek yogurt" on supermarket shelves is strained yogurt, and each brand has its own degree of thickness. In the Middle East, yogurt is called *laban* and it is prepared by fermenting milk with a yogurt starter then incubating it for a specific length of time to achieve the desired acidity. You can buy regular yogurt and strain it yourself to the desired thickness of *labneh* or you can use Greek yogurt, which thickens faster. Avoid using "Greek-style" yogurt, as it may well have thickeners in it, such as gelatine or gum blends.

Serves 4
Preparation time: 5 minutes plus overnight straining

500g/1lb 2oz goat's milk yogurt
½ tsp sea salt

To serve:
olive oil
Wild Thyme Mixture (see left)
cucumbers, sliced
tomatoes, quartered
olives
chopped mint
Arabic Bread (see page 217)

1 Combine the yogurt and salt together. Place a colander over a bowl so that it is secure and then line the colander with a muslin cloth. Add the yogurt mixture to the cloth and then gather all the edges of the muslin and twist tightly. Tie with kitchen string. Transfer the bowl with the colander and muslin bag to the fridge to sit overnight or for up to 24 hours.

2 The following day, you will notice that the whey has separated. The strained yogurt will have become thicker – similar to a cream cheese consistency. If you'd like it thicker still, you may let it sit for a further day.

3 Transfer the strained yogurt to a serving dish and create a well in the middle. Drizzle with olive oil and sprinkle with the thyme mixture. Serve with sliced cucumbers, tomatoes, olives, mint and Arabic Bread.

SAVOURY YOGURT SHAKE

Yogurt drinks, known as *lassi* in India, *doogh* in Iran, *tahn* in Armenia and *ayran* in Turkey, Syria and Lebanon, abound in the East. *Ayran* and *doogh* are very popular drinks across the region and are very simple to make. Thinning down yogurt with water and seasoning it with salt makes a refreshing drink that combines thirst-quenching water with the powerful digestive aid of yogurt and the restoring benefits of essential salts, which are perspired during the hot Levantine summers. Unlike its counterparts, *ayran* and *doogh* are never served sweetened, although *doogh* can be fizzy if made with carbonated water. Esteemed as the ultimate drink for washing down a Spiced Lamb Flatbread Pizza (see page 107), this shake also reaps incredible rewards for the stomach if drunk first thing each morning, with or without mint, as preferred. It prevents stomach infections, diarrhoea, constipation, ulcers and bowel inflammation, amongst other things.

Serves 4
Preparation time: 5 minutes

500ml/17fl oz/2 cups Greek yogurt
1 tsp sea salt
2 tsp dried mint (optional)
300ml/10½fl oz/1¼ cups cold sparkling (optional) water
ice (optional)

1 Put the yogurt, salt and mint, if using, in a large jug with 300ml/10½fl oz/1¼ cups cold water (use sparkling if you want a fizzy shake) and whisk vigorously for about 1 minute. Pour into four individual glasses over ice, if you like.

SUPPLIERS

Online Middle Eastern UK

Melbury & Appleton
www.melburyandappleton.co.uk

Arabica Food and Spice Company
www.arabicafoodandspice.com

Specialty UK

Arganic Oil
Tel: 020 8150 1203
www.myarganic.co.uk

Artisan Grains
www.artisangrains.co.uk

Ethnic Grocers
Levantine
Damas Gate
81-85 Uxbridge Road
London W12 5BY
Tel: 020 8743 5116

Green Valley
36 Upper Berkeley St
London W1H 7PG
Tel: 020 7402 7385
www.green-valley.co

TFC Dalston Ltd
89 Ridley Road
London E8 2NP
Tel: 020 7254 6754
www.tfcsupermarket.com

Moroccan

Le Maroc
94 Golborne Road
London W10 5PS
Tel: 020 8968 9783

Iranian/Persian

Khayam Supermarket
149 Seymour Place
London W1H 5TL
Tel: 020 7258 3637

Persepolis
28-30 Peckham High Street
London, Greater London SE15 5D
Tel: 020 7639 8007

INDEX

Author's Acknowledgments Luck (the Universe) has blessed me with people who truly believe in what I am doing and who have dedicated themselves to the cause in one way or another. None of this would have been realized without them, be it working with me directly, recipe testing, giving me guidance, nurturing me, being a pillar of support, editing, sharing their recipes and knowledge, informing and inspiring this book and more. Thanks to my husband Chris, sisters Joslin and Adla, brother Eli, father Antoine, mother Cynthia, cousin Patrick, my aunt Amouleh and my uncle Elias, my "twin" cousin Melanie, parents in-law Jim and Joyce, my aunt Joumana and uncle Adnan, cousin Monica and niece Vanessa. Thanks also to Šárka Babická, William Dobson, Grace Cheetham, Alison Bolus, Krissy Mallett, Bishnu Khadka, Dhabia, Wid and Suham Al Bayaty, Mazen Jabado, Bashar and Anwar Younis, Abi Blake, Elias Abu Nader, Aoife Cox, Jason Lee, Lama Khatib Daniel, Sukruti Staneley, Harold McGee, Greg Malouf, Claudia Roden, Margaret Shaida, my loyal blog readers and now, you, for buying this book and cooking the recipes.